LIT CRIT £4—
12/23
W

CAMBRIDGE STUDIES IN ROMANTICISM 52

BYRON, POETICS AND HISTORY

D1375677

Jane Stabler offers the first full-scale examination of Byron's poetic form in relation to historical debates of his time. Responding to recent studies of publishing and audiences in the Romantic period, Stabler argues that Byron's poetics developed in response to contemporary cultural history and his reception by the English reading public. Drawing on extensive new archive research into Byron's correspondence and reading, Stabler traces the complexity of the intertextual dialogues that run through his work. For example, Stabler analyses *Don Juan* alongside *Galignani's Messenger* – Byron's principal source of news about British politics while in Italy – and refers to hitherto unpublished letters between Byron's publishers and his friends revealing a powerful impulse among his contemporaries to direct his controversial poetic style to their own political ends. This fascinating study will be of interest to Byronists and, more broadly, to scholars of Romanticism in general.

JANE STABLER is Lecturer in English at the University of Dundee. She is the author of *The Longman Critical Reader* on *Byron* (1998) and *Burke to Byron, Barbauld to Baillie 1790–1830* (2001).

CAMBRIDGE STUDIES IN ROMANTICISM

General editors
Professor Marilyn Butler   Professor James Chandler
University of Oxford   *University of Chicago*

Editorial board
John Barrell, *University of York*
Paul Hamilton, *University of London*
Mary Jacobus, *University of Cambridge*
Kenneth Johnston, *Indiana University*
Alan Liu, *University of California, Santa Barbara*
Jerome McGann, *University of Virginia*
David Simpson, *University of California, Davis*

This series aims to foster the best new work in one of the most challenging fields within English literary studies. From the early 1780s to the early 1830s a formidable array of talented men and women took to literary composition, not just in poetry, which some of them famously transformed, but in many modes of writing. The expansion of publishing created new opportunities for writers, and the political stakes of what they wrote were raised again by what Wordsworth called those 'great national events' that were 'almost daily taking place': the French Revolution, the Napoleonic and American wars, urbanisation, industrialisation, religious revival, an expanded empire abroad and the reform movement at home. This was an enormous ambition, even when it pretended otherwise. The relations between science, philosophy, religion and literature were reworked in texts such as *Frankenstein* and *Biographia Literaria*; gender relations in *A Vindication of the Rights of Woman* and *Don Juan*; journalism by Cobbett and Hazlitt; poetic form, content and style by the Lake School and the Cockney School. Outside Shakespeare studies, probably no body of writing has produced such a wealth of response or done so much to shape the responses of modern criticism. This indeed is the period that saw the emergence of those notions of 'literature' and of literary history, especially national literary history, on which modern scholarship in English has been founded.

The categories produced by Romanticism have also been challenged by recent historicist arguments. The task of the series is to engage both with a challenging corpus of Romantic writings and with the changing field of criticism they have helped to shape. As with other literary series published by Cambridge, this one will represent the work of both younger and more established scholars, on either side of the Atlantic and elsewhere.

For a complete list of titles published see end of book.

BYRON, POETICS
AND HISTORY

JANE STABLER

CAMBRIDGE
UNIVERSITY PRESS

CAMBRIDGE UNIVERSITY PRESS
Cambridge, New York, Melbourne, Madrid, Cape Town, Singapore, São Paulo, Delhi

Cambridge University Press
The Edinburgh Building, Cambridge CB2 8RU, UK

Published in the United States of America by Cambridge University Press, New York

www.cambridge.org
Information on this title: www.cambridge.org/9780521111850

© Jane Stabler 2002

This publication is in copyright. Subject to statutory exception
and to the provisions of relevant collective licensing agreements,
no reproduction of any part may take place without the written
permission of Cambridge University Press.

First published 2002
This digitally printed version 2009

A catalogue record for this publication is available from the British Library

Library of Congress Cataloguing in Publication data
Stabler, Jane.
Byron, poetics, and history / Jane Stabler.
p.   cm. – (Cambridge studies in Romanticism; 52)
Includes bibliographical references and index.
ISBN 0 521 81241 0
1. Byron, George Gordon Byron, Baron, 1788–1824 – Knowledge – History.
2. Literature and history – Great Britain – History – 19th century.   3. Byron, George Gordon
Byron, Baron, 1788–1824. Don Juan.   4. Historical poetry, English – History and criticism.
5. Don Juan (Legendary character) in literature.   I. Title.   II. Series.
PR4392.H5 S73   2002
821′.7 – dc21   2002022286

ISBN 978-0-521-81241-2 hardback
ISBN 978-0-521-11185-0 paperback

For NHR
and MGQR

all these things – like most things are a lottery – it may be as well at
least to have the ticket drawn.

(BLJ, X, pp. 92–3)

Contents

Acknowledgements

My work has involved many debts of gratitude and it is a pleasure to acknowledge them here. I am grateful to the staff of the following institutions: the Bibliothèque Interuniversitaire of Lille, the Bibliothèque Nationale in Paris, the British Library, the Bodleian Library, the Brotherton Library, Dundee University Library, Edinburgh University Library, Glasgow University Library, the House of Lords Record Office, the National Library of Scotland, Stirling University Library, St Andrews University Library, the Special Collections Department, University of St Andrews. Like many other people who have worked on Byron, I am indebted to Virginia Murray for her kind help in locating manuscripts and I would like to thank JOHN MURRAY for permission to consult and quote from material in the John Murray Archive. I would also like to thank the Earl of Lytton for permission to consult and quote from the Lovelace Papers deposited in the Bodleian Library.

A section of Chapter Two appeared in *Essays in Criticism* 50.4 (October 2000), 306–28, and is reprinted by permission of Oxford University Press. A version of the first part of Chapter Three appeared in *Translation & Literature* 3 (1994), 47–65, and is reprinted by permission of the editors and Edinburgh University Press. A version of one section of Chapter Four appeared in *The Byron Journal* 26 (1998), 39–49 and is reprinted by permission of the editor.

I have received kindly encouragement and advice from many friends and colleagues during the writing of this book. I would particularly like to thank Alex Alec-Smith, Michael Alexander, Bernard Beatty, Alison Chapman, Peter Cochran, Robert Crawford, Richard Cronin, Jonathan Cutmore, Tom Duncan, Peter Easingwood, Fiona Gaman, Marilyn Gaull, Jo-Anne George, Jill Heydt-Stevenson, Abi Holt, Gwen Hunter, Peter Isaac, Molly Lefebure, Ralph Lloyd Jones, Malcolm Kelsall, Sally Kilmister, Peter Kitson, Gregory P. Kucich, Michael O'Neill, Sarah Poynting, David Robb, Andrew Roberts, Bill Ruddick, Victor

Skretkowicz, Jean Spence, Jim Stewart, Peter Vassallo, Stephen Wall, Rob Watt, Tim Webb, Mary Wedd, Jonathan Wordsworth, Keith Williams and Duncan Wu. My family, my husband's family, Drummond and Vivian Bone, David Fairer, Lawrence and Mary James, Seamus Perry and Nicola Trott have offered generous hospitality, vigorous conversation and good cheer over many years and they have seen my work on Byron through all its digressions.

I am deeply indebted to Drummond Bone, Richard Cronin, David Fairer, Andrew Nicholson, Nicholas Roe and Susan Wolfson for reading and commenting on different chapters at various stages. Their scholarly expertise, generously shared knowledge and shrewd criticism have greatly improved the book; any clumsiness or errors which remain are my responsibility. I benefited from the work of two anonymous Cambridge University Press readers and owe the first one in particular a great deal for his or her detailed editorial observations and suggestions. I am most grateful to Rose Bell and Rachel De Wachter for seeing the book through the press. Finally I would like to thank Josie Dixon, former commissioning editor of Cambridge University Press, for her initial interest in the book and her successor, Linda Bree, and the Cambridge Studies in Romanticism Series Editors for carrying the book forward with continued enthusiasm.

Note on texts

All quotations from Byron's poetry unless otherwise stated are taken from *CPW*. *Childe Harold's Pilgrimage* and *Don Juan* are referred to by canto and stanza numbers; all other poems are referred to by line reference or stanza and line reference.

Plays are referred to by act, scene, and line. The edition of Shakespeare used is *The Arden Shakespeare*, second series, general editors: Harold F. Brooks, Harold Jenkins and Brian Morris (London and New York: Methuen, 1951–82). All references to *Paradise Lost* are taken from Milton, *Paradise Lost*, (ed.) Alastair Fowler, 2nd edn (Harlow: Longman, 1968; repr. 1982): references are to book and line numbers.

All references to the *OED* are to the *Oxford English Dictionary*, 2nd edn, prepared by J.A. Simpson and E.S.C. Weiner, 20 vols. (Oxford: Clarendon Press, 1989).

All quotations from the Bible are from the Authorised Version.

Abbreviations

BLJ	Lord Byron, *Byron's Letters and Journals*, (ed.) Leslie A. Marchand, 13 vols. (London: John Murray, 1973–94)
CPW	Lord Byron, *The Complete Poetical Works*, (ed.) Jerome J. McGann, 7 vols. (Oxford: Clarendon Press, 1980–93)
ELH	*English Literary History*
GM	*Galignani's Messenger*
GLG	*Galignani's Literary Gazette*
HLRO	House of Lords Record Office
OED	*Oxford English Dictionary*
PMLA	*Publication of the Modern Language Association of America*
RR, A	Donald H. Reiman (ed.), *The Romantics Reviewed: Contemporary Reviews of British Romantic Writers, Part A: The Lake Poets*, 2 vols. (New York and London: Garland Publishing, 1972)
RR, B	Donald H. Reiman (ed.), *The Romantics Reviewed: Contemporary Reviews of British Romantic Writers, Part B: Byron and Regency Society Poets*, 5 vols. (New York and London: Garland Publishing, 1972)
RR, C	Donald H. Reiman (ed.), *The Romantics Reviewed: Contemporary Reviews of British Romantic Writers, Part C: Shelley, Keats, and London Radical Writers*, 2 vols. (New York and London: Garland Publishing, 1972)
SEL	*Studies in English Literature*

Introduction: Byron and the poetics of digression

More delicate than the historians' are the map-makers' colors.
Elizabeth Bishop, 'The Map'

In April 1816 Byron's plans to leave England were well under way. He had commissioned the Napoleonic carriage which would carry him across Europe and on 21 April the deed of separation from Lady Byron was completed. Byron signed-off from his marriage with an epigram which 'the lawyers objected to . . . as superfluous':

> A year ago you swore, fond she!
>   'To love, to honour', and so forth:
> Such was the vow you pledged to me,
>   And here's exactly what 'tis worth.[1]

This bitter full stop is a textual manifestation of the experience of severance, but Byron's disengagement from the English public was not quite so terminal. Hidden among the well-known details of his departure – the selling of his library and the histrionic claims that his friends had forsaken him – is the record in the House of Lords Proxy Book for 1816 which states that from 3 April 1816 'George Earl of Essex hath the proxy of George Lord Byron.'[2] In other words, while flaunting his intention to shake the dust of England from his shoes, Byron was also preparing to re-engage with English politics via a different route. One abrupt change of direction is shadowed by an alternative and, in this case, opposite course of action. This discontinuously continuous relationship with England colours Byron's life history and also his poetics.

Our experiences of reading, teaching and studying Romantic poetics have been enriched over the last two decades by critical attention to historical context and gender. In the last five years, a resurgence of interest in form, genre and poetics has enabled us to reflect on how selective some of those early definitions of 'historical context' were. The recovery of socio-political and cultural contexts sometimes tended to overlook the aesthetics of Romantic period works. More recently, however, critics have begun to unite the traditional strengths of close formal analysis with attention to the shaping dynamics of historical contexts.

Following Stuart Curran's absorbing study of the Romantic poets' uses of traditional poetic forms within eighteenth-century generic boundaries, Richard Cronin, Michael O'Neill, Jerome McGann and Susan Wolfson have redirected attention to the ways in which a text's relationship with its readers may sculpt and energise form.[3] Cronin's *In Search of the Pure Commonwealth: The Politics of Romantic Poetry* (2000), O'Neill's *Romanticism and the Self-Conscious Poem* (1997), McGann's *The Poetics of Sensibility: A Revolution in Literary Style* (1996) and Wolfson's *Formal Charges: The Shaping of Poetry in British Romanticism* (1997) have in different ways redirected attention to the aesthetic and affective contours of Romantic poetry, highlighting the extent to which poetic form had been neglected in earlier revisionary historicist studies of the period.

The recovery of women writers in the Romantic period has also provoked a reassessment of the aesthetic audacity of the canonical Romantic poets. The technical virtuosity of women writers, coupled with their decorous reticence within well-defined generic categories, are now seen to have inspired some of the formal experiments of the 'Big Six'. While Francis Jeffrey praised Felicia Hemans for her 'serenity of execution', however, he identified Byron's poetry with the disturbing experience of being 'at once torn and transported'.[4] The tension between continuity and rupture associated with Byron's poetry by Jeffrey and his contemporaries emerges subsequently as a determining characteristic in Elizabeth Barrett Browning's 'Stanzas on the Death of Lord Byron' and Felicia Hemans's 'The Lost Pleiad'.

For Barrett Browning and Hemans, Byron is associated with a violent collision of presence and absence. 'He *was*, and *is* not!', Barrett Browning's poem begins, using Spenserian stanzas to circle round 'The awful tale of greatness swiftly o'er' (l. 34).[5] Similarly, for Hemans, the myth of the lost Pleiad preserves Byron's absent presence: 'And is there glory from the heavens departed? – / O! void unmark'd!'[6] Although the poem identifies steady feminine value in the 'Unchanged' sister Pleiads who 'Still hold their place on high', it keeps returning to the moment of fracture when Byron's orb 'started' away: 'Hath the night lost a gem?'; 'Couldst thou be shaken?'

The shock of Byron's death in Greece was registered as yet another textual fissure in William Hazlitt's *The Spirit of the Age*. News of the poet's death literally interrupts the essay, creating a 'void' marked by a constellation of asterisks. Inscribing in print this sense of abrupt departure, displacement and interruption, Hazlitt, Barrett Browning and Hemans drew on a new syntax of disruption which was already marked as Byronic. Such instances when the reader is jolted out of secure knowledge can only be addressed in a line-by-line encounter with the text, not through any generalised overview. Byron's unsettling uses of the fragment, satire, mixed or medley forms, obtrusive allusion and Romantic irony are all moments when the reading process is disturbed by his art of digression.

'The matter of digression is the key to Byron's method', Jerome McGann states, but we cannot fully understand this method if we confine our notion of digression simply to conversational deviation from the plot.[7] Rather, Byron's digressions comprehend multiple challenges to a placid readerly experience. Throughout his poetic career, Byron developed an ever-shifting repertoire of strategies for changing the subject. While popular contemporaries such as Walter Scott, Felicia Hemans, William Wordsworth and LEL perfected reassuring modes of readerly address, Byron's relationship with his public was marked by abrupt transitions and discontinuities. Even within the perceived sameness of the Byronic hero in the oriental tales, Byron aggravated his audience. 'I suppose you have read Lord Byron's Giaour', Anna Barbauld remarked in a letter to her friend, Mrs Beecroft (anticipating the discussion between Anne Elliot and Captain Benwick in Chapter 11 of *Persuasion*):

– and which edition? because there are five, and in every one he adds about fifty lines; so that the different editions have rather the sisterly likeness which Ovid says the Nereids had, than the identity expected by purchasers of the same work. And pray do you say Lord Bӯron or Bẙron? . . . And do you pronounce Giaour hard *g* or soft *g*? And do you understand the poem at first reading? – because Lord Byron and the Edinburgh Reviewers say you are very stupid if you don't, and yet the same Reviewers have thought proper to prefix the story to help your apprehension.[8]

Barbauld shrewdly envisages a publishing ploy behind the teasing serpentine release of *The Giaour*. Its narrative toying with an audience has provoked much critical debate, but most of this has tended to buttress a reconstruction of the Byronic hero. The effect of narrative unpredictability on the reader and the reader's subsequent part in the construction of meaning, registered at the time, were rapidly overshadowed by the potency of biographical myth.[9] It has taken a long time, but this traditional focus on the character of the poet-hero has been challenged by the in-creasingly diverse contextualising energies of historical criticism.

For Byron's most sophisticated historicist critics, his digressive tech-niques called attention to the poems' self-reflexive relationship to their historical moment. Voicing the post-colonial concerns of the later 1980s, Nigel Leask considered 'Romanticism's sense of its own problematic *modernity*' exhibited in self-conscious antiquarian techniques, 'placing the "original" ballad within a discontinuous historical or geopolitical field and posing questions about the moral and cultural significance of heroic and epical values in the context of a "progressive" present'.[10] Leask argued that 'Byron's critique of empire broadens out into a critique of modernity itself', and he developed Truman Guy Pratt's 1957 reading of *Lara* by suggesting that the 'narrative anxiety' of that poem predicts the 'dark mythic forces of Fascism and totalitarianism'.[11] Leask's notion of a disruptive European modernity 'cut loose from tradition' anticipated Jerome Christensen's suggestion that 'the modernity of *Juan*'s dispensa-tion is that neither the narrator nor anyone else can claim on cognitively reliable grounds to be its father. The narrator must forcibly institute the grounds of his own authority, summoning as he does so the maddening aporia of self-legitimating authority.'[12] In Christensen's reading, 'cutting loose' from tradition paradoxically generates an acutely self-conscious reliance on tradition, as we can see in his discussion of the ' "Carpe diem" ' exhortation of *Don Juan* canto xi: ' "Life's a poor player," – then "play out the play," ' (xi. 86):

> The quotation marks are what Hazlitt calls an 'infliction of the present' on the incorporated maxim, the sign of a time when the existence of the 'common place' is itself at stake ... The citation attempts to generate for the maxim a normative transcendence of the moment of audition.[13]

As we shall see, placing quotation marks at 'the moment of audition' has implications for the reader as well as for the status of quoted mate-rial. Christensen's isolation of the 'aporia of self-legitimating authority' affects both reader and narrator; the reader of Byron's poetry is always implicated in this heightened awareness of the 'now' of the text. From the beginning of Byron's career, an increasingly risky relationship between poet and reader generated the meaning of the poem as they collabo-rated – or not – in realising textual digressions within a tightly controlled formal patterning.

Christensen's emphasis on *Don Juan* as context rather than as an au-thored text extended Jerome McGann's foundational work on the moral and generic parameters of digression within Byron's epic style. McGann's accounts of Byron's digressions depended upon 'the biographical substructure' of a mythic personality in *Fiery Dust* (1968) and the 'total field' of 'history, tradition, facts' in *Don Juan in Context* (1976).[14] Based on his perception of 'local consequences . . . injected into the larger field of the poem as a whole', McGann's unifying of Byron's style under a philosophical or moral ideal gradually but inevitably sacrificed a realisation of Byron's poetry at the level of the reading experience, a level I think we now need to recover.[15] As with Christensen, the critical conception of the whole ('the key words' or 'the most significant stylistic elements') tended to eclipse the particularity of the reading experience.[16]

While McGann discussed the digressive form of the English cantos of *Don Juan* 'in order to explain, if not to justify, Byron's procedure', the 'formalities of explanation' themselves come under scrutiny in James Chandler's thoughtful and ultra self-conscious scrutiny of Romantic texts in *England in 1819: The Politics of Literary Culture and the Case of Romantic Historicism* (1998).[17] Chandler developed a method of 'performative self-consciousness' to examine Byron's modernisation of epic form. In the novelistic *Don Juan*, Chandler suggested, Byron followed Scott in creating a new form of contemporaneity which itself anticipated the manoeuvres of Byron's historically self-conscious commentators in the late twentieth century. Identifying a tension between what is 'perspicuous' and what constitutes the 'labile ironies' in *Don Juan*, Chandler approached the texture of the poem's historical moment.[18] His 'work of explanation' ends when the critic finds himself 'suspended' in contradiction. By focusing on some of those points of contradiction and suspense, *Byron, Poetics and History* re-examines the poem's relationship with its reader at particular historical moments.[19]

The omnipresence of post-modern narrative in film, television and advertising has ensured that in the 1980s and 1990s the notion of the reader as co-producer became widely accepted in popular culture as well as literary criticism. Locating Romantic self-reflexiveness in relation to post-modern film narrative, William Galperin has examined the ways in which Romantic texts question an omniscient authorial position and acknowledge their own materiality. Efforts to make Byron into a modernist or post-modernist, he argued, derive from Byron's 'virtual exclusion from the more liberal, humanistic conceptions of the romantic achievement . . . by critics such as M.H. Abrams and Harold Bloom'.[20] Galperin's fascinating deconstructive analysis of *Childe Harold's Pilgrimage* and *Don Juan* suggests that *Don Juan* might be less deconstructively 'advanced' than aspects of the first cantos of *Childe Harold*:

> If the most mature aspects of *Childe Harold's Pilgrimage* represent a resistance
> to writing ... and to the totalizing visions writing ordinarily serves, then *Don
> Juan* would seem to confirm Byron's claim that his earlier poems were more
> advanced than anything he had produced subsequently ... For all of *Don
> Juan's* various subversions, it is also the case that these are circumscribed by
> writing. [21]

In this critique of *Don Juan's* 'notable faith in writing', literary production
is exclusively author-centred, omitting any reference to the poem's anxieties about its readers. Galperin's separate discussions of *Childe Harold's
Pilgrimage* and *Don Juan* overlook the way that the later cantos of *Don
Juan* revisit Byron's earlier poems in an ironic manner (which Galperin
might well have connected with post-modern film and music). Both the
narrator of *Don Juan* and the director of *Chinatown* (to use Galperin's
cinematic example) use unexpected returns and recurrences to test and
modify the relationship between reader and text.

In her stimulating analysis of an absent presence in *Don Juan* (more
present for the poem's first readers than it is today), Moyra Haslett has
explored the scandalous associations of the Don Juan legend in Byron's
own time. Her book offers an illuminating survey of Regency attitudes
to male and female libertinism, concluding with parallels between Don
Juan and Baudrillard's definition of the 'consummate seducer'.[22] The
effect of the theoretical coda is to place both these texts in an a-historical
continuum of 'masculinist ideology': 'The subversive potential of both
Don Juan and *De la séduction* collapses under, as indeed it returns to, the
conventional asymmetry of the sexes' (*Byron's* Don Juan, p. 288). Here
we witness the surrender of the particular to the general which typifies
considerations of the poem where formal texture is neglected: amidst
all the meticulously researched detail about *Don Juan's* cultural contexts,
there is no room for any discussion of the seductive potential embodied
in feminine rhyme or the movement of *ottava rima*. The monograph's
neglect of poetic form is emphasised by Clarendon Press's ironing-out
of the irregularities of *ottava rima* with a justified left-hand margin.

Turning from historical considerations of Romantic poetry to more
philosophical critical approaches, many theorists of Romantic irony
have contemplated the impact of Byron's self-reflexive digressions. Irving
Babbitt famously saw Byron's sudden transitions as an egotistical impo-
sition on the reader: 'It is as though he would inflict upon the reader
the disillusion from which he has himself suffered. By his swift passage

from one mood to another (*Stimmungsbrechung*) he shows that he is subject to no centre. The effect is often that of a sudden breaking of the spell of poetry by an intrusion of the poet's ego.'[23] Babbitt's account of the working of Romantic irony in Byron's *Don Juan* depicts the reader at the mercy of the whims of the poet rather than participating in the breaks and qualifications in the poetic surface. It is a classic high Modernist conception of the arrogant artist, and it is unable to admit the possibility of the poet spilling tea or responding to reviews. Although the quotidian actions of the poet might seem the province of the biographer, they have as much impact on the production of texts as broader cultural contexts and help us to recover the nervous vulnerability of Romantic texts to their readers.[24] The legacy of Friedrich Schlegel's Romantic irony, in particular, has had the effect of elevating the poet to a god-like status, as if to fill the theological gap created by its first premises. It becomes a form of transcendence, rising infinitely above everything finite and accidental and is just as remote from the materiality of Byron's scrawled instructions to his publisher as Roland Barthes's conception of the author as textual 'function'.

In a later account of Romantic irony, Anne K. Mellor connected Byron's 'exuberant *mobilité*' with the texts of Yeats, Joyce and Nabokov which '*play* between order and chaos' and allow the reader to participate in 'liminality'.[25] For Mellor, the texts of Byron and other Romantic ironists offer 'pleasure, psychic health, and intellectual freedom'; more than this, 'Romantic irony . . . can potentially free individuals and even entire cultures from totalitarian modes of thought and behaviour.'[26] Mellor's Romantic irony is a positive inverse of Jerome McGann's Romantic ideology – a kind of global, democratising process which liberates texts and readers across continents. Yet, we may be wary that this generous, liberal panoply is nevertheless a-historical in its treatment of literary modes, and inattentive to other crucial textual dynamics.

In Mellor's early work – as also in the influential studies of the 1970s and 1980s by Paul de Man, Geoffrey Hartman, Tilottama Rajan and David Simpson – Romantic irony helped to efface consideration of historical context and gender. While appearing to celebrate the possibilities of undecidability and openness, it tended to consolidate a male-dominated canonical Romanticism rooted in high Modernism. For Mellor, Byron the Romantic ironist was 'Schlegel's hero, the urbane man of liberal imagination and tolerance' (*English Romantic Irony*, p. 31). Likewise, Tilottama Rajan presented Byron's approach to 'radical modernism' as an heroic quest: 'In *Don Juan* he tries to become a modern poet and to make irony into a *modus vivendi*. But ... in that very process he declares the need for the resolution forged by Keats and Shelley, whose final poems reach beyond Byron's precisely because they do not reach as far.'[27] Rajan described the self-irony of *Don Juan* as a momentary apprehension of the high Modernism of Wallace Stevens, insulating art from natural or historical process (*Dark Interpreter*, p. 137). Her searching study of Keats and Percy Bysshe Shelley in the light of modern existentialism suggested that it was the hitherto unquestioned domination of high Modernism by male theorists which led to the relative neglect of what we might see as the 'feminine' aspects of Byron's poetic texture and (until recently) literature across the Romantic period.

The poet appeared again as masculine Enlightenment hero in Frederick Garber's eloquent and compelling study of Byron as a Romantic ironist. Garber argued that Byron's discursive variety 'is strung on an obsessive singleness of seeing, a vision of the world's radical discordance and of the fearsome and pervasive threat that discordance poses to all the symmetries of the self'.[28] In this reading, Romantic irony was aligned (as in Babbitt's reading) with Swiftian satire as a way of countering the 'destructive ironies of the world' and answering 'assaults on the self'.[29] Garber acknowledged that Swift was 'as devious' as Byron in his 'implication of the reader', but was primarily concerned with the 'mastery' of the ironist's performance in the 'perpetual making and remaking of self and text'.[30] This emphasis drew what Garber calls the 'commonplaces' of illusion-breaking and sudden shifts of tone into a unified and stringently Modern project: 'His purpose was to purify the language of the tribe.'[31] Garber's quest for stability is a traditional one, close to William Empson's much earlier anchoring of ambiguity: 'The object of life, after all, is not to understand things, but to maintain one's defences and equilibrium and live as well as one can.'[32] The importance of critical control over digressive and discordant possibilities is, of course, a masculine ideal which has persisted since Plato banned poets from his Republic.

Among all the deconstructive explorations of Romantic irony, Michael G. Cooke was the only critic to suggest that it might be a mode receptive to 'new potential and new risks ... inseparable from the feminine figure'.[33] Once we shake ourselves free from the demand that poetry and criticism should express a manly, unified purpose, we can discover the possibilities of affiliation between Byron's poetics and a more feminised aesthetic theory. In particular, I consider the role of 'feminine Caprice' as vital to Byron's digressive mode and an important adaptation of his eighteenth-century Popean legacy in the light of a very different sense of the readership.

Previous discussions of Byron's digressive relationship with the reader through historical self-consciousness or intertextuality exemplify similar critical procedures: the critic selects a premise for comparison and proceeds to decontextualise the modern text and Byronic text as if historical contingencies of reception might threaten critical continuity. Hermione de Almeida's linkage of Byron's and James Joyce's 'serious attempt to emulate and rival' Homeric myth typified this transcendent assumption about the stability of poetic form. 'By seeming to digress', de Almeida observes, 'Byron and Joyce show the domination of their immortal minds.'[34] Literary modes and figures of speech are bound to recur in later and still later works of literature, but as they reappear, they acquire different meanings which are contingent on historical contexts and the role of the reader.

Although it is an instinctive and entrancing critical gesture to trace parallels between different writers, it is of limited critical usefulness to point out that bits of Byron are like bits of Joyce, or Auden, or Nabokov, or Melville or Muldoon (although the temptation to record these resemblances remains very strong and at times, irresistible). What I think we recognise when we make such a-historical connections (the reader's version of literary allusion) is the way that certain textual manoeuvres invite contingency into the text, leaving more room for the reader within the activity of composition. To put it another way, in the process of reading, we tend to experience texts as the author's contemporary (whereas when we reflect critically on them, we place them historically). That experience of contemporaneousness and historical difference is one of the most distinctive qualities of reading Byron.

This book examines, in a necessarily speculative manner, the ways in which Byron's digressive contingency is historically rooted and develops in relation to particular readers. Although Byron imagines a future readership ('But ye – our children's children! think how we / Showed *what things were* before the world was free!'), the aim of this book is not to explore what Andrew Bennett calls 'the culture of posterity', but to examine how networks of anticipated and actual reading responses affected Byron's texts at the time of composition and publication.[35] One context which has dominated discussion of Byronic digression since the nineteenth century is the concept of poetic *mobilité* which Byron discussed in his famous footnote about Adeline in *Don Juan* canto xvi. In subsequent criticism, however, this concept has resulted in the unifying of diverse effects under the imprint of a biographical personality and distracting attention from the reader's experience of the 'painful and unhappy attribute'.[36]

Closer attention to the texture of Byron's poetry at the level of the reading experience helps to recover the dialectical relationship between Byron's readers and his mobile poetic surface. For this reason, I have chosen to focus my book on Byron's satirical works, especially *Don Juan*. Satire is a notoriously digressive mode and its hybridity was one reason Stuart Curran excluded it from his study of Romantic poetic form. Since Curran's work, however, Frederick L. Beaty, Stephen C. Behrendt, Steven E. Jones and Gary Dyer have published important studies which correct the critical neglect of satire in Romantic culture.[37] Building on their research, this book considers some of Byron's less well-known writing from *Fugitive Pieces* (1806), *Hours of Idleness* (1807), *Hints from Horace* (1811 and 1820–1), the *Letter to John Murray Esqre.* (1821) and *The Age of Bronze* (1823), revealing the ways in which Byron's art of digression developed in response to various readers – whether individual acquaintances, critics, or the English reading public as variously conceived between 1812 and 1823 (including the ghostly existence of an ex-readership).

My book is concerned to recover the vitality of formal matters in Byron's poetry, but this consideration of form is intended to be alert also to the contingencies of readerly participation and the historical matrices of literary composition. Andrew Elfenbein's *Byron and the Victorians* set out to 're-examine the historicity of influence' and 'to suggest how historicising the workings of influence, with particular reference to Byron, enables a rethinking of the significance of Victorian texts'.[38] Whereas his work offers a valuable analysis of Byron's relationship with the later nineteenth century, *Byron, Poetics and History* is more concerned with Byron's immediate impact on early nineteenth-century readers. The main focus of Elfenbein's study was writing of the inner self, so that although he successfully complicated the concept of the Byronic hero in Victorian literature, he devoted little attention to the ways in which Victorian writers received the materiality of Byron's *ottava rima* writing. In his chapter on Carlyle, for example, Elfenbein concentrated on Teufelsdröckh as a means of supplanting the Byronic hero with the character of a professional intellectual. By contrast, my book points forward to a re-examination of the 'labyrinthic combination' of *Sartor Resartus* or the 'glaciers' Ruskin found in Robert Browning's poetry, and the 'holes', 'ledges', 'bits' and 'breaks' Browning himself defended.[39]

In common with the earliest dedicated studies of digression in Byron's writing by E.D.H. Johnson, William T. Ross and Joel Dana Black, critics in recent years have all relied on a paradigm which places digression in relation to a totalising conception of the completed work.[40] By tracing the different manifestations of Byronic digression in momentary paren-thetical asides and fleeting signalled allusions to other texts or contextual events, I argue that Byron's digressiveness challenged eighteenth-century moral ideals of aesthetic completion such as taste or harmony, and emerg-ing nineteenth-century aesthetic ideals of organic unity. We need to re-cover the abruptness and discontinuity of Byron's generic deflections on the printed page before we can appreciate the reader's response to mo-ments of textual indeterminacy as a crucial part of the meaning of the poem. In this respect, Wolfgang Iser's dynamic account of the response of the reader to certain texts has been very useful to me, although I do not follow Iser's view that textual indeterminacy decreases as the reader makes his or her choice about how to proceed. In my reading of Byron's *Don Juan*, for example, I believe that digressions keep the reader aware of alternative routes so that a sense of indeterminacy is heightened even as a choice about interpretation is made.[41] Byron's poetics of digression invites his readers to negotiate the general and the particular in an in-finitely more complex way than in the writing of some of his critics, asking us to reconsider how we relate concepts of parts and whole. In so doing, Byron's textual procedures might be seen to anticipate the theoretical debate about the value of imaginative activity in an intellectual climate of utilitarianism which John Whale has recently identified in the writing of Hazlitt, Coleridge and Mill.[42] The present book identifies Byron's focus on individual aesthetic response in the digressive modes of juxta-position, transition and intertextuality, and examines these in relation to the shifting historical contexts which helped to shape their meaning.

To attend to formal texture, historical context and reader response, I use familiar reader-centred and author-centred approaches. The book begins with separate reader- and author-oriented sections before moving towards an approach which brings them together. The first chapter is reader-centred; it offers a fresh examination of Byron's contemporary reviews, focusing particularly on the ways in which Byron's writing was perceived to disturb its readers through sudden turns, transitions and allusions. This instability was not only identified with the later *ottava rima* (the dominant later nineteenth-century view of Byron), but was detected by Byron's contemporaries from an early date in the first two cantos of *Childe Harold's Pilgrimage* (1812). Here, satiric interpolations and whimsical prose notes were condemned for disrupting what the reader expected from poetry. I argue that although these forms of digression provoked

hostility among Byron's readers, they quickly became an identifiable part
of his poetic and political identity – so much so, indeed, that his later
experiments with *ottava rima* verse appeared to have been predicted by
his readers.

Digressive poetics may be traced back to a range of literary traditions.
My second chapter offers a literary context for Byron's forms of disruption, looking back to eighteenth-century writers who preceded him
in their use of self-reflexive narrative, juxtaposition and parodic quotation. The chapter is author-centred, foregrounding the work of Charles
Churchill, Laurence Sterne and Matthew Prior. I also suggest that prologues written for specific theatrical productions also provided Byron
with another model for digressive mediation between text and audience,
and so modified his use of closed heroic couplets in a way which would be
fully realised in *The Age of Bronze*. The materiality of Byronic digression,
I argue, created a form of theatre (somewhat different from the 'mental
theatre' of *Manfred*) in which textual disruption was co-produced by
poet and audience, at first resisting, but gradually incorporating a much
greater receptiveness to historical matter.

Chapter Three investigates a section of Byron's audience in more detail, considering the role of some of the specific readers addressed in
Hints from Horace, and treating the poet as a 'reader' of his own earlier
work. The 1811 and 1820–1 texts of *Hints from Horace* bridge Byron's early
and later verse without imposing an over-simplified trajectory of development onto his career. The chapter reconsiders *Hints from Horace* as a
dialogue between Byron's early and later critiques of the Lake School,
which turned into a debate between Byron and his friends about the
politics of publication. This chapter also considers the construction of
'Byron's Pope' and suggests that the different receptions of Pope's *mobilité*
amongst Byron, his publisher and other English readers help to define
the changing face of the readership which influenced Byron's poetry
throughout his career. Analysis of different digressive characteristics in
Hints from Horace suggests that Byron's quotation of other texts creates a
chiaroscuro of intertextuality quite distinct from other kinds of Romantic
allusion. An examination of unpublished letters from the John Murray
Archive charts some of the hitherto concealed details of the poem's historical moment, and explores the poem's interventions in a public debate
about literary taste.

Byron's later work on *Hints from Horace* coincided with his break from
John Murray in 1822 over the publication of *Don Juan*, and the continuation of that poem under John Hunt's imprint. My fourth chapter
mixes author- and reader-centred approaches to the digressive texture

of *Don Juan*, particularly in the harem episode (canto VI) and the siege cantos (cantos VII and VIII). Building on the idea of theatrical resources introduced in Chapters One and Two, and the idea of poetic chiaroscuro discussed in Chapter Three, I offer a close reading of the effects of Shakespearean drama in *Don Juan*, showing how the reader may, or may not, recognise this strand and co-produce its metamorphosis into sexual comedy. Modifying earlier readings of *Don Juan* which have identified Byron's allusion as a means of establishing narrative control and personal stability, this book suggests that various configurations of Shakespearean drama in Byron's work transfer the focus of instability on to the response of the reader. The reader's response to the riskiness of this procedure is, I argue, a vital aspect of Byron's poetics of digression.

The fifth chapter builds on the argument of Chapter Four, suggesting that while digression offers a poetics of indeterminacy, aesthetic form is always shaped by context. This chapter is concerned with the intermingling of the 'low' cultural field of contemporary journalism with the 'high' cultural field of literary allusion in *Don Juan*. In particular I use new archive research to identify interwoven reports from the newspaper *Galignani's Messenger* in satiric passages in the poem. I suggest that editorials from this newspaper inflect Byron's references to England in the English cantos, and that this should qualify a prevailing view, elaborated by E.D.H. Johnson, McGann and Graham, that Byron was sadly out of touch with and nostalgic about English society.[43] This chapter also examines the contiguities between Byron's textual instability and various tropes of femininity in the poem, developing recent feminist analyses of *Don Juan* by Caroline Franklin, Moyra Haslett and Susan Wolfson.[44] The chapter closes with a reading of Byron's 'frozen champagne' stanzas in canto XIII which beautifully illustrate the intricate, shifting layers of Byronic digression and suggest some of the contingencies in the poem's address to its community of readers. This individual instance of digression exemplifies how *Don Juan* renders the concrete details of its historical period as literature, while simultaneously leaving the literary texture of the poem open to the random particulars of the world. Byron's hospitality to the uncertainties of historical events invites a comparison with post-Modern theories of textuality in which the reader is engaged in the undecidability of a surface rather than in the interpretation of symbols; but to label Byron as a post-Modernist runs the risk of distorting his historical particularity.[45]

The sixth and final chapter focuses on *The Age of Bronze*, examining the fascinating implications of Byron's return to this traditional form of satire at a moment when he was also engaged with the *ottava rima* satire of

Don Juan's English cantos. The chapter looks at the ways in which Whig factionalism shaped the direction of Byron's satire and responses to the poem. In particular, I argue that Byron's formal experiments with *The Age of Bronze* and *The Island* in between cantos XII and XIII of *Don Juan* represent a political stance rather different from the accepted view of Byron's aristocratic Whig poetic identity. Building on my discussion of the Pope/Bowles controversy in Chapter Three, I examine what Byron's last turn to couplet satire tells us about critical differences between his work and Pope's, and how his use of a feminine digressive persona in *Don Juan* is tested and affirmed in his last digressive swerves.

Throughout this book there is a deliberate concentration on local effects rather than any over-arching survey of Byron's complete works. The main reason for this is that poetic texture in Romantic literature and Byron's work in particular has been relatively neglected. A study which directs close attention to small-scale formal matters will always invite the objection that it lacks an adequate concept of the general. As the first chapter of this book demonstrates, this response permeated the classically-informed reviews of Byron's poetry in his own time. Since the reviews of Francis Jeffrey and William Roberts, Byron has not been short of critics who have unified his digressive poetics under their own religious or political preoccupations. My book attempts to correct an imbalance in those studies which, with a few exceptions, have set out to regulate Byron's digressions and to systematise the strange conjunctions of violence and polish in his poetics. This book adopts an approach which is more sensitive to the local, the contingent and the individual case.

'When a man talks of system', Byron wrote of Leigh Hunt, 'his case is hopeless.'[46] For the reasons I give below, literary theory informs this book non-systematically. It will be obvious that post-structuralist theoretical models have enabled us to talk about the liberating pleasure of digression in a way which was not possible for Byron's contemporary reviewers. Bakhtinian ideas about carnival and chronotype have been employed productively in Byron criticism for several years. Julia Kristeva's reading of Bakhtin on Menippean discourse helpfully opens up the value of scandal and eccentricity in language: 'This discourse is made up of contrasts ... It uses abrupt transitions and changes; high and low, rise and fall, and misalliances of all kinds ... It is an all-inclusive genre, put together as a pavement of citations.'[47] The French feminist writings of Julia Kristeva, Luce Irigaray and Hélène Cixous together with the later work of Roland Barthes all offer models for a positive assessment of Byron's destabilising textual practices. In particular, the idea of readerly and writerly acceptance of risk draws on what Cixous has defined as a feminine libidinal economy, while the weaving metaphor I invoke to describe Byron's poetic texture is indebted to the feminist poetics of Irigaray, Nancy K. Miller and Alice Jardine.[48] However, the complete ideological matrix of each writer would in each case reproduce 'their' Byron, not mine. Throughout the book I aim to keep formal contours in touch with historical contexts and instead of advancing a theoretically systematised thesis, my study interweaves discussions of and encounters with individual case studies.

Any adequate theoretical model for Byron's textual digressiveness would need to capture some – or all – of the following characteristics: a delight in form; an awareness of how history inflects form; a sensitivity to the changing regard of the reader; an awareness of multiple paths available through a work of literature but not all taken; a sense of relativity and responsibility; an alertness to particularity and scale; an appreciation of affirmative forms of indeterminacy. Distinguished writing on Byron this century has touched on some of these needs; Jerome McGann, for example, has described the 'generosity' of Byron's writing in arguing that the dynamic driving Byron's writing is inadequately represented as a 'dialectical form':

> *Don Juan* does something more than set in motion Byron's version of Kierkegaard's either/or problematic. The poem's contradictions ... deconstruct all truth-functions which are founded either in (metaphysical) Identity or (psychological) Integrity. In their place is set a truth-function founded (negatively) in contradiction itself, and (positively) in metonymy: to the negative either/or dialectic, *Don Juan* adds the procedural rule of 'both/and.'[49]

What we have in Byron's writing, McGann suggests, is 'a third being . . . the awareness of the unresolved characters of original opposition.'[50] I have argued that in digressive allusion this 'third being' is an invitation to the reader to make the casting vote, while preserving the awareness that there is always another way to move forward. It is important to stress that *Don Juan* does not offer infinite 'unresolvability' but emphasises readerly and writerly responsibility. Byron's poetics offers the possibility of an affirmative texture of indeterminacy because its meaning is not located in transcendence of the text, but in the local negotiations between the text and its reader.

Here modern French theory falls short of Byron's technique; feminist theory, for example, relies too extensively on Lacanian assumptions. This means that the critic is occupied by asking to what system does any

reading subscribe – rather than asking what any reading might create.
In digressive allusion, the reader's potential to create offers a way of
questioning the Lacanian 'Law', as I suggest in Chapter Five. A problem
with Derridean theory in relation to Byron's poetry is almost the opposite
one, that while deconstructive '*jouissance*' is suggestive of the affirmative
dynamic of Byron's 'ever-varying rhyme', deconstructive resistance to
'rule-governed scenarios' is not.[51] An *ottava rima* stanza is 'a rule governed
scenario', and the materiality of *Don Juan*'s language can work as political
agency precisely because the reader is invited to limit textual *jouissance*.
We feel this pressure, for example, in the multiplicity of puns in the siege
cantos which ensnare us in the lush and sinister way of Andrew Marvell's
'The Garden'. Derridean deconstruction can offer suggestive models for
a dynamic of disruption, undecidability, and moments where reader and
writer are be-labyrinthed in language, but its elating momentum defers
forever the urgency of readerly discrimination, construction and responsibility for one's decisions, all of which are vital to the fabric of *Don Juan*.

The texture of Byronic digression enables us to reconsider the relationship between the general and the particular, not just in Byron's work,
but in our readings of all Romantic poetry. There has been a growing
post-Derridean awareness, shared by both Marxist and formalist critics,
that subversion cannot exist – or exist effectively – throughout a text.
'Pure difference ... is as blank and tedious as pure identity ... there
can be no talk of difference or dissonance without some provisional con-
figurating of the particulars in question', Terry Eagleton has remarked.
Frank Kermode makes the same point in defence of mythic wholeness:
'without routine, without inherited structures, carnival loses its point;
without social totalities there are no anti-social fragments.'[52] Andrew
Bowie argues that philosophical oversights by post-modern thinkers such
as Lyotard and Derrida were anticipated by the Romantic philosopher,
Johann Georg Hamann, who 'arrives at his position through a desire to
celebrate difference as the endless articulation of the diversity of God's
universe. God gives him the moment of identity, which makes difference
significant, and which his post-structuralist heirs wrongly think they can
do without.'[53] As I argue in Chapter Three, Byron's poetics asks the
reader to come to terms with the relation of disruptive particularity to
'inherited structures' and the shadow of a universe of order. It is this
urgent involvement of the reader in questions of organisation which, I
argue, constitutes the political force of Byron's poetry.

Provisional and fleeting points of contact between Byron and post-
structuralist writing may be helpful in our attempts to define the

characteristics of a remarkable and complex literary intertexture. In the end, however, Byron's writing resists the totalising discourse of any one theoretical model. It is difficult above all to relate Byron's poetics to models which take no account of the formal properties of poetry. Although Byronic texts challenge the law of genre (as early nineteenth-century reactions to his poetry show), they are energised conceptually and practically by strict adherence to verse structure and resist the disintegration of formal difference which comes with novelisation. Rhyme cannot be endlessly deferred, and poetic form and genre still stand as recognisable, historical presences to which we respond, albeit less violently than Byron and his contemporaries. If we recover the cultural dynamics of, for example, the Pope/Bowles controversy (1819–26), we shall be closer to an element of the Romantic period which makes the works composed at that time so different from one another and so separate from our own time. By bringing the relationship between form, context and reader to a crisis, Byron's digressive poetics challenges us to rethink our assumptions about stability and change in literature and to be aware of the relative, historical state of any critical position. If Romantic literary criticism is going to perform any meaningful dialogue with a wider audience it needs to be at least as attentive to readers as Romantic poets themselves were. It also needs to account for the momentary experiences of pleasure and surprise engendered by reading Romantic poems. As J. Paul Hunter observes, 'theory has a crucial place ... Still, one has to find a theory appropriate to the text, and that may also involve finding an appropriate theory for the form.'[54] This book is an endeavour in that direction.

CHAPTER ONE

'Scorching and drenching': discourses of digression among Byron's readers

Max Beerbohm's picture of 'Lord Byron, shaking the dust of England from his shoes' (1904) captures the exquisitely self-conscious turn away from the English public Byron was seen to have made in April 1816. That moment of departure also signalled a turning-point in his reputation – or so the familiar outline of his career has led us to believe. The separation scandal is usually presented as the definitive break between Byron, London society and the adulation of his English readership.[1] There is strong evidence, however, to suggest that Byron's readers were already alert to and unsettled by this kind of behaviour, not least because his poetics of rapid transition, modulation and subversive aside raised awkward questions from the start of his career. Critical expressions of unease offer us a reader-centred view of digressive poetics and a fresh way of approaching the unique texture of Byron's verse.[2]

Scholars of Byron's and other Romantic poets' receptions in England have, of course, noted that his work was always controversial. But they have not analysed the peculiar kinds of misgiving expressed about Byron's poetry, nor have they traced the evolving significance of this kind of critical discourse. The extensive reviews of Byron's publications during his lifetime are evidence that, for his contemporaries, digression covered a multitude of sins including misanthropic or political perversion, contradictory principles, sudden changes of tone, and personal or cultural allusions in a variety of shapes and forms. This broader understanding of digression, rather than the strict structuralist definition of a (usually lengthy) deviation from the narrative subject, enables us to see the mixture of aesthetic and political factors that made Byron's poetics so disturbing for his contemporary readers. A digression may be as short as a single word in parenthesis or quotation marks or it may extend, as it did for Byron's readers, to include most of a canto or most of a career.

One important feature of Byronic digression is that it offers its readers the experience of an encounter with awkward historical particulars coupled with the experience of conflicting textual worlds. When Byron interrupts his verse, readers are forced to accept a new thread of poetic development, while remaining aware of the relation of this new part to an altered concept of the poetic whole. While the ideal of the whole, unified work of art had been agreed by gentlemanly consensus for most of the eighteenth century, mirroring the ideal of a benign Nature, Byron's poetry raised the possibility that this ideal construction was partial and subject to accident and human intervention. 'All is exploded – be it good or bad' (l. 9), Byron wrote in *The Age of Bronze*, indicating that the stable collective sense of an 'all' had gone as well as the content of the 'all' which made up the traditional *ubi sunt* motif.

The reception of Byron's poetry during his life was a complex affair and cannot simply be glossed as massive popularity for melancholy narratives followed by ostracism for the sociable *mobilité* of *ottava rima* verse. Contemporary reviews reveal widespread concern about the unstable compounds of tone, mood and allusions in Byron's writing from the publication of the first two cantos of *Childe Harold's Pilgrimage*. This early turbulent aspect of Byron's critical reception was overshadowed in the nineteenth century by the popularisation of the Byronic hero – 'the wither'd heart that would not break' – and in the twentieth, by an emphasis on the weight of Romantic self-consciousness – 'I write, write, write, as the Wandering Jew walks, walks, walks.'[3]

Critical emphasis on nature, sublimity and the transcendent mind reinforced the classification of late Byron as an 'anti-Romantic' or psychological oddity. M.H. Abrams famously omitted Byron from his discussion of Romantic literature in *Natural Supernaturalism* (1971) 'because in his greatest work he speaks with an ironic counter-voice and deliberately opens a satirical perspective on the vatic stance of his Romantic contemporaries'.[4] This segregation seemed natural and inevitable because it fulfilled the 'either/or' canons of criticism that had always characterised the reception of Byron's work. But Abrams need not have read Byron's irony as the 'deliberate' undermining of Romantic vision: his choice of the musical metaphor 'counter-voice' suggests the co-existence of two or more voices in juxtaposition; 'the action of placing two or more things side by side' (*OED*) offers the possibility of oscillation or simultaneity.

Byron's 'counter-voice' questioned both traditional morality agreed by social consensus and the emergent aesthetic of individual sincerity defined against society. Nineteenth-century readers feared that Byron's juxtaposition of serious and comic elements would automatically undermine

all moral seriousness including the integrity of personal and social relationships. This worry contributed to the idea of Byron's 'perversion',
the term used by Francis Jeffrey to characterise the perniciously active
influence of *The Giaour* over its readers:

The sterner and more terrible poetry which is conversant with the guilty and
vindictive passions, is not indeed without its use both in purging and in exalting
the soul: but the delight which it yields is of a less pure, and more overpowering
nature; and the impressions which it leaves behind are of a more dangerous and
ambiguous tendency. Energy of character and intensity of emotion are sublime
in themselves, and attractive in the highest degree as objects of admiration; but
the admiration which they excite, when presented *in combination* with worthless-
ness and guilt, is one of the most powerful corrupters and perverters of our moral
nature; and is the more to be lamented, as it is most apt to exert its influence
on the noblest characters. The poetry of Lord Byron is full of this perversion.
(*RR*, B: II, p. 847; my italics)

Jeffrey used the literal and technical meaning of 'perversion' – 'to turn
round or about, turn the wrong way, overturn . . . to subvert' (*OED*). His
phobia about 'combination' represents the conservative fear of hybridity,
doubt and 'ambiguous tendencies' which may be traced back to Old
Testament injunctions against mixture: 'Thou shalt not sow thy vineyard
with divers seeds . . . Thou shalt not plow with an ox and an ass together.
Thou shalt not wear a garment of divers sorts, as of woollen and linen
together' (Deuteronomy 22.9–11).

   In the course of Byron's poetic career, Jeffrey's very precise use of the
idea of perversion was overlaid by the more generalised apprehension of
moral depravity – a process which continued throughout the nineteenth
century. John Addington Symonds's essay on Byron (1880) displaced the
active sense of perversion in Byron's writing with the view that the poet's
judgement had been 'prematurely warped' before he began to write
poetry and that his 'perverse ideas' were reflexes of self-defence acquired
as a child.[5] By re-examining the first responses to Byron's poetry, we can
recover the textually de-familiarising effects of digression and the ways in
which it brought to a crisis the relationship between poet and reader in
early nineteenth-century Britain. The rest of this chapter focuses on the
cultural significance of digression in the period between the appearance
of the first two cantos of *Childe Harold's Pilgrimage* (1812) and the last
complete cantos of *Don Juan* (1824).

   Byron began his 'years of fame' with an apology for 'variation'. His
first draft of *Childe Harold* involved more abrupt changes of tone, incongruous material and digressive allusions to contemporary social and

political circumstances than the version which was finally published, but the digressive tendency of what remained, even after censorship, caused a stir amongst reviewers.[6] Their varying degrees of critical objection depended on a number of factors including the political affiliation of the periodical and its intended readership. In June 1812 the *Critical Review* (at this time moderately Whig) was one of several to question Byron's invocation of James Beattie as a model:

The use of the burlesque in this poem is, we think, not sufficiently justified by the opinion of Dr. Beattie, which the author has quoted in his preface. The general complexion of the work is serious, and even melancholy. The occasional bursts of humour are, therefore, unpleasant, as breaking in too abruptly upon the general tone of the reader's feelings. What mind can, without very disagreeable sensations, turn on a sudden from the ridiculous picture of the Convention, before alluded to, to the contemplation of the Childe Harold's melancholy mood, and again to the description of a Cockney-Sunday? The latter is, also, pourtrayed in a style of *hackneyed*, not to say vulgar, ridicule, which could not have been much relished, even in a work of lighter composition. (*RR*, B: II, pp. 616–17)

This critique reveals a subtle link between the canons of classical criticism, social class and the criteria of Christian moral judgement: 'vulgarity' or a mingling with quotidian detail is regarded as a shocking intrusion.

During Byron's lifetime, the emphasis of literary criticism was shifting away from general rules of literary taste towards an interest in the psychological effects of literature on individual readers. This shift is manifest in the critical essays of Anna Barbauld, the preface to Joanna Baillie's *A Series of Plays* (1798), and later, the Shakespearean criticism of Samuel Taylor Coleridge, William Hazlitt, and Thomas De Quincey. But eighteenth-century stylistic proscriptions lingered on besides the newly evolving attention to the individual. Critics like the Earl of Shaftesbury, Edmund Burke, Dr Johnson, Lord Kames, George Campbell, Sir Joshua Reynolds and James Beattie had all decreed that 'incongruity' and 'harsh combinations' were to be avoided as departures from established literary form. According to eighteenth-century critical discourse, unexpected juxtapositions – 'turning on a sudden' – would be condemned by the classically-educated reader as a lapse of decorum. For many nineteenth-century critics, in addition, abrupt juxtapositions of pathos and humour appeared as a form of social transgression that might corrupt readers – especially increasing numbers of non-classically educated women.[7]

One of the effects of Byron's writing was to bring the reader to question Johnsonian constructions of normative decorum and taste in poetry. This clash of different cultural values is encapsulated by Maria Edgeworth's description of a party in 1822 at which *Don Juan* was read aloud by Edward Ellice – much against the better judgement of those present:

He *would* read passages of Don Juan to us and to tell you the truth the best of us & Lady Elizabeth herself could not help laughing. Lady Hannah turned her face almost off her shoulder and picked the embroidered corner almost out of her pocket handkerchief and she did *not* laugh.[8]

Edgeworth's letter offers graphic evidence – 'to tell you the truth' – of how unacceptable it was for women to share in public the humour of Byron's poem. The account of Edgeworth and 'the best of' her female companions physically struggling to suppress their laughter shows how values of order and propriety (the embroidered pocket handkerchief) came to be 'unpicked' by Byron's verse. In this instance, the force of the conflict was embodied by the strong reaction of the audience; more often, however, a sense of disjunction, of cultural values buckling under the force of poetic collision, was displaced on to Byron himself.

Voicing a Protestant, dissenting point of view in June 1812, the *Eclectic Review* regarded the asides in *Childe Harold's Pilgrimage* as a flaw in the Childe's characterisation:

There are, however, some inconveniences attending this arrangement of the several parts, appropriated to the author and to the hero of the poem. Sometimes the Childe forgets (accidentally, we believe,) the heart-struck melancholy of his temper, and deviates into a species of pleasantry, which, to say the truth, appears to us very flippant, and very unworthy of the person to whom it is attributed. (*RR*, B: ii, p. 706)

As with Edgeworth's parenthetical 'to tell you the truth', the reviewer's effort 'to say the truth' points to an awkwardness in attempts to define reaction. Byron's 'inconvenience', his 'deviance' and 'species of pleasantry', failed to keep within eighteenth-century conventions of witty incongruity epitomised, for example, in the ultra-conservative essays of James Beattie.[9]

By contrast, the more forward-looking critic William Hazlitt's 'Essay on Wit and Humour' (1818), explored the positive aesthetic fascination of 'juxta-position':

it is the mirror broken into pieces, each fragment of which reflects a new light from surrounding objects; or it is the untwisting chain of our ideas, whereby each link is made to hook on more readily to others than when they were all bound up together by habit.[10]

Hazlitt's stylistic desire to escape from reactionary 'habit' was, of course, something of an anomaly and, as we shall see, Hazlitt was less sure about the value of Byronic fragmentation when it confronted him on the page rather than as an abstract idea. In 1812 readers often attributed Byron's early poetic inconsistencies to 'accidental' misjudgements rather than to a deliberate 'untwisting' of the chain of ideas. However, a hint of the instability which shadowed early readings of Byron is evident when the *Eclectic* applied to Byron what Johnson said of Dryden, that he treads 'upon the brink of meaning where light and darkness begin to mingle'.[11] Having quoted extensively and approvingly from *Childe Harold* to illustrate its 'beauties' the reviewer noted reluctantly that

Lord Byron labours under a very unfortunate mistake as to his gifts and qualifications as a satirist . . . Can it be believed, that the author of the passages we have quoted could write such stanzas as the following? [I. 69–70] Can any thing be more flippant than the foregoing passage? – unless, indeed, it be the ingenious personification of the imp 'Convention,' . . . or the following caustic animadversions on a book called Ida of Athens, the production of a Miss Owenson, who, it seems, is just now a popular writer of novels. (*RR*, B: II, p. 709)

Caught between the desire to chastise Byron for an *ad hominem* attack on a woman and the instinct to patronise a woman novelist, this reviewer identified authorial instability in *Childe Harold*. The *Edinburgh Review*, the *Critical Review* and the *Quarterly Review* all objected to 'those attacks on private feeling' in Byron's notes to the poem, joining the *Eclectic* in finding in Byron's notes 'animadversions' and incongruities which reinforced the wayward digressiveness of the poem's text.[12] Some of the poet's endnotes expressed the topical satire which Murray had advised Byron to suppress – for example the 'expressions concerning Spain and Portugal which', Murray said, 'do not harmonize with the now prevalent feeling'.[13] Murray's sense of a consensus of 'prevalent feeling' points to a new version of the eighteenth-century 'public sphere'. This consensus of domestic 'feeling' rather than Enlightenment debate was partly the result of Britain's war with France.

Internal rupture in the shape of civil war or civil disobedience is particularly threatening when national frontiers are also at risk. As we witness in relations between press and government today, it is still deemed 'bad form' to draw attention to blunders in British foreign policy while British troops are risking their lives abroad. But this is exactly what Byron's poem did. Murray's acute audience sensitivity anticipated the risk of satiric infection in what was otherwise a very popular genre. As Gary Dyer has recently demonstrated, satire persisted throughout the Romantic period,

but it was less present in public or literary discourse than in Pope's or
Swift's day. Dyer also points out that both Neo-Juvenalian and Neo-
Horatian verse satires tended to support a conservative outlook either
because they were anti-Jacobin or quiescent.[14] Byron's satiric interruptions were therefore doubly unexpected because they turned a conservative form against the Tory government of the day.

By far the most hostile reaction to the first cantos of *Childe Harold* came
from the *Antijacobin Review* in a politically-motivated attack on the
'fractious, wayward, capricious, cheerless, morose, sullen, discontented,
and unprincipled' character of the Childe (*RR*, B: 1, p. 11). For this iras-
cible reviewer, the digressiveness of anti-Establishment poet/hero fractured the poem:

> We object, then, to the political prejudices, to the unpatriotic defects, and to the
> irreligious principles, of this bastard of the imagination. He arraigns wars, gen-
> erally, and indiscriminately, confounding the just with the unjust, the defensive
> with the offensive, the preservative with the destructive, not with the judgment
> of a sage, but with the settled moroseness of a misanthrope. (*RR*, B: 1, p. 11)

As the review progressed, similar accusations were extended to Byron's
style and to his politics. Byron's comparison of British and Turkish gov-
ernments was dismissed as the product of 'unsettled principles and wayward mind' (*RR*, B: 1, p. 18). In the period preceding the Reform Act in
1832 the Tory press applied this tag indiscriminately to reformist Whigs
like Sir Francis Burdett and Burkean radicals like William Cobbett. Its
appearance in reviews of Byron's early work indicates that his style was
perceived as a threat to established social hierarchies.

Just as Byron identified himself with frame-breaking in the political
forum of the House of Lords, his refusal to discriminate in matters of
style was equated with democratic principles, while the 'straying' plot and
'mingled' character of the hero were presented as the 'bastard' images of
a liberal imagination.[15] The *Antijacobin* extracted the stanzas on Cintra
(1. 24–6) and quoted Byron's note with the following comment:

> The loose sneers, and sarcastic remarks, which an author, who suffers no restraint
> from principle, may introduce in the course of a poetical narrative, where they
> appear to be merely *incidental*, are calculated to do more mischief, because
> the ordinary reader is not on his guard against them; than laboured treatises,
> composed for the avowed purpose of attacking the settled order of things in any
> state or government. (*RR*, B: 1, p. 13)

Dated August 1812, this is one of the earliest political readings of Byron's
digressive poetics. It is clear that the reviewer was concerned about the

'rant of democracy' (for example 1. 37–44), but his concern extends to the politics of poetic style and the seemingly 'incidental' way in which this material is introduced into poetry: 'the bard seems determined, that the delight which his genius is able to impart shall be marred by the un-seasonable intrusion of his offensive sentiments' (*RR*, B: 1, pp. 15; 14). For this reason, the *Antijacobin* and other reviews italicised offending phrases in their extracts of Byron's poetry, enhancing the effect of an uneven poetic surface.

Byron's sentiments were 'offensive' because they questioned British foreign policy in a genre which was usually the vehicle for patriotic celebration. From the 1790s onwards, war in Europe provided the conditions for the travel poem in English to become a vehicle of cultural consolidation in which the stimulus of different landscapes and societies introduced reflections on the preferability of home. If satire did occur in the travel poem, it was at the expense of other nations. Henry Fox, the son of Byron's Whig mentor, remarked in his diary during a stay in Italy in 1823, 'the whole object of an Englishman when once ferried over Pas de Calais is to compare every thing he sees to the diminutive objects he has passed his existence with, and to make a sort of perpetual justification of his own superiority'.[16] Byron's satire in text and notes directed against British non-achievement and mis-management abroad undermined the expected ideological basis of the literary tour. Anna Barbauld provoked similar outrage when she published the satire *Eighteen Hundred and Eleven*. She was accused of transgressing generic propriety by producing Juvenalian satire, but critics like J.W. Croker also responded to the shock of a 'tour' of a London fallen into ruins, cultural corruption and moral decay. For Byron's reviewers the liberal and oppositional sentiments voiced directly in his poem were reinforced by the unpredictable turnings and inconsistencies of his style.[17]

Byron had claimed that the first two cantos of *Childe Harold* were experimental, a comment which encouraged most reviewers to anticipate greater completion and unity in his next production. Byron thwarted their expectations by producing a 'voluntarily mutilated' composition in full knowledge of the 'general horror of *fragments*'.[18] Besides the choice of poetic form the *Antijacobin* detected a more dangerous instability of 'ambiguity' in *The Giaour*:

It is not that any marked absence of religious or moral principle is betrayed in any particular passages; but that there is a doubt left on the reader's mind by the loose and ambiguous manner in which allusions are made, in different places, to topics of the nature referred to. (*RR*, B: 1, p. 30)

Doubt is dangerous. Byron's 'ambiguity' represented a threat to the religious and political status quo. His line, 'Even bliss -'twere woe alone to bear' was particularly objectionable, noted the reviewer, because

woe and bliss are incompatible; the moment woe comes, bliss is expelled from the heart; they cannot dwell together in the human bosom. We are not converts to the justice of the poet's general position. (*RR*, B: 1, p. 34)

Again, it is the experience of simultaneity which is seen as threatening. Hostile criticism of Byron's style derived from a negative moral assessment of indeterminacy or relativism. The *Antijacobin* succeeded in associating Byron's textual 'incompatibilities' with immaturity, malice, and (eventually) madness. They were delighted to point out that Byron's dedication of *The Corsair* to Thomas Moore represented a personal *volte-face*: 'he does not condescend to state to the public one single reason for the revolution which has taken place in his sentiments ... This is treating the public rather cavalierly' (*RR*, B: 1, p. 41). Stylistic instability could be accounted for by an author 'whose opinions and whose principles are as unsettled as the wind; and who seems to take delight only in venting the splenetic effusions of a restless, wayward, and perturbed imagination' (*RR*, B: 1, p. 41). But their obsessive depiction of these characteristics suggests that reviewers were challenged by a poetry of disparate parts which questioned the construction of a consistent whole.

The organisation of works of art very easily tilts into discussions of general principles with political implications. Aesthetic oddity or singularity may be condemned because, as John Barrell has pointed out, it 'is always the sign of an adherence to private concerns, and an imperfect awareness of one's duties to the public'.[19] In the seventh *Discourse*, Sir Joshua Reynolds remarked that 'the arts would lie open for ever to caprice and casualty, if those who are to judge of their excellencies had no settled principles by which they are to regulate their decisions, and the merit or defect of performances were to be determined by unguided fancy'.[20] The tradition of Reynoldsian criticism is consistently and solidly opposed to whatever is capricious, variable or transient. When Byron's poetry arrived on the public scene, Reynolds's fears about instability and flimsiness were seen to be embodied in the shape of an influential author, the poet of 'distorted fancy' (*RR*, B: 1, p. 44), whose characters embodied the same offensive mingling of attributes: 'a more hideous assemblage of detestable qualities were never surely compressed before within so small a space', the reviewer noted of Conrad (*RR*, B: 1, p. 45).

This kind of 'delusive compound' (*RR*, B: 1, p. 429) was identified by William Roberts as originating from 'modern poetry and the German drama' (*RR*, B: 1, p. 415). In the oriental tales Byron's adoption of the fragment form and his continued elaboration of an aesthetic of sudden mixture or variety was received as dangerously European. The pre-eminent instance of instability and dislocation for Byron's contemporaries and succeeding generations was, of course, the French Revolution. Behind the often invoked 'law of nature' in Tory reviews of Byron's poetry stood the political and philosophical writings of Edmund Burke. In contemplating the fragmented narration of *The Giaour*, Roberts found himself reminded of 'those who, in the language of Mr. Burke, are expert in "arrangements for general confusion"' (*RR*, B: 1, p. 411). As Chris Baldick has shown, Burke's characterisation of the French Revolutionary 'political monster' was immensely influential throughout the nineteenth century:

Everything seems out of nature in this strange chaos of levity and ferocity, and all sorts of crimes jumbled together with all sorts of follies. In viewing this monstrous tragi-comic scene, the most opposite passions necessarily succeed, and sometimes mix with each other in the mind; alternate contempt and indignation; alternate laughter and tears; alternate scorn and horror.[21]

Burke's political preference for an organised whole was buttressed, as we have seen, by Reynoldsian aesthetics which aligned digressive characteristics with the unnatural: 'deformity is not nature', Reynolds argued, 'but an accidental deviation from her accustomed practice'.[22] The trouble was that reviewers were beginning to suspect Byron of digressing not 'by accident', but by design. Burke's account of revolutionary miscegenation consistently informed Tory criticisms of Byron's style, and was used to classify him not only with the liberal Whigs but eventually, as we shall see, with confirmed opponents of the British Establishment – Radicals and Cockneys like Leigh and John Hunt.[23]

In 1815–16 the early associations of the poet's 'wayward' interruptions with a democratic inclination were inflected by his participation in the new Drury Lane Theatre project.[24] Byron's membership of the management sub-committee complicated his relationship with contemporary readers in several major respects: it provided Byron with new models for the whimsical or capricious digressive aside, it offered his readership an image of its own role as spectator to a performance and it also emphasised Byron's role as an oppositional Whig. Public interest in the plans to reopen and run the Drury Lane Theatre under the direction of prominent Whigs like Samuel Whitbread and Lord Holland was widespread. One hitherto unexamined outcome of the scheme was that oblique references to the politicised theatrical world filtered into reviews of Byron's style.[25] Tory attacks on Drury Lane's management and mismanagement merged with responses to the public drama of Byron's separation scandal. Josiah Conder's review of *Poems* (1816) in the *Eclectic* referred to 'the mind of the artist at leisure' who 'coolly [attends] to the costume of the passions he delineates', and Conder was led to remember that

Garrick, in the most pathetic part of King Lear, had his mind sufficiently at leisure to observe the aspect of his audience, and to whisper, with a low oath, to a fellow actor, 'Tom, this will do.' (*RR*, B: II, p. 737)

The scandal of this anecdote comes in the combination of high passion and a 'low oath'. Indulgence in low behaviour was, of course, an aristocratic prerogative. 'One of the many advantages of birth is', Byron remarked to Lady Blessington, 'that it saves one from ... hypercritical gentility.'[26] To a certain extent, Byron was licensed to use 'common thoughts' and 'common words', knowing that 'what would have been deemed originality and spirit' in him would have been condemned as 'a natural bias to vulgar habits' in writers who were not part of the same aristocratic, cosmopolitan coterie.

In May 1816 William Roberts had reviewed 'Fare Thee Well' unfavourably as 'a phenomenon [of] the gloomy-gay world', written not by 'a German, or Frenchman, or Italian, but an *Englishman*' (*RR*, B: I, p. 437). Aristocratic privilege was seen to tip over into a self-indulgence increasingly under attack from the Evangelical middle-classes which formed the readership of the *British Critic*. Roberts's disquiet only increased when he came to review *Childe Harold* canto III. Amongst the 'play and pliability of Lord Byron's genius' he found a 'foul admixture' of scenes allied to 'the sport of a tumultuous assemblage of undisciplined feelings', 'wayward temper', 'fretful moods and inconsistencies', 'discordant principles' and altogether a 'strange jumble' (*RR*, B: I, pp. 439–50). Clearly, Roberts had recognised that 'play' or 'variety' were essential constituents of Byron's poetry and he continued to read such volatility as a dangerous 'sport'. Reviewing *Manfred* in August 1817, he summarised his position:

The mischief that lurks in all Lord Byron's productions is this – they are all lying representations of human nature; they bring qualities of a most contradictory kind into close alliance; and so shape them into seeming union as to confound sentiments, which, for the sake of sound morality and social security, should for ever be kept contrasted, and at polar extremities with respect to each other ... These representations go beyond mere contradictoriness of character; they involve a confusion of principle, and operate very fatally and very diffusively in strengthening prejudices, which are at the bottom of our falsest estimations of men and things. (*RR*, B: 1, p. 453)

Roberts's use of the word 'diffusively' is an indication of the breadth of influence he feared Byron to have, and his point about 'social security' shows exactly the kind of disruptive, revolutionary potential that Byron's performances were believed to contain. By 1816–17 Byron's writing had acquired a reputation for 'contradictoriness' which could be traced to characterisation, plot, Byronic 'performance' and more generally as an operating principle within the text.

Beppo and the first instalment of *Don Juan* appeared as a confirmation of Byron's most unsettling traits just at the time that *ottava rima* was recommended to the English public in a smooth and palatable form. In April 1819 the *Quarterly Review* published a detailed article on 'Narrative and Romantic Poems of the Italians'. It embraced reviews of two poems: *Whistlecraft*, by John Hookham Frere and William Rose's *The Court of Beasts*.[27] The essay was by Ugo Foscolo but 'rendered into good English' by Francis Cohen (later Francis Palgrave).[28] As an authoritative account of what the nineteenth-century English reader should expect from the Italian serio-comic form, it provides a crucial context for the publication of Byron's *ottava rima* poetry.

Although the Italian model offered a precedent for mixing mood and allusion, English adapters of the same form prided themselves on their ability to tone down sudden contrasts. In discussing the poetry of Giambattista Casti, Foscolo's article argued that during the sixteenth century the spirit of chivalry could be blended with licentiousness. 'A thousand such contradictions may be found in the history of civilized society', he wrote, but he reminded his readers, 'we cannot judge of ancient decency by a modern standard'.[29] The satirist Casti was judged to be inappropriate for the English audience of 1819:

We may or may not be purer in our morals than our ancestors were; but it is quite evident that our taste is more chaste. It therefore becomes the duty of every writer to avoid offending delicacy; and if he sins against the feeling of the age, the genius which he prostitutes will not redeem him from contempt. ('Narrative and Romantic Poems', p. 490)

Distaste for 'such contradictions' is here seen as a mark of a more refined 'delicacy'. Rose was congratulated for having 'purified his satire' so that 'his allusions to the foibles of individuals are poignant without being ill-tempered'.[30] This accords with the polite preference for Horatian, rather than Juvenalian satire recently documented by Gary Dyer, and the gradual turn away from satire as a distinct genre in the 1820s and 1830s when British culture was taming its more abrasive literary modes.[31] Similarly, the author of *Whistlecraft* was commended for 'uniting great playfulness with poetical dignity':

We hope that he will be induced to continue this style in chastening and correcting the extravagant fancies of Pulci and the romantic poets. The acumen and acquirements of the man of letters, and the originality of the poet, will undoubtedly enable him to mellow and harmonize the materials which he derives from these writers, and perhaps to create a style which, while retaining the blithesomeness and ease of his models, will become completely English, and be truly naturalized by English wit and English feeling. But he must do his best to gain the suffrages of the ladies, who, in every country, and particularly in England, are, after all, the supreme arbiters of the destiny and reputation of the new poetry. (pp. 508–9)

This passage is worth quoting at length for the light it sheds on the feminisation of culture at the time: the use of Italian digressive romance is welcomed on the understanding that it is mellowed, harmonised and made respectable for the ladies. 'English wit', as Foscolo emphasised, was distinguished by its display of 'correct' morals (p. 490). This represents a considerable curbing of the energies of eighteenth-century digressive writing, and we can see how the culture of moral serenity, guarded by 'ladies' as the signifiers of 'reputation' was becoming dominant well before the Victorian period: 'Women the ultimate Oracles of Morals', Coleridge's notebook records gloomily in 1804.[32]

Byron's *Beppo* was cited once in Foscolo's article as a modern counterpart to the parodies of Niccolo Forteguerri, sharing the ability to present commonplace remarks 'with fresh graces'.[33] Considered as a one-off in the tradition of Ariosto's romance, the anonymous *Beppo* might appear innocuous but as soon as it was known to be by the author of *Childe Harold*, critical responses became markedly more hostile. When it reviewed *Childe Harold* canto IV in July 1818, the *Gentleman's Magazine* objected to the way 'Lord Byron closes a well-written preface on general topicks with a sudden plunge into politicks, painful to the admirers of the man of genius' (*RR*, B: III, p. 1112). The abruptness of the 'plunge' had become so recognisable as a Byronic trope that it enabled the *Gentleman's Magazine* to identify the author of *Beppo* a month later:

The Poem wanders on from digression to digression, occasionally pointed, or even sour and satiric, but chiefly in the easy and listless style in which verse is allowed to fashion sentiment ... The Poem has been given to a large parentage;

but from some peculiar expressions, from its ardour in praise of foreign beauty, and its rapid turn from festivity to satire, we presume it to be Lord Byron's. (*RR*, B: III, p. 1115)

Josiah Conder suggested that the poem cohered 'by no other law than that of *juxta-position*' and returned to his picture of Byron as the disingenuous actor when he analysed the meditation on Rome in canto IV: 'in the midst of his enthusiasm, [Lord Byron] is still cool enough to be able to digress to his own domestic affairs; like the tragic actor, who, in the very paroxysm of his mimic agonies, has his feelings perfectly at leisure for a whispered joke' (*RR*, B:, II, pp. 756–7).

The same sudden switches 'from festivity to satire' had led William Roberts in May 1818 to describe *Beppo* as 'a burlesque upon Lord Byron's manner ... for the resemblance between the solemn banter, and epicurean sarcasm which mark every page of the Childe Harold, and the derisory ease and ironical pleasantry with which all serious things are treated in this poem of Beppo, is most successfully preserved' (*RR*, B: I, p. 456). Roberts objected in particular to 'little facetious, frolicsome attacks' which he saw as a dangerous species of 'French ridicule' (*RR*, B: I, p. 457). He followed this up by attacking canto IV of *Childe Harold's Pilgrimage* for its modern quality, 'bred out of the French revolution' and its 'most unnatural and contradictory [union of] the false philosophy of the continental schools, with all its anti-social and disorganizing principles, a creed ... subversive of all established discipline' (*RR*, B: I, p. 462). Again we can see that the resistance to '*dis*organization' adopts Burke's line on the French Revolution as something which destroyed the organic cohesiveness of society. Anything which touched on principles of organisation was received in the light of the upheaval it might cause to British social stratification.

Political objections can account for some of the outrage, but it is important to distinguish between political prejudice and the form it adopted in reviews. Byron's power to unsettle was not felt solely by the Tory critics. Hazlitt's review of *Beppo* in the *Yellow Dwarf* in March 1818, criticised 'the bitterness of the satirist' whom he depicted 'digressing from his digressions' (*RR*, B: V, p. 2335). But his criticism of *Childe Harold* canto IV went beyond mild rebuke to attack Byron for 'indigestion of the mind ... Politically and practically speaking', Hazlitt asserted, 'a house divided against itself cannot stand' (*RR*, B: V, p. 2336). His comments here may reflect a wider concern about the messiness of opposition politics which fed, as we shall see, into Byron's digressive intertextuality in *Don Juan*. Although he discerned in the early Wordsworth a 'levelling muse', a

voice of nature which could challenge the establishment, Hazlitt found
the versification and style of *Childe Harold* to be counter-productive –
'as perverse and capricious as the method or the sentiments' – and he
objected both to the 'alternate mixture of enthusiasm and spleen' and to
the disjointed mode of composition:

> There is here and in every line an effort at brilliancy, and a successful effort; and
> yet, in the next, as if nothing had been done, the same thing is attempted to be
> expressed again with the same effort of labour as before, the same success, and
> with as little appearance of repose or satisfaction of mind. (*RR*, B: v, pp. 2336–8)

Hazlitt's dislike of a 'mass of discordant things' (*RR*, B: v, p. 2338),
here contradicts his ability to appreciate the 'broken mirror' brilliance
of human wit. In Byron's case he seems to have been disturbed because
'alternate mixture' dissipates the capacity of the human mind to be an
agent of political change.

Interestingly, Hazlitt's objections were not shared by Byron's Whig
mentor, Lord Holland who in 1818–19 was attempting to draw Byron
back into moderate Whig politics (rather than Hobhouse's reformist
variety). An unpublished letter from March 1818 suggests that Holland
had identified positive political action in *Beppo*:

> Among many other good things in Beppo the excellence of your politicks ought
> not to be overlooked – Nothing can be worse than the system pursued since
> you left England – Arbitrary principles supported by the most hypocritical
> professions & the employment of spies to create the treason it was convenient
> to suppose have been resorted to by Government & sanctioned by Parliament
> till a positive disunion between the upper & lower classes of society seems really
> likely to be the consequence – In this state of things I have more than once
> regretted that your proxy was extinct with last session & half reproached myself
> with not sending you another – However I did not venture to do so till I had
> consulted Hobhouse whom I had expected every day but who did not arrive till
> lately – He tells me you would like to sign & I enclose it – It must be sealed with
> your arms or crest.[34]

Holland held Byron's proxy for the remainder of the session from 27 April
1818, but it was not renewed after that and the increasing gulf between
Holland House and Byron's politics and aesthetics will be discussed in
a later chapter.[35] Holland's political approval for *Beppo* suggests that
he saw the conversational, digressive style of the poem as a method of
countering the 'disunion between the upper & lower classes of society'
promoted by the Tory government. Byron's use of *ottava rima* renders

small scale accident in the texture of the poem as if to counter the larger scale uncertainties which afflict individuals under 'arbitrary' regimes. Holland's paternalistic dislike for 'positive disunion', however, follows the moral and political preference for a united whole which we have seen in Byron's other readers.

Holland's appreciation of *Beppo* was also informed by his aristocratic enjoyment of the robust wit of Dryden, Swift and Pope. Representing the conservative instincts of the more middling class of readers, John Murray expressed pleasure in Byron's new medley style through a conventional analogy with Shakespeare's changeability, but his letter also reveals a thinly veiled anxiety:

Mr. Frere is at length satisfied that you are the author of 'Beppo'. He had no conception that you possessed the protean talent of Shakespeare, thus to assume at will so different a character. He, and every one, continues in the same very high opinion of its beauties. I am glad to find that you are disposed to pursue this strain, which has occasioned so much delight. (Smiles, *A Publisher and His Friends*, 1, p. 393)

Murray then added cautiously 'Do you never think of prose?' He was inclined, perhaps, to be wary of Byron's protean potential. As we shall see in Chapter Three, Murray attempted in vain to steer Byron's digressiveness into a more commodifiable form while friends like Douglas Kinnaird enjoyed Murray's discomfort. Meanwhile, in the *Quarterly Review* Foscolo's taste-shaping essay was followed by an advertisement for new poetic publications. The anonymous final entry was '*Don Juan* 4to. 1 l. 11 s. 6d.'[36] Byron's notorious poem arrived on the public scene at the very moment when *ottava rima* had been recommended to English readers in a 'naturalized' verse form. It was doomed never to gain 'the suffrages of the ladies'.

The consternation of Byron's friends and publisher when they read *Don Juan* has been well-documented. But an important response to the first cantos, not widely known, is contained in a letter to John Murray by Francis Cohen postmarked 16 July 1819 which Murray shared with Byron. Cohen was a trusted adviser who had been a regular contributor to the *Edinburgh* and the *Quarterly* (including his translation of Foscolo's article on Italian narrative poetry discussed above). Coming from someone who had experience of Italian verse, the letter allows us to see why Byron's contradictions were regarded as a departure from both English and Italian precedent. 'Like Shakespeare', Cohen wrote, 'he shows that his soul can soar well into the seventh heaven & that when he returns into this body he can be as merry as if sublimity ne'er was known.':

but Lord B. should have been grave & gay by turns; grave in one page & gay in the next; grave in one stanza, & gay in the next; grave in one line, & gay in the next. And not grave & gay in the same page, or in the same stanza, or in the same line. – If he had followed <Pulci more closely> Ariosto more closely, he would have produced a masterpiece & not a sport of fancy. Nothing can be better calculated to display the talent of a great poet, than a composition admitting of a ready transition from fun & drollery to sublimity & pathos, but then they must be interchanged, they must not be mixed up together: they must be kept distinct – though contemplated jointly. If we stand on a mountain we gladly view a storm beating on one side of the horizon & dark clouds impending & the sun shining bright & calm in the other quarter of the heavens, but we are never drenched & scorched at the same instant whilst standing in one spot.[37]

In correcting his mention of Pulci and substituting the name of Ariosto, Cohen is following the English preference for romance over satire. His letter to Murray tells us that it is the frequency of Byron's transitions which disturbed contemporary readers: to change tone 'by turns' (of the page) would have been acceptable but transitions which threaten proper tonal segregation are not. Cohen's tactile 'drenched & scorched' metaphor emphasises that, like other readers, he was responding to a surface texture, not to metaphysical depths.

There have been several studies of the reception of *Don Juan* in England but the obsessive critical preoccupation with the poem's surface texture and its relationship with Byron's earlier poems has been overshadowed by the poem's content. A few early reviewers felt that the satiric strain of the poem licensed its heterogeneous mixture. One writer for the *Literary Gazette* applauded the 'singularly felicitous mixture of burlesque and pathos', and used a Shakespearean image to characterise Byron's genius: 'like the dolphin sporting in its native waves, however grotesque, displaying a new hue and a new beauty, the noble author has shewn an absolute controul over his means' (*RR*, B: IV, pp. 1412; 1410). Such 'control', however, soon came to be seen as threatening. Contemporary criticism of the poem built on the patterns of inconsistency which had been perceived in Byron's writing since 1812, and which were recognised as threats to Burkean and, later, Coleridgean organic principles of criticism:

the occasional profanity which defiled his graver, and the indecency which stained his lighter productions, are here embodied in the compactness of a system, and have been madly exalted from their station as humble though repulsive accessories of his theme, to be its avowed end, purpose and consummation. (*RR*, B: ii, p. 799)

It was the suspicion of a 'system' at work which caused much of the hostility. As David Simpson has shown, the aversion to 'systems' often came from a Tory suspicion of abstraction and theory associated with the French Revolution.[38] This prejudice was usually combined with a celebration of English (Shakespearean) irregularity, but Byron's systematised disorder confounded national stereotypes. Far from finding a humane Shakespearean plurality when they encountered Byron's poetic irregularity at close quarters, reviewers decried his methodical process of 'degrading' human experience. Blame was frequently attached to Byron's distance from his readers and his own work as if, like Stephen Dedalus's artist, he could be seen 'indifferent, paring his fingernails'.[39] 'Byron' became a signifier for a paradoxical mixture of extreme separateness from society, an aloof and isolated authorship together with a textual experience of simultaneity, or contradictory areas of experience '[jumbled] in one undistinguished mass' (*RR*, B: iii, p. 1181). It is as if readers felt Byron to be in a realm of untrammelled space beyond his poems while they were relegated to an urban existence of crush and clamour. William Roberts, for example, argued that the poem's simultaneity destroyed the possibility of readerly empathy:

it delights in extracting ridicule out of its own pathos. While it brings the tears of sympathy into the eyes of the reader ... a heartless humour immediately succeeds, showing how little the writer participates in the emotion he excites. Skilful to play upon another's bosom, and to touch with mysterious art the finest chords of sensibility himself, he is all the while an alien to his own magical creation. (*RR*, B: i, p. 490)

The poet's detachment was recurrently contrasted with the reader's baffled experience of palpable disjunction. The fame of Byron's misanthropical heroes, however, has since overshadowed the way in which the style of the poem itself was felt to be misanthropical.

Don Juan was regarded as a work of deliberate provocation by evangelical Tories like Roberts, but – surprisingly, perhaps – also by educated liberals and reformists. In the circle of writers that included Leigh Hunt and John Keats, for example, there is evidence of strong resistance to Byron's mingled style. On 20 September 1819 Richard Woodhouse (who may be taken as a barometer of taste for educated readers with strong

liberal sympathies) wrote to John Taylor about Keats's proposed alterations to 'The Eve of St Agnes':

[Keats] has altered the last 3 lines to leave on the reader a sense of pettish
disgust, by bringing Old Angela in (only) dead stiff & ugly. – He says he likes
that the poem should leave off with this Change of Sentiment – it was what he
aimed at, & was glad to find from my objections to it that he had succeeded. –
I apprehend he had a fancy for trying his hand at an attempt to play with the
reader, & fling him off at the last – I shd. have thought, he affected the Don Juan
style of mingling up sentiment & sneering: but that he had before asked Hessey
if he cod. procure him a sight of that work, as he had not met with it, and if the
'E. of St A.' had not in all probability been altered before his Lordship had thus
flown in the face of the public.[40]

Keats may have adopted a Byronic mode to forestall criticism of his
work as weak and sentimental: he was determined to write 'for men'
and *Don Juan*, as Moyra Haslett has recently pointed out, 'was addressed
conspiratorially to masculine intimates, but was not unaware that women
would overhear'.[41]

Under the cover of concern about how the poem might threaten
female readers, Byron's reviewers also expressed fear of an invidious
feminine style. The image of the prostituted muse combined allegations
of Byron's 'perversion' or degradation of his genius with earlier responses
to his imaginative fertility. The *British Critic*, for example, created the
image of a 'non-descript goddess' presiding over *Don Juan*:

In the first canto we saw her elegant, highly talented, and graceful, and lamented
her deflection from virtue. We can trace her subsequently through each stage
of deterioration, till we find her a camp-follower at Ismail, still possessing al-
lurements of a coarse and sensual sort, and though thoroughly depraved, full of
anecdote and adventurous spirit . . . her conversation a mixture of metaphysical
scraps picked up in the course of her former education; with broader slang
and more unblushing indecency, than she had as yet ventured upon. (*RR*, B: 1,
pp. 339–40)

Reviewers had hinted before at a feminine prolixity in Byron's style:
'The muse of Lord Byron is so extremely prolific, that if she does not
actually bring forth *Twins*, her offspring succeed each other with such
wonderful rapidity, that it becomes almost impracticable to complete the
examination of the beauties and deformities of one, before another bursts
upon us.'[42] A feminine mutability had been detected in his digressive
characteristics, and this was confirmed by the triviality of *Beppo* which
Jeffrey called 'a mere piece of lively and loquacious prattling . . . upon
all kinds of frivolous subjects, – a sort of gay and desultory babbling'

(*RR*, B: ɪɪ, p. 889). *Don Juan*, however, extended fickle caprice into harlotry and the concept of the prostituted muse led to criticism of the increasing 'infection' of the poem (*RR*, B: ɪv, p. 1426).

What prompted this violent dislike was the fear that *Don Juan* could nihilistically undermine all political and philosophical positions. The radical publisher William Hone protested about the 'character' of the poem, claiming in 1819 that *Don Juan* 'keeps no terms with even the common feelings of civilized man ... It wars with virtue, as resolutely as with vice.'[43] Hone's troubled response parallels that of Byron's friend Hobhouse who criticised 'the whole turn of the poem' because he felt that those opposing the corruption of the Establishment should uphold an unimpeachable moral standard.[44] While classically educated aristocrats might enjoy the wit of the poem, they could not cope with the politics of *Don Juan* and the liberals and radicals who might have welcomed the politics were thrown by the poem's asides on religious and moral codes. The poem was indeed 'non-descript'.

The perversion of national genius by hybrid foreign influences was, of course, increasingly threatening to an imperial power. Byron's *Don Juan* recalled the protean variations of Shakespeare without the security of English national pride: 'it is true', wrote William Roberts,

that this existence is a medley of joy and sorrow, close upon each other's confines; and that moral and pathetic representations of life in prose or verse proceeding in correspondence with the reality, admit of being chequered by grave and gay, pensive and playful moods; but they must not be suffered to run into one another and disturb each other's impressions. Sorrow is engrossing – nor can the heart at the same time lend itself to two opposite emotions. (*RR*, B: ɪ, p. 490)

Roberts attempted to distinguish between a just imitation of the varied human lot and Byron's world of contradiction where constant collisions and qualifications of experience led to a sense that no stable emotional states existed. In the background of this criticism is Johnson's appreciation of Shakespeare which provided a pattern for acceptable mixture. Shakespeare's plays, according to Johnson, exhibit 'the real state of sublunary nature':

which partakes of good and evil, joy and sorrow, mingled with endless variety of proportion and innumerable modes of combination; and expressing the course of the world, in which the loss of one is the gain of another; in which, at the same time, the reveller is hasting to his wine, and the mourner burying his friend; in which the malignity of one is sometimes defeated by the frolick of another; and many mischiefs and many benefits are done and hindered without design.[45]

Byron's digressions usurped the prerogative of nature in a way that Johnson had verged on detecting in Shakespeare: 'what he does best, he soon ceases to do ... He no sooner begins to move, than he counteracts himself; and terror and pity, as they are rising in the mind, are checked and blasted by sudden frigidity' (*Works of Samuel Johnson*, VII, p. 74). But this criticism was wholly subordinate to the overview of Shakespeare as a national genius. Byron was still alive and in Italy, apparently disowning his Englishness as in the *Letter to John Murray Esqre.* where he referred to Great Britain as 'your Country'.[46]

Byron's betrayal of class and race was confirmed by his involvement with the 'hobby-horse of Radicalism' (*RR*, B: 1, p. 335), otherwise known as the Cockney School as reconstituted in Pisa. In 1822, as soon as Byron's collaboration with Leigh Hunt on the *Liberal* was known, Tory reviewers began to trace Cockney influences in his work. Recent criticism by Richard Cronin, Nicholas Roe and Jeffrey Cox has identified and explored the reasons for the 'high' cultural resistance to Hunt's circle, but the impact of this on Byron's reputation has not been discussed.[47] In *Blackwood's* and the *British Critic* parallels between Byron and Hunt were detected in images of disharmony and opposition; 'anti-British garbage', 'unmusical drawl', 'lisping dull *double-entendres*' and 'hymning Jacobinism' (*RR*, B: 1, p. 205). Byron's rhymes in *Don Juan* cantos VI, VII and VIII were depicted in *Blackwood's* as the result of his listening to Cockney 'gibberish', and were attributed to Hunt's joint authorship by the *British Critic*. In March 1823 the *British Critic* summarised Byron to date:

To blow hot and cold from every point in the compass, to praise and abuse respectively republics and monarchies; monarchies and republics; to libel and flatter England and America, Buonoparte and Tom Paine, the king and the people, friends and enemies, men and women, truth and justice, backwards and forwards ten times over; to do all this without any excuse or bashfulness *within the continent of one work*, is really at once a symptom, a proof, and a consequence of an order of intellect, which we have no adequate terms to describe. (*RR*, B: 1, p. 321)

Beyond the pale, Byron's writing undermined the criteria of unity and harmony which had sustained Johnsonian literary criticism in England. When T.S. Eliot reluctantly turned his attention to Byron in 1937, he too was shocked by how un-English Byron was: 'I cannot think of another poet of his distinction who might so easily have been an accomplished for-eigner writing English.'[48] Byron's association with Hunt in Italy blurred clear distinctions of class and nationhood. Not surprisingly, the *British Critic* regarded Byron's association with 'accomplished foreigners' as a menace to Whigs and Tories alike:

The case is perfectly plain. Lord Byron has perceived too late that public opinion has connected him, more than he may approve, with the Riminists, or Cocknio-Carbonari, or whatever name may rejoice the ears of the literary club which he has been pleased to found at Pisa. As obvious must it have become ... that these his chosen friends are scouted both by Whig and Tory as a gang of despicable Pilgarlics, insensible alike to English prejudices, English pursuits, English humour, and the comforts of an English fireside. Alike coarse, fluttering and insignificant, their body collective has been roughly brushed away, like a nauseous flesh-fly from the front of Whiggism on which it had crawled for a while, and not even Lord Byron himself has escaped a portion of the disgrace. (*RR*, B: 1, p. 337)

If the effectiveness of a challenge to orthodoxy is to be gauged by the violence of the response, we can see how seriously Byron's illicit union with the Cockneys threatened members of the Establishment. When it reviewed *Werner* in March 1823 the *British Critic* accounted for all Byron's textual disruptions by categorising him as 'the *dupe* of Leigh Hunt':

the Aristocratico-democrat is the tame hackney scrivener of the jacobinico-radical; the macaroni simperer on the patrician properties of long fingers is linked hand in hand with the mutton fist of the sometime tenant of a gaol. (*RR*, B: 1, p. 322)

These caricatures of 'the Pisan Confederacy' were one way of dealing with Byron's 'scorching and drenching', but a few reviewers seem to have sensed that the instability of Byron's poetry could not be explained away simply in terms of politics.

Compounding moral, political and aesthetic uncertainties, Byron's problematic poetic texture was summarised in Francis Jeffrey's article on Byron's tragedies in the *Edinburgh Review* (February 1822). Jeffrey discussed the effect of *Don Juan*, distinguishing it from the 'affectiveness' of satire:

The charge we bring against Lord B. in short is, that his writings have a tendency to destroy all belief in the reality of virtue – and to make all enthusiasm and constancy of affection ridiculous ... when the satirist deals out his sarcasms against the sincerity of human professions, and unmasks the secret infirmities of our bosoms, we consider this as aimed at hypocrisy and not at mankind ... The true antidote to such seductive or revolting views of human nature, is to turn to the scenes of its nobleness and attraction; and to reconcile ourselves again to our kind, by listening to the accents of pure affection and incorruptible

honour. But if those accents have flowed, in all their sweetness, from the very lips
that instantly open again to mock and blaspheme them, the antidote is mingled
with the poison, and the draught is more deadly for the mixture! (*RR*, B: II,
p. 936)

For Jeffrey, Byron's 'theatrical exhibition' undermined not only the illusion of sincerity in the poem but the illusion of any public meaning or
coherence. Byron demonstrated 'how possible it is to have all fine and noble feelings, or their appearance, for a moment, and yet retain no particle
of respect for them – or of belief in their intrinsic worth or permanent
reality' (*RR*, B: II, p. 937). In this case *Don Juan* offered an exploration of
relativity of value for the reader. Jeffrey read in this sceptical process 'a
system of resolute misanthropy': 'all good feelings are excited only to ac-
custom us to their speedy and complete extinction' (*RR*, B: II, pp. 937–8).

What we find in Jeffrey's reaction is the fear of ambiguity and indeterminacy which had been expressed in aesthetic treatises throughout the eighteenth century and which pervaded critical resistance to
the mind which 'floats and fluctuates in cheerless uncertainty'.[49] John
Barrell has analysed some of these attitudes to fluctuation in the field
of the visual arts, and has suggested that, 'sketchiness, indistinctness,
a capricious looseness of handling – these are only allowable in works
which, because their aim is to represent the accidental, are understood
to be private pictures'.[50] If we trace this orthodoxy from painting into
the field of literature (as the language of Byron's reviewers tells us they
did), we can see that *Don Juan*'s miscible modes created a troubling simultaneity which confused public and private experience. In the sixth and
tenth *Discourses*, Sir Joshua Reynolds warned his audience about the dangers of 'peculiarities' which 'force themselves upon view'. He used the
'entangled confusion' of Bernini's Neptune as an example and discussed
the 'mischief' of dividing the work 'into many minute parts', destroying
the 'grandeur of its general effect'.[51] The language of Byron's contemporary reviews tells us that his work was perceived to have violated the
same aesthetic standard of civic cohesion. In *Don Juan*, as in his earlier
works, Byron's stylistic interruptions made the reader aware of the uncertainty of the relationship between the general and the particular as
the accidental rises up to challenge the whole.

It is open to twentieth-century readers, although it was not to Jeffrey,
to distinguish relativity from cynicism. The strand we have been tracing in the reception of Byron's poetry is significant for, as John Keats
remarked early in 1819, 'These Reviews . . . are getting more and more
powerful . . . They are like a superstition.'[52] The discourse of the reviews

helped to fix not only readers' conceptions of Byron, but Byron's conception of his readers and of the English public more widely. Byron's art of juxtaposition provoked both predictable political outrage and a less easily definable anxiety about poetry's palpable effect on its readers. The perceived theatricality of Byron's texts questioned poetic ideals of organic unity and sincerity of address, challenging the new orthodoxies of nineteenth-century poetic production.

After Byron's death in 1824 it became easier for retrospective accounts of his career to unify division under the sign of biography. Thomas Moore followed the pattern of Hunt's defensive criticism in creating as smooth an image as possible, surrounding Byron's writing with a protective gloss of biographical commentary.[53] Byron's 'habit of forming ... incongruous juxtapositions' was coupled with a 'natural tendency to yield ... to every chance impression, and change with every passing impulse'.[54] By stressing the experience of schism in Byron's childhood and the 'strange assemblage of contrary elements, all meeting together in the same mind' in 1818, Moore prepared the way for readings of *Don Juan* as case-history: 'the most powerful and ... painful display of the versatility of genius that has ever been left for succeeding ages to wonder at and deplore' (*The Works of Lord Byron* (1832–3), IV, p. 122). It was Moore's version, I would argue, which fixed the view of Byron as a 'painful mixture' (VI, p. 235) of personal misfortune and psychological oddity for the rest of the nineteenth century.

A little known, but fascinating variant on this commodification of Byron is supplied in a meditation by Samuel Taylor Coleridge, whose critical legacy was that quest for unity, depth, symbol and religious certainty in literature which diminished Byron's more troubled poetic surfaces. Coleridge's account of Byron was recorded by Seymour Teulon Porter, the boy at the chemist's shop in Highgate where Coleridge purchased his laudanum. He recalled that in July 1824 while watching Byron's funeral procession from the door of the shop Coleridge arrived and spoke on 'topics suggested by the scene of that hour':

Byron's unhappy youth; the extraordinary issue of it in his prodigious works & his numerous & great public merits; his great & special claims on his countrymen's generous if discriminative appreciation; the delightful fact that even then, at that so early period after his death, the funeral ceremonies indicated that in the future, according to the noble wont of the English people, Byron's literary merits would seem continually to rise, while his personal errors, if not denied, or altogether forgotten, would be little noticed, & would be treated with ever softening gentleness.[55]

How much of this is Coleridge, and how much Porter, we cannot tell, but the indication it gives of 'ever softening gentleness' catches the feminisation of culture which we have begun to trace and suggests how it was that Byron's unique poetic texture, the experience of simultaneous 'scorching and drenching', came to be obscured by more harmonious nineteenth-century cultural forms like biography, patriotism and religious belief.

To a certain extent, new poetic forms are always perceived to create a physical rupturing of the reader's experience. In June 1801, for example, the *Monthly Monitor* had attacked *Lyrical Ballads* for the 'studied abruptness' of the poems 'which makes them assume the appearance of mere fragments'. The political inference of this style led the reviewer to suspect Wordsworth and Coleridge of a 'wayward spirit of discontent ... calculated to diffuse the seeds of general dissatisfaction' (*RR*, A: II, p. 687). Over a century later, W.B. Yeats struggled with Ezra Pound's *Cantos*, finding 'grotesque fragments', 'unbridged transitions' and 'unexplained ejaculations'.[56] The advent of Modernism in the early nineteenth and again in the early twentieth century possesses a distinctive texture, but the meaning of the texture is entirely dependent on literary and historical contexts. In order to understand the reading experience of Byron's contemporaries, we need to look at what shapes the unexpected was expected to take.

CHAPTER TWO

'Breaches in transition': eighteenth-century digressions and Byron's early verse

Seventeenth-century scientific empiricism was famously hostile to 'all the amplifications, digressions, and swellings of style' which the Royal Society of London condemned as resulting in 'only mists and uncertainties'.[1] By the first decades of the eighteenth century, however, positive appraisals of digressions were appearing in rhetorical theory. Shaftesbury described a style of 'deviations and excursions' as the prerogative of the gentleman and poet in his *Characteristicks* (1711), and Longinian theory offered another way of reading abrupt change or discontinuity in poetry as the product of sublime inspiration. But the art of digression remained controversial, often highlighting an insecurity in literary criticism more generally. Alexander Pope used digressive footnotes in *The Dunciad* (1729) to parody the academic scholarship of Lewis Theobald. This technique anticipated the anti-Jacobin satire of Gifford, Canning, Frere and Mathias in the 1790s. All these writers, however, used digression to support the concept of ideal beauty: even the labyrinthine gothic library of *The Dunciad* shadows the orderly classical edifice of all civilised knowledge.

In eighteenth-century critical discourse, digression was presented as structural beauty, an integral part, whereby the poet temporarily departed from a poem's ostensible subject, but discovered in the process of digressing a hidden connection with the main subject. Digression was, therefore, a way of reinforcing a concept of the unified whole: like the operation of divinity it moved in a mysterious way. Anna Barbauld summarised this digressive decorum in her preface to Akenside's *The Pleasures of Imagination*:

Many of these pieces . . . owe all their entertainment to the frequent digressions. Where these arise naturally out of the subject . . . they are not only allowable but graceful; but if forced, . . . they can be considered in no other light than that of beautiful monsters, and injure the piece they are meant to adorn.[2]

As we have seen, Byron's digressions were received by contemporary critics as 'monsters' (not always beautiful, by any means), and subsequent critics have also found them difficult to categorise. In tracing the relationship between theories of digression and transition in the eighteenth-century long poem, Richard Terry usefully distinguishes between the use of digression to affirm hidden continuity, and digression as 'an autonomous textual unit'.[3] Byron's critics have frequently assimilated digression to the theory of harmonious totality and, in so doing, have overlooked the element of juxtaposition which is essential to Byronic digression. Throughout the eighteenth century, the evaluation of digression was entwined with questions about how poetry could deal with cultural and social manifestations of transition and change.

Disputes about the timing and delivery of poetic transition inevitably returned to classical models, trying to balance the demands of emotional veracity with consideration for the reader. Tensions between the expression of feeling and formal organisation were focused on the ode. William Congreve's 'discourse on the pindarique ode' (1706) had characterised some recent lyrics as 'a Bundle of rambling incoherent Thoughts, express'd in a like parcel of irregular Stanzas which also consist of such another complication of disproportion'd, uncertain and perplex'd verses and Rhimes'.[4] Congreve rejected the frequently cited precedent of Pindar, 'for tho' his Digressions are frequent, and his Transitions sudden, yet there is ever some secret connexion which tho' not always appearing to the Eye, never fails to communicate itself to the Understanding of the Reader'.[5] The appeal to 'understanding' was, of course, an affirmation of the shared outlook of classically educated gentlemen whose taste could be relied upon to guard social 'connexion'. James Beattie was sure that incongruous allusion would never 'force a smile' from a gentleman 'except it surprise him in an unguarded moment' and the laws of genre helped to prevent any such 'unguarded moments'.[6]

In the *Rambler* in 1751 Samuel Johnson complained that poets were using the 'accidental peculiarity' of ancient writers to free lyric poetry from all laws, 'to neglect the niceties of transition, to start into remote digressions, and to wander without restraint from one scene of imagery to another'. This pandered to a weakness in the uncultivated reader whose attention is 'more successfully excited by sudden sallies and unexpected exclamations, than by ... more artful and placid beauties'.[7] In 1762, however, Goldsmith's revision of Newbery's *The Art of Poetry on a New Plan* celebrated the ode's new loosening of restraint: 'Fired ... with his subject', the lyric poet 'disdains grammatical niceties, and common modes of speech, and often soars above rule ... This freedom ... consists chiefly in sudden transitions, bold digressions, and lofty excursions.'[8] Nevertheless Goldsmith, too, looked for an underlying coherence where the poet is 'led naturally to his subject again, and like a bee, having collected the essence of many different flowers, returns home and unites them all in one uniform pleasing sweet' (II, p. 41). Apparent disjunction was expected to prepare the way for deeper resolution.

Revisiting the question of proper transition in the ode in 1783, Hugh Blair was concerned about the mental stability of the poet who 'becomes so abrupt in his transitions; so eccentric and irregular in his motions ... that we essay in vain to follow him ... The transitions from thought to thought may be light and delicate, such as are prompted by a lively fancy; but still they should be such as preserve the connection of ideas, and show the Author to be one who thinks, and not one who raves.'[9] The threat of individual insanity to the community is comically embodied in Jane Austen's Henry Tilney who, when translated into the role of lover, 'talked at random, without sense or connection'.[10] But as well as the wider community, Blair also envisaged the immediate relationship between poet and reader. He was particularly concerned about how the sublime could be sustained since 'the mind is tending every moment to fall down into its ordinary situation': as soon as the author 'alters the key; he relaxes the tension of the mind; the strength of the feeling is emasculated; the Beautiful may remain, but the Sublime is gone' (*Lectures*, I, p. 66).[11] Blair judged one of the greatest threats to sublimity to be the incursion of particularity, insisting that if in sublime compositions 'any trivial or improper circumstances are mingled, the whole is degraded' (I, p. 70). Cowper also wrestled with this problem in his translations of Homer: 'It is difficult to kill a sheep with dignity in a modern language', he admitted wryly in his Preface, 'Difficult also, without sinking below the level of poetry, to harness mules to a waggon, particularizing every article of their furniture, straps, rings, staples, and even the tying of knots that kept all together. HOMER, who writes always to the eye, with all his sublimity and grandeur, has the minuteness of a Flemish painter.'[12] Homer's minutiae were problematic for a late eighteenth-century readership because quotidian detail, as Naomi Schor has observed, has always been 'part of a larger semantic network, bounded on the one side by the *ornamental*, with its traditional connotations of effeminacy and decadence, and on the other, by the *everyday*, whose "prosiness" is rooted in the domestic sphere of social life presided over by women'.[13]

Early nineteenth-century questions about how to represent the intricate fluxes and refluxes of the human mind were informed by eighteenth-century theories about the association of ideas.[14] For Hume, the words 'transition' and 'association' were almost interchangeable, but transition in a work of art ought to strengthen the ties of community. In a just composition, he argued, 'the passions make an easy transition from one object to another' and prompt the kindling of sympathy, 'But were the poet to make a total digression from his subject ... the imagination, feeling a breach in the transition, would enter coldly into the new scene.'[15] English taste could warm to eccentric digression, such as the progress of Sterne's *The Life and Opinions of Tristram Shandy*, but in this case, changeability was contained under the unifying sign of Irish personality. For a similar reason, the capriciousness of John Wolcot's (Peter Pindar's) verse was popular as a humorous (if vulgar) adaptation of classical precedent: 'A Desultory way of writing, / A hop and step and jump mode of inditing, / My great and wise relation Pindar, boasted.'[16] Peter Pindar's buffoonery was clearly just that, and so did not present any threat to the law of genre; his self-indulgent rambling simply elaborated the extravagant potential of sensibility.

Poetry of sensibility made much of the waywardness of the sentimental traveller. Thomas Warton, William Lisle Bowles, Charlotte Smith and Samuel Taylor Coleridge all deployed self-consciously 'desultory' lines as a vehicle of individual feeling. In the 1790s desultory writing was rapidly associated with radical sensibility and feminine susceptibility.[17] In its 'New Morality' attack on the culture of tender radicalism, *The Anti-Jacobin* praised fellow satirist T. J. Mathias for his 'manly vigour' and 'patriot warmth' which 'wakes and points the desultory fires' (ll. 52–54).[18] Although desultory forms could render faithfully the transitions of the suffering human mind, they lacked the masculine virtues of order, discipline and rational control. It was in the spirit of a manly rebuke that Mackintosh condemned Burke's narrative of the French revolution as 'desultory'.[19]

Byron's writing was condemned as 'desultory' by reviewers long before he acknowledged the description in *Don Juan* canto xv (stanza 20); the pedigree of Byron's mingled poetic surface was, however, uncertain. While Byron himself was evidently and self-consciously an aristocrat, his poetic voice was dangerously hybridised and feminised. It focused a nexus of critical uneasiness about digressions, 'unblushing allusions', transitions, juxtapositions and minute detail. In order to clarify Byron's break with tradition, we need to look more closely at the disruptive textuality of some of Byron's eighteenth-century models.

No poet offers more of a digressive parallel than Charles Churchill, the satirist who 'blazed / The comet of a season' and whose grave in Dover Byron visited the evening before he left England.[20] Andrew Bennett has recently discussed Byron's poem 'Churchill's Grave' as an unteasing of the myth of posterity, but Churchill's use of digression in verse also opens up the art of 'mingling' to 'confuse a Newton's thought' (l. 23).[21] The poem's composition dates from the summer of 1816 when Byron was reading Wordsworth at Shelley's instigation. Anticipating Coleridge's criticisms of Wordsworthian abruptness in *Biographia Literaria*, Byron set out to imitate Wordsworth's style, 'its beauties and its defects'.[22]

With a blend of sentimental encounter ('of sorrow and of awe') and parody ('Because my homely phrase the truth would tell'), Byron sets up a double relationship with his readers. The poem mixes alternately rhyming lines and couplets, shadowing both Wordsworth's *Lyrical Ballads* style and Churchill's Miltonised couplets: the meditative pace is that of Wordsworth's 'Michael' or *The Excursion*, but this 'natural homily' is presented as a knowing performance. We are given the melancholy erasure of human achievement 'Through the thick deaths of half a century' (l. 10), juxtaposed with the opportunistic Sexton's hints that he would like a tip. After struggling to 'extricate remembrance' of the grave's significance, the Sexton manages to dredge up 'the twilight of a former Sun' and eventually he supplies the simple and moving reason why 'frequent travellers turn to pilgrims so': 'the man of whom you wot ... / Was a most famous writer in his day, / And therefore travellers step from out their way / To pay him honour' (ll. 29–32).

This is an explanation, but it is also a mystery. The desire to step out of one's way to visit a 'name no clearer than the names unknown' (l. 6) introduces an invisible notion of value which challenges (rather than circulates with) the transaction between Byron and the Sexton.[23] Byron invokes Churchill, I think, not only because of the circumstantial parallel of a season's fame, but because Churchill's relationship with his audience existed on a cusp between formal verse satire and sentimental epistolary conversation which was as risky and combative as Byron's own position in 1816. This curious mixture is 'Literally Rendered' in the poem and the doubleness of the mode of address captures Byron's critical sense of his precarious textual and social position.

Churchill had been recognised as an element in Byron's style at the very start of his publishing career. The *Eclectic*'s review of *English Bards and Scotch Reviewers* found that Byron's 'indiscriminate' revenge indicated he had been taking 'a course of *Churchill*'.[24] Peter J. Manning has discussed the importance of Charles Churchill's poetry for Byron's early satire,

reading Byron's deliberate echoes of Churchill as a means of appealing
to literary tradition in an audience which could no longer be relied
upon to recognise classical allusion.[25] As well as providing a model of
vituperative force, Churchill also offered a precedent for interrupting the
flow of verse to the reader with urgent or humorous asides. Byron seems
to have realised the potential of this technique early on, even though
one of Churchill's most influential editors presented such disruptions as
aesthetic flaws.

In the account of Churchill's life prefacing his edition, William Tooke
established a way of reading Churchill's stylistic irregularity as an accident of personal history: 'The anxiety arising from domestic infelicity
unhinged his mind though naturally of a firm texture, and seemed to
give an entirely new bias to his disposition'.[26] The abruptness of this
'plunge' into 'an abyss of misery' (*The Poetical Works of Charles Churchill*
(1804), I, p. xvii), coupled with reports of Churchill's loss of faith in
'Christianity as by law established' and his trouble with creditors may
have encouraged Byron's identification with the poet in 1816.[27] More
significantly, Churchill's poetry offered an acute awareness of the public,
textual interface of private scandal:

> Ah! what, my Lord, hath private life to do
> With things of public nature? Why to view
> Would you thus cruelly these scenes unfold . . . ?[28]

In the two-volume 1804 edition of Churchill's poetry (listed in the 1816
sale catalogue of Byron's library), Tooke used his notes to suggest that
Churchill's digressive asides were an 'accident' of composition – a view
which seems to have prevailed throughout the nineteenth century.[29] The
main 'blemish' of the poet's style, according to Tooke, was his personal,
abusive censure of individuals. Tooke classed Churchill as a Juvenalian satirist and made it clear that it was his 'roughness' and 'commonplace' qualities which kept him 'below the first rank'.[30] Personal allusions
were regarded as errors, whereas classical allusions were accepted as the
currency of 'every writer of taste':

Though not unacquainted with the poets of ancient and modern times, the
Editor has seldom presumed to notice the passages of preceding writers, which
his author has occasionally imitated or borrowed; to every reader of taste they
will readily suggest themselves, and thus an idle accumulation of notes will have
been avoided ... [the Editor] will be better pleased with being reproached
for the scantiness of information than for the admission of one superfluous
note.[31]

Tooke's preface suggests that he regarded 'superfluous' prose notes as stylistic imperfections, much as he disapproved of the 'general irregularity' of Churchill's conduct and of Churchill's 'indulgence' in the 'license of digression'.[32] Byron's higher esteem for the satirist is evident in his comparison of Churchill's *Times* with Dryden's *Annus Mirabilis* in correspondence with Lord Holland when asked to help out with the Drury Lane Address.[33] Byron adopted and developed the textual features which Tooke described as Churchill's 'most obvious . . . blemishes'. While Churchill's 'years of fame' have been cited as relevant contexts for Byron's meditations on posterity, the texture of Churchill's verse satire has not been analysed in detail, and an exploration of its idiosyncrasies helps to define the rough ride of which Byron's readers complained.[34]

Like much eighteenth-century verse, Byron's early poetry displays an emphatic use of personification – a traditional method of gaining universality for satire. Churchill and Byron, however, share an inclination towards more detailed and tangible personifications, suggesting a pull towards the fabric rather than the figurines of didactic poetry.[35] In Churchill's *Gotham* (1764) a playfully idiosyncratic voice emerges to interrupt the poem before it is properly underway:

> Far off (no matter whether east or west,
> A real country, or one made in jest,
> Not yet by modern Mandevilles disgrac'd,
> Nor by map-jobbers wretchedly misplac'd,)
> There lies an island, neither great nor small,
> Which, for distinction sake, I Gotham call.
>
> (ll. 1–6)

As well as being an outrageous parenthetical interruption, these lines flaunt the marginalisation of the poet. Thomas Lockwood suggests that *Gotham* presents Churchill as a legislator: 'whereas Pope represents the author's isolation as enforced, Churchill accepts or even welcomes it and tracks down its relativistic implications'.[36] But Gotham is off the map in a way which reminds us that, unlike Byron, Churchill was writing at a time when the edges of England (notably Scotland) were dangerously peripheral. Churchill collaborated with John Wilkes on the *North Briton* and to some extent, his digressive licence is the flaunting of an aggressive English chauvinism. While Byron would borrow Churchill's meandering digressive line, his experience of British imperialism in Napoleonic Europe and his sympathy with oppressed Celtic peoples questioned rather than supported English nationalistic celebration.

Churchill bullied and harassed his readers with parenthetical asides which were designed to pre-empt and forestall their objections. This desire to incorporate and quell audience heckling in the text is evident in the way qualifications are planted in Churchill's *Independence* (1764) from the first line:

> Happy the bard (though few such bards we find)
> Who, 'bove controulment, dares to speak his mind.
>
> (ll. 1–2)

The deliberate disruption of the verse texture in these lines demonstrates the roughness of the 'independent voice'. Not surprisingly, Hogarth's 1763 print of Churchill ('The Bruiser') depicted him as a club-wielding bear.[37] With Wilkes, Churchill perfected the expression of an outsider's voice, proclaiming an authentic Englishness which had been betrayed by the ruling party. Churchill's aggressive Whiggish stance bolstered a strong, patriotic sense of identity while simultaneously criticising the status quo. In later years Byron sought to retain the idiom of independence and liberty, but would (eventually) cut loose from the Whiggish conception of the whole.

The Journey, which was left in manuscript at Churchill's death, exemplifies in even more exaggerated form the obtrusiveness of the satirist's intelligence through the deflections of a self-interrupting narrator:

> Some of my friends, (for friends I must suppose
> All, who, not daring to appear my foes,
> Feign great good will, and, not more full of spite
> Than full of craft, under false colours fight)
> Some of my friends, (so lavishly I print)
> As more in sorrow than in anger, hint
> (Though that indeed will scarce admit a doubt)
> That I shall run my stock of genius out.
>
> (ll. 1–8)

This passage displays many of the digressive modes later employed by Byron: the repeated beginning of a phrase (or poem), thwarted linear progress, qualification, commentary on the process of composition, use of proverbial expression from *Hamlet* and conversational after-thought. In *The Ghost*, Churchill attempts to extricate himself from a digression using 'But, to return' three times in thirty lines, a device which Byron exploits in *Beppo*: 'To turn, – and to return; – the devil take it! / This story slips forever through my fingers' (ll. 497–8). This self-reflexive narratology, of course, finds a prose counterpart in the writing of Laurence Sterne, and Churchill insisted that his use of a modish Shandean form should reinforce his oppositional politics.

The first two volumes of *Tristram Shandy* were published in 1760 and at the time Churchill was writing, Sterne's novel was at the peak of its popularity. Although this aspect of his satire has been seldom discussed, Churchill was clearly interested in the possibility of a digressive prose model for verse:

> But though to poets we allow,
> No matter when acquir'd or how,
> From truth unbounded deviation,
> Which custom calls Imagination,
> Yet can't they be suppos'd to lie
> One half so fast as Fame can fly;
> Therefore (to solve this Gordian knot,
> A point we almost had forgot)
> To courteous readers be it known,
> That, fond of verse and falsehood grown,
> Whilst we in sweet digression sung,
> Fame check'd her flight, and held her tongue,
> And now pursues, with double force
> And double speed, her destin'd course.
>
> (*The Ghost* III, ll. 503–16)

The reference to Imagination as a sort of deviation, the graphic display of deviation in parenthesis, the use of the adjective 'sweet' to characterise the experience of digression, and the reference to the 'knot' are all Shandean traits. *The Ghost* experiments with Sterne's modes of narration and, correspondingly, it was the poem least admired by Tooke:

> The metre is rugged, and on the whole inferior to that of 'The Duellist;' and though many fine passages occur, the rambling, digressive manner in which the whole poem is written, seldom invites to a re-perusal. (*The Poetical Works of Charles Churchill* (1804), II, 10)[38]

In spite of widespread assumptions (like Tooke's) that digression should be seamless and contribute to the coherence of the long poem, Churchill's interruptions insist on opacities of language, the haphazard process of reading, and the 'sportive' persona of the poet. This is evident in *The Ghost* where the poet complicates our progress through the text by attempting to '[lug] in' material from other texts:

> Men of sound parts, who, deeply read,
> O'erload the storehouse of the head
> With furniture they ne'er can use

> Cannot forgive our rambling Muse
> This wild excursion; cannot see
> Why Physic and Divinity,
> To the surprise of all beholders,
> Are lugg'd in by the head and shoulders;
> Or how, in any point of view,
> Oxford hath any thing to do:
> But men of nice and subtle learning,
> Remarkable for quick discerning,
> Through spectacles of critic mould,
> Without instruction, will behold
> That we a method here have got
> To shew what is, by what is not;
> And that our drift (parenthesis
> For once apart) is briefly this.
>
> (*The Ghost* IV, ll. 107–24)

Of course, the next section is by no means brief. Churchill versified recurrent apologies for his digressions, and cultivated his association with the hapless Shandean narrator who is constitutionally unable to restrict himself to a linear narrative. We find the same unwieldy textuality in *Don Juan* canto VI, 'Kind reader! pass / This long parenthesis: I could not shut / It sooner for the soul of me' (VI. 56). The manuscript of canto VI in the British Library reveals the faint trace of an opening mark of parenthesis just before 'I could not shut ...', suggesting the extent to which, for Byron, opening an aside became a reflex of composition.

In his illuminating discussion of the use of brackets in *Childe Harold's Pilgrimage* and *Don Juan*, John Lennard followed the rhetorical lead of A.B. England in emphasising the relationship between Byron's parenthetical asides and verisimilitude.[39] Lennard was sensitive to the reader's role in digression, but saw it as an essentially passive one, concluding that Byron's parentheses soothe the reader into compliance:

To a considerable extent the use of lunulae ... becomes a mannerism, serving, like grunts of agreement on the telephone, as phatic communication, reassuring the reader that the 'line' is still open, that the private, mercuric Byron is still there.[40]

Contemporary reviews indicate that the contrary was the case and that Byron's bracketed asides worked to check and modify the poet–reader relationship, reinjecting tension rather than offering reassuring returns. The contingencies of publication and critical reception are inextricably linked with formal signifiers of the arbitrary and accidental in the printed text. Byron and Churchill presented their falls into parentheses both as a way of succumbing to the fluxes and refluxes of the mind and as a renegotiation of the contract between poet and reader:

> After my promise made in rhime,
> And meant in earnest at that time,
> To jog, according to the mode,
> In one dull pace, in one dull road.
> What but that curse of heart and head
> To this digression could have lead?
> Where plung'd, in vain I look about,
> And can't stay in, nor well get out.
>   Could I, whilst Humour held the quill,
> Could I digress with half that skill;
> Could I with half that skill return,
> Which we so much admire in Sterne,
> Where each digression, seeming vain,
> And only fit to entertain,
> Is found, on better recollection,
> To have a just and nice connexion,
> To help the whole with wondrous art,
> Whence it seems idle to depart;
> Then should our readers ne'er accuse
> These wild excursions of the Muse;
> Ne'er backward turn dull pages o'er
> To recollect what went before.
>   (*The Ghost* III, ll. 959–80)

Churchill here invokes the idea of organic digression 'to help the whole' only to reject it in favour of something more obstreperous. The reference to the book as a material article and to the reader's experience of turning back pages are self-conscious adaptations of Sterne's running commentary on the course of *Tristram Shandy*:

– We'll not stop two minutes, my dear Sir, – only, as we have got through these five volumes, (do, Sir, sit down upon a set – they are better than nothing) let us just look back upon the country we have passed through.[41]

By referring to 'the skill ... which we so much admire in Sterne', Churchill links the reader's experience of digression in *Tristram Shandy* and the experience of digression in his own work. Sterne, however, appears as the more traditional writer, upholding the decorum of parts contributing to a whole as opposed to the 'wild excursions' of Churchill's Muse: Sterne's digressions create a potential space for 'better recollection', while Churchill's only produce the abruptness of a 'plunge'. Nevertheless, while deprecating his art, Churchill satirised literary critics as a 'pack' intolerant of whatever does not connect:

> When loose Digression, like a colt unbroke,
> Spurning connexion and her formal yoke,
> Bounds through the forest, wanders far astray
> From the known path, and loves to lose her way,
> 'Tis a full feast to all the mongrel pack
> To run the rambler down and bring her back.
>
> (*Gotham* II, ll. 205–10)

Digression is here a female figure and the hint of sexual promiscuity in 'loose' is emphasised by the traditional association of wantonness in the image of the 'colt' like Sterne's 'unbacked filly', or Swift's 'fancy [getting] astride on his reason'.[42]

Swift and Sterne veer towards a relativism which is just held in check; Churchill and Byron, on the other hand, flirt in a much riskier way with the texture of moral and aesthetic relativity. While digression figures as a journey in the eighteenth-century models we have been examining, Byron's writing takes this literary trope a stage further by mingling it with the historical actuality of travel across war-scarred Europe. Although Sterne does not always characterise digression as feminine, both Churchill and Byron attribute feminine characteristics to digressive behaviour, a point which will be explored later in the book. It is important to recognise, however, that – as with their party politics – Byron's and Churchill's sexual politics were not identical: Churchill produced violent anti-homosexual satire in *The Times* while Byron's hospitality to homo-erotic as well as heterosexual innuendo increases rather than restricts the range of possible readings.

Besides the charm of the parenthetical aside, Churchill's verse encouraged attention to the physical peculiarities of the speaker through satirical expansion of an insignificant 'stage direction' (Churchill was also a playwright):

> Here Trifle cough'd, (for coughing still
> Bears witness to the speaker's skill,
> A necessary piece of art,
> Of rhet'ric an essential part,
> And adepts in the speaking trade
> Keep a cough by them ready made,
> Which they successfully dispense
> When at a loss for words or sense)
> Here Trifle cough'd, here paus'd.
>
> (*The Ghost* II, ll. 541–9)

Byron deploys a similarly acute observation of personal mannerism in *Don Juan* canto VI, when Baba attempts to evade the direct questions of Gulbeyaz:

> But there seemed something that he wished to hide,
>   *Which* hesitation more betrayed than masked; –
> He scratched his ear, the infallible resource
> To which embarrassed people have recourse.
>
> (VI. 100)

Churchill's use of the mock-heroic device of stock-piling similes and a feigned difficulty in choosing the most suitable one to carry the narrative forward is also taken up by Byron:

> He said, and ceas'd; the chamber rung
> With due applause from ev'ry tongue:
> The mingled sound (now, let me see –
> Something by way of simile)
> Was it more like Strymonian cranes,
> Or winds low murmuring when it rains,
> Or drowsy hum of clust'ring bees,
> Or the hoarse roar of angry seas?
> Or (still to heighten and explain,
> For else our simile is vain)
> Shall we declare it like all four,
> A scream, a murmur, hum, and roar?
>
> (*The Ghost* II, ll. 605–16)

In Alexander Pope's use of poetic lists every detail is a necessary part of the whole. By contrast, Churchill and Byron use lists less to encapsulate the quality of the subject and more to focus on the difficulty of conveying it to the reader. Following Churchill's emphasis on authorial indulgence, Byron's *The Vision of Judgement* offers a menu of similes from which the reader is invited to choose, culminating in the shifting likenesses of the shadow Junius, the author who is '*really, truly,* nobody at all' (l. 80). This politicised manifestation of indeterminacy displaces sublime uncertainty on to the role of the reader and dismantles the integrity of the Popean collection. In *Don Juan* canto VI, the reader is given 'similes ... gathered in a heap' from which to 'pick and chuse' a description of a sleeping girl in a harem. While Sterne instructs the reader to 'clear up the mist which hangs upon these three pages', Byron's readers possess a far greater potential to augment the obscurity of the poem.[43] The invitation to select appropriate images is made not to refine the accuracy of a description, but so that both writer and reader may prolong and enjoy the various possibilities: different literary textures are sampled and appreciated; the movement through the text becomes a shared receptivity to let and hindrance. As Gary Dyer has shown, in the course of the eighteenth century this attention to the physical properties of the text and the materiality of language threatened to undermine the moral basis for satire in truthtelling.

Churchill and Byron demonstrate a keen interest in the multiple meanings of language, particularly the processes of euphemism and punning.[44] They both engage the reader in discussions about the 'tastefulness' of different words and delight in the way that fashionable shifts in meaning might interrupt narrative stability. As with parenthetical asides, there are continuities between Churchill's and Byron's juxtapositions of literary allusions with topical social or cultural material. In 'An Epistle to William Hogarth', Churchill attacked Hogarth's serious composition 'Sigismund' by using a borrowed form of address from *Paradise Lost*, one that was unsignalled by marks of quotation, but too famous for the audience to miss:

> But, O, how much unlike! how fall'n! how chang'd!
> How much from Nature and herself estrang'd!
> 　　　　　　　　　　　　　　　(ll. 501–2)

The woeful moment of recognition and alienation is transferred brilliantly from the fallen angels in Hell to the public's first viewing of a picture. Churchill conveys both the fall of Hogarth's reputation, and the failure of the composition to exhibit the power of its subject. In the satire *The Ghost*, Dr Johnson was also translated to the realm of the eternally vanquished:

> Pomposo, with strong sense supplied,
> Supported, and confirm'd by Pride,
> His comrades' terrors to beguile
> 'Grinn'd horribly a ghastly smile:'
> Features so horrid, were it light,
> Would put the devil himself to flight.
> 　　　　　　　　　(*The Ghost* ii, ll. 683–8)

Churchill relished the excessive nature of his epic insults, and the use of quotation marks here invites the reader to recognise the poet's sources and experience the shock of the connection. His desire for readerly participation in the construction of satire, however, coexists (like Byron's) with disdain for the mass readership. *The Rosciad* satirises the grotesquerie of audience taste by associating theatrical novelty with the perverse creations of Milton's Hell:

> Monsters, with tails of ice, and heads of fire;
> Gorgons, and Hydras, and Chimeras dire.
> Each was bestrode by full as monstrous wight,
> Giant, dwarf, genius, elf, hermaphrodite.
> The Town, as usual, met him in full cry;
> The Town, as usual, knew no reason why.
>
> (ll. 673–8)

Churchill's verse challenged the audience to discriminate between high and low culture (a division which was still available to him, but much less secure for Byron). The allusion to *Paradise Lost* contrasts epic gravity with dramatic buffoonery, and suggests the volatility of audience taste. Byron employed the same satirical devices, but his creative recasting of epic culture slides into a questioning of the cultural hierarchy which was so much more certain in Churchill's time: Byron confounds the source of his allusions with the new context where his predecessors had more simply contrasted the two. This is in part a response to the changing power of the readership.

As numbers of readers grew in the later eighteenth century, the reception of poetry was less confined to an easily recognisable 'public sphere' of coffee house society. *The Dunciad* (1743) used digression to reflect the monstrous growth of a 'literary lower empire'. For Byron, the extent of this empire was never simply confined to the environs of Grub Street. We can detect a certain amount of social animus, but also uncertainty in Byron's use of digressive quotations which mix the old and new styles of the literary marketplace. By the time Byron picked up the 'grey goose-quill', a digressive style was no longer the sole territory of Shaftesbury's educated gentleman. Aiming directly at the new markets for leisure and luxury, novelists had adapted far more quickly than contemporary poets to the complex stratification of the reading public.

While Churchill's verse offered one eighteenth-century verse model for digressive communication with the reader, Byron found extensive authorial asides in eighteenth-century novels. Sentimental poetry offered a heightened awareness of the body, and the narrators of sentimental prose added to this a self-reflexive consciousness of literature as artifice. Attentiveness towards the reader was driven by moral concern, as John Mullan has explained:

In an age in which narrative fiction was suspected by many, even of its more enthusiastic consumers, of being suggestive, improper, promiscuous, novels were thick with descriptions of how narratives should be attended to and interpreted. They constantly concerned themselves, technically and moralistically, with the effects of telling stories.[45]

If we analyse eighteenth-century modes of direct address to the reader, we observe satire and sentiment working in parallel ways rather than in opposite directions.[46] In satirical and sentimental writing the reader is recognised as a risk in the production of meaning. This awareness may lead to gentle authorial nudges or a more laboured attempt to guide and correct, but in all cases the uncertainty of the reader's response is tacitly acknowledged. What separates Byron's digressive writing from the arabesque flourishes of his forerunners is his gradual acceptance of the chance element in the reader's reception of his work. Aware of many different audiences from an early age – including the coterie of Southwell, the House of Lords, Scotch reviewers, the audience at Drury Lane, the female 'arbiters of taste', and the various recipients of his letters – Byron developed a mode that was capable of wooing, including and discarding readers. Instead of refining 'mechanisms of control' (Empson's check on ambiguity), Byron gradually incorporated risk as part of the digressive texture of his writing, translating the aristocratic pastime of seduction into a textual encounter.

'To the Earl of [Clare]' (1807), written when Byron was nineteen years old, illustrates an early self-conscious use of digression between aristocratic men:

> Now [Clare] I must return to you,
> And sure apologies are due.
>   Accept then, my concession;
> In truth, dear [Clare], in fancy's flight,
> I soar along from left to right,
>   My Muse admires digression.
>
>   (ll. 67–72)

But in this verse epistle Byron's digressive topical references extend to the literary marketplace in footnote gossip about the middling class of readers and the row between Francis Jeffrey and Thomas Moore.

A Bard, (Horresco referens,) defied his Reviewer to mortal combat; if this ex-ample becomes prevalent, our periodical Censors must be dipt in the River Styx, for what else can secure them from the numerous Host of their enraged assailants. (*CPW*, I, p. 372)

This leads the reader away from general verse reflection on 'critic sar-casm' to a specific incident (the farcical duel between Moore and Jeffrey); memory of this event is in turn overtaken by a frivolous classical allusion.

The tone of the footnote is arch, making display of erudite wit, and it shows an interest in the volatile relationship between poets and reviewers well before *Hours of Idleness* was dissected in the same 'Northern review'. The verse epistle has, of course, a long tradition of wide-ranging reference, but the promiscuity of Byron's topical and literary allusions tests and surpasses the limits of that tradition by overflowing into prose and the distracting physical particulars of specific historical incident.

Byron's familiar, conversational style and the medley of different formal modes within one work continued the loosening and hybridisation of verse which began, for example, in the work of Matthew Prior. Prior's poetry (like Churchill's) embodied apparently conflicting forces of eighteenth-century poetry, ranging between tender pastoral lyrics and frisky burlesque.[47] Whereas Churchill's mode of address was wary and sometimes irritable, Prior's conversational style was tolerant and sinuous, embracing (rather than colliding) old and new modes:

> Examples I could cite you more;
> But be contented with these four:
> For, when one's proofs are aptly chosen
> Four are as valid as four dozen. . . .
> For some in ancient books delight;
> Others prefer what moderns write;
> Now I should be extremely loth,
> Not to be thought expert in both.[48]

Prior offers a bridge from the coterie verse of the 'mob of gentleman' to the accommodating, familiar style of subscription poetry. His middling mode of address proved extremely popular and the 1717 collection attracted more subscribers than Pope's translations.[49]

In a recent reappraisal of Prior's contribution to sentimental literature, Blanford Parker observes that 'Prior stands with Gay as the most perfect manipulator of conversational tone' in the period, but that his verse rejects an 'Augustan' unity of purpose.[50] Whereas Pope and Mandeville 'sought a new economy of motivation to explain the apparent diversity of human actions, Prior remained agnostic to the end about the twists and turns of the human mind'.[51] In this way, Prior's verse conveys some of the same strains of relativism and independence that emerged in Churchill. The narrative and epistolary voices which emerge from their verse are not the confidently centralised accents of Dryden or Pope. In Prior and Churchill, digressive stops and starts are not the badge of courtly privilege or imitative excellence, but a kind of conversational individualism designed to appeal to a fickle, ambitious class of purchasers.

Their paradoxical creation of an independent voice which entails varying, multiple and subtle degrees of dependence on the reader was played
out across Byron's career and he cited the bawdy extremes of Prior's
poetry to suggest that English taste had lost its stylistic identity.

Two key modes of Byronic digression – parenthetical asides and signalled topical or literary allusions – allow us to see how the allegedly
opposite modes of satirical and sentimental writing developed parallel
relationships with the reader.[52] In his two 'Farewells' to Malta and to
Hobhouse, Byron uses bracketed asides so that a tone of playful scep-
ticism may modify without completely subverting an otherwise elegiac
voice.[53] The genre of the valediction has a tradition of loving itemi-
sation or concentration on the physical qualities of place or person to
be quitted. Byron departs from this formula, using parenthesis to suggest a counter-genre of relief at departure. In the 'Farewell Petition to
J[ohn] C[am] H[obhouse] Esq.', Byron embarks on an eight-line list
of the sufferings endured by Fletcher, translating his manservant into a
series of objections, resistances, and complaints. The figure of Fletcher
is gradually replaced by a catalogue of things: 'The Vizier's galliot, and
Albanias' rocks / All Asias' bugs, and Pera's sable Pox'.[54] Byron's poem
becomes absorbed in details for their own sake. They are not listed to
create a cohesive pattern or picture, but occur simply as a trail of association in which the sound of the words is the main shaping agency. This
incorporation of encyclopaedic detail into verse is accompanied by an
amused self-consciousness: the poem continues by drawing attention to
itself as literature; talking about the 'paths of Sale', quoting Pope (who
addresses Bolingbroke as 'philosopher, and friend') and foregrounding
the difficulties of verse-writing:

> Tell him, my guide, Philosopher, and Friend,
> Who cannot love me, and who will not mend,
> Tell him, that not in vain I shall essay
> To tread and trace our 'old Horatian way',[55]
> And be (with prose supply my dearth of rhymes)
> What better men have been in better times.
>
> (ll. 34–40)

The parenthetical aside hints at the prosaic side of Hobhouse, which
Byron teased and appreciated. It also lifts editorial deliberation into
the poem, mediating between verse and marginal prose commentary,
and playing-up the drama of finding a rhyme. The bracketed interruption displays Byron's awareness of formal discipline while simultaneously
placing such rules under comic strain.

In *An Essay on Man* (the source of Byron's Popean allusion), Pope claimed to have chosen 'an Epistolary way of writing' because his subject matter 'approacheth to prose'.[56] Byron pushed this model further. As in many of Byron's later poems, the promise to close comes some time before the poem stops: 'Here let me cease,' occurs thirteen lines before the last line. The interim is filled with projections of publication:

> Go, get thee hence to Paternoster Row,
> Thy patrons wave a duodecimo!
> (Best form for *letters* from a distant land,
> It fits the pocket, nor fatigues the hand.)
>
> (ll. 47–50)

Attention to the book as physical object was not a new literary device in 1810, nor was the suggestive innuendo which accompanies Byron's address, but Byron transposed an emphasis on the mechanics of book production into incongruous literary modes, drawing attention to the text as a commodity and questioning the reader's position in a wider culture.

The 'Farewell to Malta' similarly abandons the sentiment of leave-taking for a series of parenthetical interpolations which focus attention on comically mundane details. The poem parodies loco-descriptive farewells, and by an accumulation of common nouns suggests that the poet's destination might be anywhere:

> I go – but God knows when, or why,
> To smoky towns and cloudy sky,
> To things (the honest truth to say)
> As bad – but in a different way.
>
> (ll. 21–4)

The specificity of place is here juxtaposed with the colloquial surrender of detail in 'God knows when, or why', but the brackets enclose a (duplicitous) reminder of truth and honesty. In this 'Farewell', Malta (the addressee) is displaced by the whimsical thought processes of the poet, who can

> ... only stare from out my casement,
> And ask, for what is such a place meant?
> Then, in my solitary nook,
> Return to scribbling, or a book,
> Or take my physic while I'm able
> (Two spoonfuls hourly by the label).
>
> (ll. 49–54)

This last parenthesis has the effect of jolting the reader out of a list-less survey and into the comedy of specificity with another reminder of duty and discipline. The exactitude of the digressive aside discharges the obligation of rhyme by embracing scrupulously detailed irrelevance. Though Byron referred to the poem as 'a copy of Hudibrastics', intended only for private circulation, it was published in 1816 in *Poems on His Domestic Circumstances* (sixth edition). Byron professed puzzlement in 1811 when the verses caused disquiet ('I am sure there is nothing to annoy any body, or a single personal allusion throughout'), but it is easy to see how the casual specificity of this poem – especially the rhymes around 'Mrs Fraser' – might have been received in the context of the Separation Scandal.[57]

Hudibrastics, anyway, had always been a form of stylistic brinkman-ship: the palpable disruption of Hudibrastic rhymes was captured by Dryden when he distinguished them from 'manly' satire and described the way 'the quick returns of rhyme, [debase] the dignity of the style ... it turns earnest too much to jest, and gives us a boyish kind of pleasure. It tickles awkwardly with a kind of pain, to the best sort of readers: we are pleased ungratefully, and ... against our liking.'[58] The efforts of the 'awkwardly tickled' reader to accommodate these rhymes have the same distancing effect as parenthetical allusion: in both ma-noeuvres, the poem mocks the authoritative precision of 'precedent' and throws its trust onto the transient relationship created with the reader. Rapid private circulation, rumoured report and pirated publication all contributed to associate Byron's casually digressive style with sexual or moral misdemeanour. As we saw in the first chapter, however, read-ers were also unsure how much of Byron was real, or to what extent he was asking them to participate in a cynical market-oriented perfor-mance which clashed with the newly fashionable modes of confessional sincerity.

At the same time that a taste for sentimental literature of emotional candour was gradually edging out more robust eighteenth-century wit, writers of dramatic comedy developed a compromise mode of address which anticipated Byron's parodic manipulation of precursor texts. Spe-cially commissioned prologues and epilogues for stage plays abandoned dramatic illusion as the playwright spoke to his or her audience directly. These addresses juxtaposed the immediate physical conditions of the theatre and actors with allusions to well-known dramatic scenes or to speeches with historical significance. Charles Dallas, Byron's first literary mentor, dabbled with theatrical writing, and in a letter from Patras in 1810, Byron discussed the intimate and often antagonistic relationship between playwright and theatre audience:

[Dallas] had a farce ready for the stage before I left England, and asked me for a prologue, which I promised, but sailed in such a hurry I never penned a couplet. – I am afraid to ask after his drama for fear it should be damned, Lord forgive me for using such a word, but the pit, Sir, you know the pit, they will do those things in spite of merit.[59]

His reference to a prologue that should have been penned in couplets points to the tradition of Goldsmith and Sheridan (among Byron's favourite sources for quotation, according to Marchand).[60] A brief discussion of some of their modes of allusion may help to place the voice that emerged in Byron's digressive literary allusions, and its peculiar effect of familiarity and estrangement.

Prologues and epilogues to new productions were published in local newspapers, national periodicals and printed editions of the play. The vigorous relationship between topical satire and dramatic occasion predated what Byron would find flourishing in the improvisatory theatre of Italy and reminds us that the relationship between playwright and audience in Georgian theatres was much more part of the performance than in our own time. In the epilogue to *The Good-Natured Man*, for example, Oliver Goldsmith compared the author's discomfort watching his play from the pit to Lear's tragic suffering in the storm:[61]

> While oft, with many a smile and many a shrug,
> He eyes the centre, where his friends sit snug;
> His simpering friends, with pleasure in their eyes,
> Sink as he sinks and as he rises rise;
> He nods, they nod; he cringes, they grimace;
> But not a soul will budge to give him place.
> Since then, unhelped, our bard must now conform
> 'To bide the pelting of this pitiless storm'.
>
> (ll. 25–32)

The audience is pointed towards the unexpected similarity of the comparison (as in metaphor) but also recognises the ludicrous aspect of the comparison (the dimension which metaphor usually suppresses).[62] It is not clear how the speaker of the epilogue conveyed the presence of quotation marks to the audience; presumably a pregnant pause would have helped to indicate allusion. In Goldsmith's epilogue to *The Sister* a stage direction dictates that the speaker should slow down to enable the audience to recognise *Hamlet*:

> What if I give a masquerade? I will.
> But how? ay, there's the rub (pausing) – I've got my cue:
> The world's a masquerade! the maskers, you, you, you.
>   [To Boxes, Pit, and Gallery]

It can be assumed that well-known speeches from Shakespeare would be as instantly recognisable as they are today. Literary quotation was a familiar game for educated readers and, as Jonathan Bate has pointed out, books of Shakespearean extracts played an important part in a child's schooling.[63] It seems likely that eighteenth-century dramatists drew on a common stock of Shakespearean allusions that were kept in the public ear by continual and competitive efforts of allusion. Goldsmith's epilogue to *She Stoops to Conquer* allowed the actor playing Harlequin to experiment with the roles of Lear and Richard III:

> Shakespeare himself shall feel my tragic rage.
> 'Off! off! vile trappings!': a new passion reigns!
> The maddening monarch revels in my veins.
> Oh! for a Richard's voice to catch the theme:
> 'Give me another horse! bind up my wounds! – soft –
>   'twas but a dream.'
> Aye, 'twas but a dream, for now there's no retreating:
> If I cease Harlequin, I cease from eating.
>
>   (ll. 20–6)

The edited highlights of Shakespearean tragedy worked to satirise a popular perception of tragic theatre, but they also reinforced the canons of popular taste and bolstered patriotism. The same moment from *Richard III* appeared in a prologue to Sheridan's *The Camp*, satirising George Colman's revival of a tragedy by Beaumont and Fletcher about Boadicea:

> She starts, she wakes, she quivers, kneels, and prays,
> 'Side saddle, my Horse! ah! lace up my Stays!
> Soft, soft; 'twas but a Dream . . .'[64]

These couplet collages deployed signalled allusion to focus on the material concerns of the production; personalities of the cast, rival productions, special effects and financial disputes. The epilogue to Sheridan's *School for Scandal*, for example, written by George Colman the Elder, revelled in an extended parody of *Othello*:

> The Transient Hour of Fashion too soon spent,
> 'Farewell the tranquil mind, farewell Content!
> Farewell the plum'd Head – the cushion'd Tete,
> That takes the Cushion from its proper seat!
> The spirit stirring Drum! – Card Drums I mean –
> Spadille, odd Trick, Pam, Basto, King and Queen!
> And you, ye knockers, that with Brazen Throat
> The Welcome Visitor's Approach denote,
> Farewell! – all Quality of high Renown,
> Pride Pomp, and Circumstance of glorious Town!
> Farewell! your revels I partake no more,
> And Lady Teazle's occupation's o'er!'
> – All this I told our Bard – he smil'd and said 'twas clear
> I ought to play deep Tragedy next year:
> *(Dramatic Works,* I, p. 443, ll. 7–20)

Whereas the direct quotations in Churchill's verse usually involved a simple substitution of one satiric target for another, the intimacy of the dramatic prologue established a more conversational, shared appropriation of a common source. In the social space of the theatre, the audience would be expected to recognise and respond to familiar allusions in a different context. Byron's writing used these sudden shifts of reference to transfer what Charles Lamb called 'this secret correspondence with the company before the curtain' from the raucous social space of the theatre into the communion between poet and reader.[65]

Byron was forced to meditate on the art of the prologue when he was commissioned to produce one himself, and he turned for a model to Colman the Elder:

– There are but two decent prologues in our tongue – Pope's to Cato – Johnson's to Drury Lane, this with the Epilogue to the 'Distrest Mother' & I think one of Goldsmith's, and a prologue of Old Colman's to Beaumont & Fletcher's Philaster are the best things of the kind we have.[66]

Byron had been asked to fête the opening of the new Drury Lane Theatre for Lord Holland, whose committee had rejected all the addresses submitted in open competition. Holland seems to have envisaged Byron's role as that of celebrity guest who could 'excuse us with the public for breaking faith with the poetasters'.[67] Byron's projected models, however, suggested a less conciliatory approach to audience sensitivities. Colman's prologue to *Philaster* (1763) had been controversial at the time because it launched a scathing attack on modern taste. After leaving England, Byron, too, would force his readers to confront their own forms of censorship, but at this stage in his career he yielded to the pressure to revise. Lord Holland remembered that Byron was 'singularly good-humoured and even docile in correcting, curtailing, or lengthening any passage at my request'.[68]

As with the changes to *Childe Harold* cantos I and II suggested by Dallas and Murray, Byron's obligations to the senior Whigs controlling the Drury Lane Theatre meant that his satirical allusions were expunged.[69] The 'Address' Byron finally produced is dutifully muted, although in the manuscript variants we can see how earlier drafts had employed the more controversial tradition of Goldsmith, Sheridan and Colman. At one point, Byron returned to the much-quoted ending of *Richard III* to satirise the contemporary audience's preference for animals on stage:

> the drama late deplores
> That late she deigned to crawl upon 'all fours'
> When Richard roars in Bosworth for a horse
> If you command – the *Steed* must come in course

These lines were dropped at Whitbread's request. Similarly, a topical reference to the rumoured madness of George III was removed from the final version:

> Though fled the Queen, our Monarchs still remain
> Yes, here 'old Lear shall be King again'.[70]

This turning of allusion allows the audience two forms of recognition: the identification of the precursor text and the application of the text in a new context. As an art thriving on the contrast between two conceptual frames of reference it is similar to political caricature, but requires more imagination from its readers who have to identify and complete the allusive process.

One of the distinctive features of Byron's mode of digressive allusion is the unmissable use of quotation marks to signal the appearance of another text. Although he frequently asked for assistance in punctuating poems, most of the quotation marks which appear in his published works were present in Byron's first drafts. Conscious use of quotation marks is foregrounded in Byron's 'Parenthetical Address, by Dr. Plagiary' which was first published in the *Morning Chronicle*. It refers to an incident at Drury Lane when, in defiance of the rejection by Holland's committee, the aggrieved son of Dr Busby attempted to read aloud his father's rejected address. The Busby family quickly became a public joke and Byron's parody entered the public domain without censorship. His preface is of particular interest because it foregrounds the use of signalled allusion:

Half stolen, with acknowledgements, to be spoken in an inarticulate voice, by Master — at the opening of the next new theatre. (Stolen parts marked with the inverted commas of quotation, thus, '—').

By drawing attention to his 'stolen' sources, Byron makes the parody irresistible. In the 'Parenthetical Address', lines from Dr Busby's original are quoted and undercut relentlessly through juxtaposition with Byron's mock-editorial commentary. Although all satiric parody is bound to be linguistically self-aware because its target is another form of rhetoric, Byron's mode of interrupting precursor texts has a peculiarly material effect; most commonly, for example, his quotations draw out sexual innuendo:

> 'These we invoke – your sister arts implore',
> With 'smiles', and 'lyres', and 'pencils', and much more.
> 'These if we win, the Graces too we gain';
> Disgraces too! 'inseparable train!'
> 'Three who have stolen their witching airs from Cupid',
> (You all know what I mean unless you're stupid).
>
> (ll. 29–34)

The effect of Byron's repeated interventions in Busby's address is to suggest an 'inseparable train' of 'much more'. He deflates Busby's attempt at sublimity by insisting on the physical associations which are suspended in polite address. This process continues throughout Byron's poems, and is not limited to those works which were wholly or mainly works of literary satire. By releasing a fuller train of association than we might expect in allusion, the experience of reading Byron's verse threatens tonal stability and inevitably, generic stability. In this way, Byron's digressions might be said to disturb the reader's generic 'competence' in a more violent, local way than the generic innovations identified by Alastair Fowler as common to each literary epoch.[71]

Signalled allusions in canonical Romantic poems are few and far between. Byron's contemporaries chose allusions of a quieter and more assimilative variety, apparently sharing Thomas De Quincey's opinion that quotation marks created a disagreeable interruption in the course of reading:

There is good reason for rejecting the typographical marks of quotation: they break the continuity of the passion by reminding the reader of a printed book.[72]

Nevertheless we can trace limited use of the eighteenth-century prologue mode in works by Percy Shelley and William Wordsworth. *The Witch of Atlas* (written August 1820) was prefaced by six *ottava rima* stanzas 'To Mary', culminating in a critique of Wordsworth:

> Wordsworth informs us he was nineteen years
>   Considering and retouching Peter Bell;
> Watering his laurels with the killing tears
>   Of slow, dull care, so that their roots to hell
> Might pierce, and their wide branches blot the spheres
>   Of Heaven, with dewy leaves and flowers; this well
> May be, for Heaven and Earth conspire to foil
> The over busy gardener's blundering toil.
>
> My Witch indeed is not so sweet a creature
>   As Ruth or Lucy, whom his graceful praise
> Clothes for our grandsons – but she matches Peter
>   Though he took nineteen years, and she three days
> In dressing. Light the vest of flowing metre
>   She wears: he, proud as dandy with his stays,
> Has hung upon his wiry limbs a dress
> Like King Lear's 'looped and windowed raggedness.'
>
>   (ll. 25–40)

Allusion in these stanzas uses the carnivalesque forms of disruption we have noted in Byron's early verse. In particular, there is an emphasis on the physical aspects of conventional metaphors: the laurels acquire downward pushing roots and an abundance of thick undergrowth. Wordsworthian metre is imaged as a corset for controlling the flesh, whilst the signalled allusion to *King Lear* insists on the nakedness of Peter Bell's body. Once we enter the main body of the poem, however, Shelley's allusions instantly settle into something quieter and more assimilative.

The preface to *The Witch of Atlas* was not published with the rest of the poem in 1824 because Mary Shelley was wary of the controversy such an overt attack on Wordsworth might arouse.[73] By this time the Establishment reviewers revered him as a figure of patriarchal simplicity. His progress into sage respectability had been, in part, self-authored. In 1814 the 'Prospectus' to *The Excursion* was printed in italics and inside inverted commas: within this formal invocation was a signalled allusion to *Paradise Lost*:

> *I sing: – 'fit audience let me find though few'*
>   *So prayed, more gaining than he asked, the Bard,*
> *Holiest of Men. – Urania I shall need*
> *Thy guidance, or a greater Muse, if such*
> *Descend to earth or dwell in highest heaven!*[74]

This allusion to Milton typifies the traditional spirit of the prologue: announcing 'the design and scope of the whole Poem' (*The Excursion*, p. x), Wordsworth invoked literary forefathers in order to situate his new work. But his form of allusion grants very little creative scope to the reader. Byron's response to the 'Prospectus' was, therefore, to open up a trail of Miltonic associations suppressed by the older Wordsworth:

> I will venture to assert that the Sale of the Paradise lost was greater in the first four years after it's publication than that of 'the Excursion' in the same number – with the difference of nearly a Century & a half between them of time, & of thousands in point of general readers notwithstanding Mr. Wordsworth's having pressed Milton into his Service as one of those not presently popular, to favour his own purpose of proving that our Grand-Children will read *him* – the said William Wordsworth ... he may have a sect, but he will never have a public, and his '*audience*' will always be '*few*' without being '*fit*', except for Bedlam.[75]

Byron's point was that Wordsworth had 'pressed Milton into his service' to shore up personal reputation. Wordsworth's politically disingenuous comparison adorned his own apostasy with Miltonic constancy. Byron's digressive quotation of Wordsworth exacted revenge by turning Wordsworth's solemnity into senility, insisting on the literalness of ' "*few*" ', and on the bodily connotation of ' "*fit*" ', and relocating Wordsworth's audience in Bedlam. The complexity of quoted quotation is signalled by both italics and inverted commas, emphasising the multiple layers of appropriation.

The use of quotation marks to signal allusion enforces a choice about allusion for the reader. If in general we see allusion as a threshold to another text, Byron's art of signalled allusion leads the reader over that threshold. The obligation on the reader might be seen to qualify the extent of imaginative free-play or indeterminacy usually associated with intertextuality. But while freedom might be curtailed in one direction, it is extended in another. As well as the types, frequency of allusion is greater in Byron's poetry than in his contemporaries' work.[76] His interceptions of other texts foreground what Peter Manning has called the 'politics of physical presentation, of dedications, appendices, prices, sizes of volumes, illustrations, and other contextual matters'.[77] As we shall see, reading with this sort of awareness is both a social and political activity.

An immediate problem in discussing allusive poetics is a lack of critical vocabulary to describe the variety of modes employed by the poet.[78] In the editorial introduction to *The Complete Poetical Works*, McGann states that he has 'tried to identify all of Byron's explicit literary allusions and

echoes, and as many of his less explicit ones as [he has] recognised'
(*CPW*, I, p. xliv). The editorial criteria for distinguishing between an
explicit allusion and an explicit echo are, however, not divulged. Mc-
Gann's other forms of reference are 'Echoes ...', 'Echoing ...', 'The
poem deliberately recalls ...', 'recalling ...', 'Perhaps recalling ...', 'Alluding to ...', 'a misquotation of ...', 'The stanza refers to ...', 'Cf ...'.
Sometimes the commentary is simply a line reference to another text.
This suggests McGann's sensitivity to Byron's multiple uses of other texts
while suggesting that it has not proved possible to devise an editorial system to accommodate these nuances. Nuances would doubtless be lost if
such a system were devised, and a concern of this book is to explore the
differences between Byron's modes of allusion while suggesting that the
vital digressive element in his poetics comes from the protean nature of
this sort of intertextuality.

In his 1970 article on 'The Art of Allusion' Manning traced three
Shakespearean reference points in the final paragraph of *English Bards and
Scotch Reviewers*. His selection indicates the instability of Byronic allusion:
one allusion comprises an unsignalled quotation from *Henry IV*, another
is direct quotation from *Hamlet*, and the third is a much more distant
verbal echo of *Macbeth*. Manning (like Jonathan Bate) refers to all of
these as 'allusions' but the effect on the page and on the poem would
seem to be different in all cases. Why did Byron signal the quotation
from *Hamlet* but not the extract from *Henry IV*? Another misquotation
from *Hamlet* earlier in the poem goes unmarked: 'Oh! what a noble heart
was here undone,' (l. 835), while Byron signals the smaller appropriation
from *Macbeth* by placing it in direct speech: '"hold, enough!"' (l. 735),
and in the 'Postscript' to Jeffrey, Byron used quotation marks at every
opportunity. It may be that the placement of these markers is entirely
arbitrary (an idea to which we shall return), but one effect of the uneven
distribution of acknowledgement is to question the idea of stable literary
reputation.[79]

The marking of the allusions defamiliarises their content, whilst the
various degrees of fidelity to the source place all references in a condition of dubiety. Byron puts his direct quotation of a Bowles 'dwarf
Epic' in inverted commas (perhaps inviting a distant recollection of
Virgil) –

> The lofty numbers of a harp like thine:
> 'Awake a louder and a loftier strain.'
>
> (ll. 350–1)

– but this treatment was also accorded to the splenetic outbursts of the critic:

> While REYNOLDS vents his 'dammes, poohs', and 'zounds',
> And common place, and common sense confounds.
>
> 　　　　　　　　　　　　　　(ll. 568–9)

Literary criticism was foregrounded in this poem not only because Byron was satirising the literary Establishment, but also because the poem dramatised the relationship between poetry and its readers, newly aware of the power various readers have to determine the meaning of a work:

> 'Why slumbers GIFFORD?' once was asked in vain:
> Why slumbers GIFFORD? let us ask again.
>
> 　　　　　　　　　　　　(ll. 819–20)[80]

The first question acknowledged a source ('New Morality' in the *Anti-Jacobin*), but the reiteration (without marks of quotation) can neither wholly discard this context nor wholly belong to it. The repetition encourages the reader to confront the difference between a line with a marked source and the same line without acknowledgement. It is also a way of realising the reader's desire for unity: the first quotation could be random, but the second represents the start of a pattern. In both instances the peculiarity of a marked allusion which 'forces itself upon the view' as Reynolds feared, turns our attention to questions of reception.

Discussing Byron's allusions in *Don Juan*, Manning suggests that the 'shadowy presences' of alluded-to texts 'augment Byron's voice by locating him within his tradition … through him a whole tradition is summoned and renovated'.[81] In *English Bards and Scotch Reviewers*, however, allusion is less of a reassuring figure because the authority of 'a whole tradition' is constantly interrogated. Byron's intertextuality may therefore pre-empt a Barthesian paradigm of the fictional:

> It is the instability of the placing of the quotation marks that decisively constitutes the fictional and renders it unrecuperable. The ideal text would be 'a text with uncertain quotation marks, with floating parentheses' … in which each undecidable component would work like a mouthful of good wine … where 'the mouthful swallowed does not have quite the same taste as the next mouthful taken'.[82]

In *English Bards and Scotch Reviewers*, each allusion becomes a troubling digression in which the reader is asked to risk his or her perspective on tradition: is '"en masque"' (l. 655) as significant as '"penetrable stuff"' (l. 1050)? What separates remembered words from an invitation and remembered words from *Hamlet*?

The link between configurations of allusion and digression has been touched on by Harold Bloom's paradigm of how influence works through poetic generations. In Bloom's model of conflict between authorial forefather and son, intertextual tension is eventually resolved and rebellious digression is superseded by a new totality.[83] Bloom concentrates on Byron's Prometheanism and, following Ridenour, emphasises the metaphor of the Fall in Byron's poetry. He is therefore less concerned with the signalled allusions on the surface of Byron's verse than with the moments where he believes that Byron is '[moving] in the poetic world of Wordsworth and Shelley'.[84] Like Byron's contemporary reviewers, Bloom occasionally vents critical frustration at the way Byron resists assimilation into the ranks of the 'Visionary Company'. Byron's digressive allusions evade Bloom's creative resettlement, keeping the whole work at the stages of swerve (or digression) away from the precursor texts and antithetical readings of them ('Clinamen' and 'Tessera' in Bloom's terms). In his discussion of the 'Big Six' and Shakespeare, Jonathan Bate suggests 'revising' Bloom's 'Revisionary Ratios' and removing the final clause from 'Tessera' ('with its antagonistic overtones') to describe the Romantics' allusive relationship with Shakespeare.[85] I would like to distinguish Byron's intertextuality from Bate's all-inclusive idea of Romantic allusion and from Bloom's paradigm of the achievement of unity and self-sufficiency: 'the attainment of a state of solitude'.[86] Byron's poetics evade both harmonious organic merger and sublime autonomy. The next chapter of the book suggests that Byron mixed literary tradition and contemporary debate to socialise the space between poet and public, leading his readers to consider the politics of digressive poetics.

CHAPTER THREE

Erring with Pope: Hints from Horace
and the trouble with decency

When Byron was accused of violating canons of correctness, his critics usually suggested that he erred from classical aesthetic ideals. Through-out the eighteenth century Horatian criticism had represented a cultural force opposed to forms of digression.[1] A review of *Tristram Shandy* in the *Journal Encyclopédique* of 15 April 1760 warned:

This is Horace's monster ... The author has neither plan nor principles, nor system: he only wishes to talk on and unfortunately one listens to him with pleasure ... Moreover, that irregular progression of ideas, so far removed from the spirit of this age, passes for intentional subtlety. The English find mystery in it and all join in admiring it.[2]

Sterne himself genuflected to this critical orthodoxy when he wrote to an early reader of the manuscript of volumes I and II of *Tristram Shandy*: 'I like Your Caution of the Ambitiosa recidet ornamenta – as I revise My book, I will shrive My conscience upon that sin.'[3] His offer to cut away 'sinful' superfluity acknowledges – albeit wryly – the traditional association between digression and transgression. Like Sterne, Byron's respect for Horatian standards of correctness coexisted with the com-position of a work which defied those notions. This chapter examines the ways in which conflicting notions of decorum in private and pub-lic contexts affect the texture, and therefore the meaning, of Byron's poetry.

Byron returned to his 1811 translation of Horace's *Ars Poetica* in 1820–1 when he was working on the fifth canto of *Don Juan*, the work he called his 'poetical T[ristram] Shandy' (*BLJ*, x, p. 150). Significantly, Byron's other model for *Don Juan* at this stage was Montaigne's essays; Montaigne had invoked a negative example from Horace's *Ars Poetica* to account for the digressive progress of his mind:

And in truth what are these *Essays* if not monstrosities and *grotesques* botched together from a variety of limbs having no defined shape, with an order, sequence and proportion which are purely fortuitous?
　　Desinit in piscem mulier formosa superne.[4]

Awareness of Horatian critical orthodoxy and a desire to exceed its generic constraints mingle in Byron's letters as well as his poetry. His complex theoretical allegiance to traditional forms, and practical subversion of them, is evident in a letter to Thomas Moore of 1 June 1818. Responding to Moore's criticisms of the enjambement between stanzas in *Childe Harold's Pilgrimage* canto IV, Byron claimed:

The fact is, that the terza rima of the Italians, which always *runs* on and in, may have led me into experiments, and carelessness into conceit – or conceit into carelessness – in either of which events failure will be probable, and my fair woman, 'superne,' end in a fish; so that Childe Harold will be like the mermaid, my family crest, with the Fourth Canto for a tail thereunto. (*BLJ*, VI, p. 46)

The unexpected termination of '"superne"' is an allusion to the image of artistic short-coming in Horace's *Ars Poetica* also borrowed by Montaigne.[5] Although Byron was prepared to see his poem damned by comparison with Horace's grotesque, other readers were unsure about whether Horatian standards ought to be applied to Byron's work.

In November 1814 the *Lady's Monthly Museum* expressed uncertainty about the criteria for evaluating *Lara*: 'To *measure* the writings of Lord Byron with the *yard* of Aristotelian and Horatian criticism', the reviewer felt, 'would be little favourable to their celebrity . . . To deviate from the beaten track as Lord Byron has done, requires no ordinary talent.'[6] This opinion takes us to the crux of a nineteenth-century aesthetic debate: might 'deviation' from the rules be a sign of genius, or was oddity merely a sign of flagrant disregard for communal discourse? Sir Joshua Reynolds had maintained that even genius ought to be recognised as 'the child of imitation'.[7] A different definition would be put forward, however, by William Hazlitt who in 'On Genius and Common Sense' argued that taste and genius made their own rules: 'In art, in taste, in life, in speech, you decide from feeling, and not from reason; that is from the impression of a number of things on the mind, which impression is true and well-founded, though you may not be able to analyse or account for it in the several particulars.'[8]

Reynolds and Hazlitt place critically different emphases on the relationship of 'small and minute parts' to the whole, Hazlitt being more interested in the gathering momentum of accumulation and Reynolds in the finished effect of the whole. For his contemporaries, Byron's writing brought to the fore this clash of neo-classical and modern frames of reference. Hobhouse experienced this collision in a particularly acute way as his classical ideals were intricately connected with his reformist Whig principles. He registered a hint of Horatian criticism about *Lara* in a letter to Byron of 11 September 1814: 'I have heard of one who prefers Lara to your last, but that all are scandalised at the possibility that such a fine fellow as Conrad could be thought to terminate in such a devil's tail as your present hero.'9 While relishing his role as a privileged insider early in Byron's career, Hobhouse was to find his loyalty to Byron tested as a personal drama about public reception unfolded.

Letters between Hobhouse and Byron play with an argot of classical allusions as well as favourite references to the stage and to novels. The bond of a Cambridge education was important to them and they seemed to take particular pleasure in declaring their shared commitment to traditional values which were perceived to be under threat. Hobhouse, for example, connected his admiration for *Childe Harold* canto IV with a respect for Popean satire. Writing to Murray from Venice on 7 December 1817, Hobhouse claimed:

Your new acquisition is a very fine finish to the three cantos already published, and, if I may trust to a taste vitiated – I say it without affectation – by an exclusive attention and attachment to that school of ancient and obsolete poetry of which your friend Mr. Gifford furnished us with the last specimen in his 'Baviad,' it is the best of all his lordship's productions. (Smiles, *A Publisher and His Friends*, I, p. 390)

This letter exemplifies an appreciation of eighteenth-century satire which would continue to play an important role in the context of *Hints from Horace*, not only in respect of the thematic content of the poem, but also because relationships between Byron, Hobhouse, Murray and Gifford influenced its texture. *Hints from Horace* offers an example of Byronic intertextuality – layers of allusion in sometimes uneasy dialogue with a number of different audiences.

The contradictory pulls of 'monstrosity' and Horatian restraint in Byron's writing were latent in the 1811 version of *Hints from Horace* and complicate the emphasis on decorum which Bernard Blackstone has seen as the leading characteristic of the work.10 *Hints from Horace* occupies a unique position in the Byronic oeuvre in that it belongs to Byron's early career and also to the period of his mature *ottava rima* poetry. The previous two chapters have explored the extent to which textual disruption was recognised as present in Byron's early writing. We have also considered the relationship between eighteenth-century digressive practices and Byron's own. *Hints from Horace* might be read as an index of the creative change between eighteenth-century digressive poetics and Byron's development of those modes. The revisions to the *Hints* also suggest how contemporary aesthetic and political debates played a crucial role in modifying Byron's later *ottava rima* satire. The focus of this chapter is, therefore, the relationship between poetics, literary history and politics.

Hints from Horace dates from March 1811: Byron thought of it both as a sequel to *English Bards and Scotch Reviewers* and as a poem to Hobhouse (*BLJ*, II, p. 43). By a strange coincidence, Hobhouse attempted in that same year a 'litteral [*sic*] verse rhyme translation of the same poem with learned notes' (Graham, *Byron's Bulldog,* p. 66) while he too was away from England. Byron expressed pride in the fidelity of his own imitation, but he also described his work as deviation, adaptation, variation and subjunction, highlighting the difference between his own poem and Horace's.[11] In the earlier version of the preface he announced: 'The Latin text is printed with the Imitation, not only to show where I have left Horace, but where Horace has left me' (*CPW*, I, p. 428).

While the tradition of imitation in English poetry welcomed the substitution of contemporary referents, the distinctive quality of Byron's version is its frequency of topical and literary allusions and the multiplicity of these variables.[12] Mary Rebecca Thayer observes that Byron's interruptions to the Horatian text

constitute a large part of the poem, and make it rather a piece of bitter satirical verse than an epistle about literature, with only an incidental element of mild satire, as is the original. The *Hints from Horace,* therefore, so far from being really Horatian in tone, rather serves to accentuate Byron's lack of sympathy with Horace.[13]

By stressing Byron's 'bitter' tone and his 'lack of sympathy with Horace', Thayer over-simplifies the complex registers and shifting tones of *Hints from Horace.* Not only is the poem 'an epistle about literature', it is also textured with different literatures which rematerialise in modified forms as they emerge from the *Ars Poetica.*[14]

It is in the prose notes in particular that we can see this very physical form of intrusion as Byron veers away from the Latin text into current literary and political quarrels. His colourful living examples acquire an autonomous energy which threatens the ideal unity of the Horatian cultural icon. In the proofs of the poem that were set up by Cawthorne in 1811, Byron's notes appear at the foot of the page. As the Latin text is printed on facing pages (as with Pope's *Imitations of Horace*), it is possible to see how Byron's English version overruns the Latin original in spatial terms and how the prose notes emphasise this tendency. The voice of the prose notes is digressive, colloquial, witty and personal.[15] As with the first two cantos of *Childe Harold's Pilgrimage*, the composition of some of the notes occurred during the first drafts of the verse. Byron's prose comments are, therefore, radically different from Wordsworth's 'Fenwick Notes' or Coleridge's marginal glosses to 'The Rime of the Ancient Mariner' which supply testimonials to unity of design and authorial purpose.

Byron's prose notes are distinctive because they foreground the immediacy of interchange between poet and reader. Whilst discussing the role of the 'atrocious reader' in *Don Juan*, Anne Barton points out that the noun 'reader' is 'entirely absent from *Childe Harold*'.[16] This applies, however, only to the text of the verse, not to the volume as a whole. The prose preface to cantos I and II states that the reception of the poem 'will determine whether the author may venture to conduct his readers to the capital of the East, through Ionia and Phrygia' (*CPW*, II, p. 3), and 'readers of romances' are teased in the notes to canto II, stanza 73, which also contain advice to 'the reader' to turn to Byron's appendix.[17] The role of the reader is similarly at issue in the notes to *Hints from Horace*, as is the process of composition itself.

The 1811 *Hints from Horace* shows how a prose voice insistently punctuates the verse with additional material detail. Horace's original text is interrupted with historically specific information on Byron's contemporaries and on the circumstances of composition:

Of 'John Joshua, Earl of Carysfort', I know nothing at present, but from an advertisement – in an old newspaper of certain Poems and Tragedies by his Lordship, which I saw by accident in the Morea. Being a rhymer himself, he will readily excuse the liberty I take with his name, seeing, as he must, how very commodious it is at the close of that couplet. (*CPW*, I, pp. 442–3)

Byron's note emphasises the contingencies of composition, the stringent demands of form, and the business of advertising and circulating literature. His use of encyclopaedic prose also records awareness of the reception of the poem. The initial subject of the prose notes is ostensibly traditional (a reference; a disputed source; a literary precedent; a note on a local antiquity), but the manner of the prose notation tends to generate further digressions from the verse. This is exaggerated by Byron's method

of introducing conversational allusions within his digressive prose
notes:

I beg Nathaniel's pardon: he is not a cobbler; *it* is a *tailor*, but begged Capel Lofft
to sink the profession in his preface to two pair of panta – psha! – of cantos,
which he wished the public to try on. (*CPW*, 1, p. 442)

Digressive notation here is a game with the reader who is expected to
enjoy the serendipity of error and slips of the pen. Another form of digression occurs when Byron offers one of his superfluous parenthetical
asides, as in the mock-fastidious reference to 'No. 31 of the Edinburgh
Review (given to me the other day by the captain of an English frigate
off Salamis)'(*CPW*, 1, p. 438). The half-forgetful, conversational trail of
association is characteristic of Byron's digressive emphasis on the contingencies of readerly reception.

Byron's awareness of words as things was signalled in the early epigraph to *Hints*, where a quotation from Fielding's *Amelia* contrasts the
exigencies of politics and poetry:

'Rimes are difficult things, they are stubborn things, Sir – I have been sometimes
longer in tagging a couplet, than writing a speech on the side of the opposition,
which hath been read with great applause all over the kingdom. – '[18]

As early as 1811, therefore, it is possible to see Byron drawing attention
to the technicalities and triumphs of poetic artifice, a process that would
become more pronounced in *Don Juan*:

> (The rhyme obliges me to this; sometimes
> Monarchs are less imperative than rhymes).
>   (v. 77)

Byron's preoccupation with the constraints of his form (particularly the
rhyme) energised his moments of discontinuity with the original Horatian
model. Letting form dictate the direction of the poem was a contraven-
tion of aesthetic propriety for which Keats was chastised when John
Wilson Croker reviewed *Endymion* in the *Quarterly*:

At first it appeared to us, that Mr. Keats had been amusing himself and wearying
his readers with an immeasurable game at *bouts-rimés*; but, if we recollect rightly,
it is an indispensable condition at his play, that the rhymes when filled up shall
have a meaning; and our author, as we have already hinted, has no meaning. He
seems to us to write a line at random, and then he follows not the thought excited
by this line, but that suggested by the *rhyme* with which it concludes. There is
hardly a complete couplet inclosing a complete idea in the whole book. He
wanders from one subject to another, from the association, not of ideas but of
sounds, and the work is composed of hemisitchs which, it is quite evident, have

forced themselves upon the author by the mere force of the catchwords on which they turn. (*RR*, C: II, pp. 768–9)

The movement of 'association' has, as we have seen, key importance in Hazlitt's definition of genius. Byron also responded to 'the mere force of the catchwords', but he does not just '[skim] the surface of things' with 'airy, intuitive faculty' (Hazlitt's image for the genius of Goldsmith).[19] Instead, Byron's insistence that readers turn and reflect on the process of association, although equally unpopular with contemporary reviewers, separates Byronic randomness from the loose Cockney meandering of *Endymion*.

From the beginning of *Hints from Horace* transgressive potential is embodied formally by digression. The association of digression and unlawful birth was popularised by Sterne's characterisation of digression as 'bastardly', and there is a hint of Sterne's presence when, in a flagrant deviation from Horace's advice, Byron inserts a requiem for Samuel Foote:

> Farce followed Comedy, and reached her prime
> In ever-laughing Foote's fantastic time,
> Mad Wag! who pardoned none, nor spared the best,
> And turned some very serious things to jest.
> Nor Church nor State escaped his public sneers,
> Arms nor the Gown, Priests, Lawyers, Volunteers:
> 'Alas, poor Yorick!' now for ever mute!
> Whoever loves a laugh must sigh for Foote.
>
> (ll. 327–34)

To compound the generic disruption, Byron incorporates a signalled borrowing from *Hamlet* which is, of course, also associated with the black page from *Tristram Shandy*. Horace's text at this point warns of the dangers of sudden turns and transitions:

> uerum ita risores, ita commendare dicaces
> conueniet Satyros, ita uertere seria ludo,
> ne quicumque deus, quicumque adhibebitur heros,
> regali conspectus in auro nuper et ostro,
> migret in obscuras humili sermone tabernas,
> aut, dum uitat humum, nubes et inania captet.
>
> (ll. 225–30)

The effect of the remembrance of Foote is to unsettle Horatian wisdom about the propriety of transitions from heavy to light material by juxtaposing tragic and comic cultural fragments. In this case both the contemporary reference and the method of inserting it conflict with Horatian decorum.

The authority of the unified organic work is also challenged by Byron's insistence on the failure and decomposition of another 'organic' production, the son and heir. Byron's most extensive digression in linear terms from the discussion of drama and literature compares the cycle of human life with the circulation and duration of books. In the *Ars Poetica*, the description of a boy's career contributes to an artistic debate about the appropriate delineation of character: in Byron's version, the rake's progress acquires a momentum of its own:

> Behold him freshman! forced no more to groan
> O'er Virgil's devilish verses, and – his own;*
> Prayers are too tedious, lectures too abstruse,
> He flies from T[a]v[e]ll's frown to 'Fordham's Mews;'
> (Unlucky T[a]v[e]ll! doom'd to daily cares*
> By pugilistic pupils, and by bears!)
> Fines, tutors, tasks, conventions threat in vain,
> Before hounds, hunters, and Newmarket Plain.
> Rough with his elders, with his equals rash,
> Civil to sharpers, prodigal of cash,
> Constant to nought – save hazard and a whore,
> Yet cursing both, for both have made him sore:
> Unread (unless since books beguile disease,
> The p[o]x becomes his passage to degrees);
> Fool'd, pillaged, dunn'd, he wastes his terms away,
> And unexpell'd, *perhaps*, retires M. A.;
> Master of Arts! as *hells* and *clubs* proclaim,*
> Where scarce a blackleg bears a brighter name!
>
> (ll. 223–40; * inserted)

The parentheses within this digression (and the prose notes (*) without) interrupt the passage to remind the reader firstly, of Byron's own ursophilia and secondly, of an unsavoury connection between the cyclical production of books and the human cycle of birth and decay. The freshman bears a strong resemblance to the young author who is 'rough with his elders' ('It will not do to call our Fathers – Fools!' (l. 430)) and whom 'conventions threat in vain' (l. 229).

Significantly, the new student is associated with images of risk in the activities around Newmarket, 'hazard' and '*hells*'. The satirical accusations of gambling reconfigure the uncertainty of the relationship between Horace's and Byron's texts. There is also a connection between the term-wasting of the undergraduate and the time-wasting of the poet in digression. Horace, it is true, displayed his consciousness of the passage of time in his conversational meanderings ('brevis esse laboro' (l. 25)), but

Byron's poem places more emphasis on his mournful awareness that the time shared by the poet and reader might always have been differently spent. As Byron's use of digression develops, we find that its self-conscious aspect intensifies: digressive poetics invite speculation about alternative routes. This may be one or other of the readerly paths through the poem, or the choice not to read the poem at all.

In a letter to James Cawthorne of 25 August 1811, in which Byron considered delaying the publication of *Hints from Horace* the first time round, he reflected that he and his friends might 'appear such pestilent scribblers':

Why, we shall want a press to ourselves, & if we go on with 'Weeks at Bath' & Travels, & Satires, & Imitations, & poems descriptive & what not, your Neighbor Mr. Eyre the trunk-maker will thrive prodigiously. (*BLJ*, II, p. 81)

Byron here plays up the casual profligacy of authorship, recognising that he is one of the 'mob of gentlemen' reluctant to suppress their 'Attic salt'. His (affected) distaste for 'this volley of Quarto's & Foolscap Octavos' was one of the satiric legacies of Pope. In *The Dunciad*, Pope had attacked the physical mass of sub-literary productions making the connection between bodily waste and the fate of failed poetry.[20] Byron's references to pastry chefs and trunk-makers in his notes to the poem were a continuation of this eighteenth-century satirical trope, but it is important to note that by including them, Byron was both augmenting the scope of the *Ars Poetica* and colliding Popean and Horatian tones with the idiom of his own time. A similar act of compression occurs when Byron translates Dryden's 'Martyrs of Pies, and reliques of the Bum' in his parodic reduction of William Wordsworth to 'Turdsworth'.[21] These divagations from Horace's text were augmented as Byron revised the poem back in England in 1811. In 1821, however, many of the digressive notes were cancelled or radically cut down.[22] Rather than seeing the later version of the poem as one in which the digressive element has been curbed, I would like to suggest that the digressive intertextuality of the 1820–1 *Hints from Horace* may be located in Byron's renewed defence of Pope and in a collateral reassessment of the role of the reader.

On 28 March 1820 Byron sent Murray 'a Screed of Doctrine' from Ravenna, and added as a postscript:

I have some thoughts of publishing the 'hints from Horace' written ten years ago – if Hobhouse can rummage them out of my papers left at his father's – with some omissions and alterations previously to be made – when I see the proofs. – – (*BLJ*, VII, p. 60)

Since Thomas Moore's editorial work on Byron's poetry, we have known that the reappearance of *Hints from Horace* was associated with Byron's involvement in the Pope/Bowles controversy. Although Jerome McGann dates the renewed interest in the *Hints* from June rather than March 1820, he shrewdly observes its significance 'in the context of his prose defences of Pope and his own *Don Juan*, and also at the time he was seriously renewing his attack upon contemporary English social and literary culture' (*CPW*, 1, pp. 426–7). Investigating these contexts in a little more detail, hitherto unpublished letters from John Murray to Byron suggest ways in which the return to *Hints from Horace* shapes a new meaning as digressive poetics were coloured by changing personal and public dynamics.

On 29 March 1820, the day after the fresh possibility of publishing the *Hints* was raised, Byron dispatched to Murray a note on Pope which was to be attached to the 'Screed of Doctrine'.[23] The accompanying letter answered Murray's of 7 March and was couched in terms of a battle to uphold taste in English writing:

I have at last lost all patience with the atrocious cant and nonsense about Pope, with which our present blackguards are overflowing, and am determined to make such head against it, as an Individual can by prose or verse – and I will at least do it with good will. – – There is no bearing it any longer, and if it goes on, it will destroy what little good writing or taste remains amongst us. – – I hope there are still a few men of taste to second me, but if not, I'll battle it alone – convinced that it is in the best cause of English literature. (*BLJ*, VII, p. 61)

For Byron the effluent metaphor ('overflowing') which appeared in *Hints from Horace* is descriptive of the work of Robert Southey in particular.[24] The changing aesthetic value of the 'overflow' figure at this time can be seen if we compare the eighteenth-century satirical characterisation of bad poetry as sewage with the Wordsworthian estimate of good poetry as an 'overflow of powerful feelings' or Byron's image of poetry as the 'lava of imagination'.[25]

No one was more sensitive to the changing tide of public taste than Byron's publisher. On 7 March 1820, Murray had written to advise Byron of the alteration he perceived in English sensibilities:

With regard to what your Lordship says as to what was permitted in a Catholic & bigoted age to a Clergyman – I humbly conceive & am surprised that you do not perceive that – religion had nothing to do with it – It was <u>Manners</u> – and they have changed – a man might as well appear without Cloaths – and quote our Saxon Ancestors – The comedies of Charles Seconds days are not tolerated now – and even in my own time I have gradually seen my favourite Love for

Love absolutely pushed by public feeling – from the stage – it is not affectation of morality but the real progress and result of refinement – and <we> our minds can no more undergo the moral & religious grossness of our predecessors that [*sic*] our bodies can sustain the heavy Armour which they wore.[26]

Murray's use of a very tactile image to claim that his own favourite play has been 'pushed' from the stage reminds us that Byron's reviewers feared the 'palpable' effects of reading his poetry. One legacy of late eighteenth-century literature of sensibility was such that early nineteenth-century readers envisaged their role as intimate participants in and moral arbiters of a work of literature. Murray's sense of the pressure of audience taste was undoubtedly sharpened by his knowledge of recent editions of English drama. In Elizabeth Inchbald's twenty-five-volume edition, *British Theatre* (1808) which Murray purchased in the 1816 sale of Byron's library, Inchbald includes three plays by Susannah Centlivre and five by herself, compared with only two plays – *Love for Love* and *The Mourning Bride* – by Congreve. *Love for Love* is prefaced by a disapproving comment on its morality. Whereas Murray accepted this change of taste as the progress of 'refinement', Byron's answer of 29 March 1820 turns into a tirade against the taste of the day, insisting that the refinement of the English stage was really a manifestation of vulgarity:

You have given me a screed of Metaphor and what not about *Pulci* – & manners, 'and going *without clothes*' . . . I differ from you about the 'refinement' which has banished the comedies of Congreve – are not the comedies of *Sheridan* acted to the thinnest houses? – I *know* (*as ex-Committed*) that the 'School for Scandal' was the *worst Stock piece* upon record. – I also know that Congreve gave up writing because Mrs. Centlivre's balderdash drove his comedies off – so it is not *decency* but Stupidity that does all this – for Sheridan is as *decent* a writer as needs be – and Congreve no worse than Mrs. Centlivre . . .

But last and most to the purpose – Pulci is *not* an *indecent* writer – at least in his first Canto as you will have perceived by this time. – – You talk of *refinement*, are you all *more* moral? are you *so* moral? – No such thing, – *I* know what the World is in England by my own proper experience. (*BLJ*, VII, p. 61)

Here we can see Byron (belatedly) joining the defence of the old comedy of manners which had been championed by Charles Lamb and William Hazlitt. In 'Whether Genius is Conscious of its Powers' (1823), for example, Hazlitt turns to Congreve after a long walk:

I had *Love for Love* in my pocket, and began to read; coffee was brought in a silver coffee pot; the cream, the bread and butter, every thing was excellent, and the flavour of Congreve's style prevailed over all.[27]

The episode is not simply about the pleasures of reading. In the rest of the essay we find Hazlitt's usual animus against the party interest of the periodical world; his delight in out-of-fashion reading material in this instance is also a challenge to contemporary shapers of opinion. Although Hazlitt and Byron differed in many things, they shared a determination to expose the hidden political agendas of supposed aesthetic or moral discourse and a desire to crush critical opponents.

Byron's attack on *decency* is consistent with his appreciation of George Colman's prologue to *Philaster* while working on the Drury Lane address.[28] Colman's prologue also accused the English public of assuming a false standard of morality:

> While modern tragedy, by rule exact,
> Spins out a thin-wrought fable, act by act,
> We dare to bring you one of those bold plays,
> Wrote by rough English wits in former days:
> Beaumont and Fletcher! those twin stars, that run
> Their glorious course round Shakespeare's golden sun,
> Or when Philaster Hamlet's place supplied,
> Or Bessus walk'd the stage by Falstaff's side.
> Their souls, well pair'd, shot fire in mingled rays,
> Their hands together twined the social bays,
> Till fashion drove, in a refining age,
> Virtue from the court, and nature from the stage.
> Their nonsense, in heroics seem'd sublime,
> Kings raved in couplets, and maids sigh'd in rhime.
> Next, prim, and trim, and delicate, and chaste,
> A hash from Greece and France, came modern taste.[29]

In this edition of Beaumont and Fletcher (in the 1816 sale catalogue of Byron's library), Weber's introduction discusses the changing standard of taste in more detail. 'Our ancestors, in the days of King James,' he explained, 'would hear, without the least offence phrases and allusions which now would be stamped with every mark of public disapprobation.'[30] While Byron was aware of these issues from the start of his career, it was not until the Pope/Bowles controversy that his critique of canons of correctness became embroiled with his personal reception and incorporated into the fabric of his poetry.

In 1820 there was a conflict between Murray's advisors, who called on what they believed to be Horatian standards of taste to oppose the publication of *Don Juan,* and Byron's own revision of Horace into an attack on the 'niceness' of the times. In a letter to Murray of 26 March

1820, J.W. Croker advised him to 'get Lord Byron to revise these two cantos [*Don Juan* III and IV], and not to make another step in the odious path which Hobhouse beckons him to pursue' (Hobhouse had, in fact, suggested a total suppression of *Don Juan*). Croker elaborated on his view to Murray:

in poetry I should think it an excellent plan – to pour out, as Lord Byron says, his whole mind in the intoxication of the moment, but to revise and condense in the sobriety of the morrow ... experience shows that the Pulcian style is very easily written ... it therefore behoves Lord Byron to distinguish his use of this measure by superior and peculiar beauties. He should refine and polish; and by *limae labor et mora*, attain the perfection of ease. (Smiles, *A Publisher and His Friends*, I, p. 416)

Croker cited the *Ars Poetica* (l. 291) to urge for restraint on *Don Juan*, whereas at the same time, Byron was rereading his translation of the Horatian text as a further reason for enlarging the scope of *Don Juan*.

Byron's intimations to Murray of his readiness for a battle against public opinion are in some measure a displacement of his anxiety about non-participation in English politics. Both Hobhouse and Kinnaird were attempting to enlist his aid in the reformist Whig cause as England appeared to be heading for revolution. On 29 March 1820 Byron warned Hobhouse (in a letter written on the same day as his fulminations against '*decency*') against 'violent' involvement with associates of the Cato Street Conspirators. One of Byron's objections to radical politics was a class-based disdain of the radical leaders' lack of a classical education:

I perceive you talk *Tacitus* to them sometimes – what do they make of it? (*BLJ*, VII, p. 63)

Byron went on to suggest wryly that his own *literary* battle was of greater consequence:

You will see that I have taken up the *Pope* question (in prose) with a high hand, and *you* (when you can spare yourself from the *Party* to Mankind) must help me: – You know how often under the Mira elms, and by the Adriatic on the Lido – we have discussed that question and lamented the villainous Cant which at present would decry him. – – It is my intention to give battle to the blackguards – and try if the 'little Nightingale' can't be heard again. – – But at present you are on the hustings – or in the Chair. – Success go with you. (*BLJ*, VII, p. 63)

But there was more than one literary skirmish going on at this time. At the beginning of April, Byron had dispatched a lampoon on Hobhouse's progress from brief imprisonment in Newgate to a seat in the House of Commons:

1

How came you in Hob's pound to cool
My boy Hobbie O?
Because I bade the people pull
The House into the Lobby O.

2

What did the House upon this call
My boy Hobbie O?
They voted me to Newgate all
Which is an awkward Jobby O.

3

Who are now the people's men
My boy Hobby O?
There's I and Burdett – Gentlemen,
And blackguard Hunt and Cobby O.

4

You hate the house – why canvass, then?
My boy Hobbie O?
Because I would reform the den
As member for the Mobby O.

5

Wherefore do you hate the Whigs
My boy Hobbie O?
Because they want to run their rigs
As under Walpole's Bobby O.

6

But when we at Cambridge were
My boy Hobbie O,
If my memory don't err
You founded a Whig Clubbie O.

7

When to the mob you make a speech
My boy Hobbie O,
How do you keep without their reach
The watch within your fobby O? –

8

By never mind such petty things –
My boy Hobbie O –
God save the people – damn all Kings –
So let us crown the Mobby O!
Yrs truly,
(Signed) *Infidus Scurra.*
M[arc]h 23 rd, 1820.

Hobhouse had been imprisoned when he admitted that he was the author of 'A Trifling Mistake in Thomas Lord Erskine's Recent Preface', a pamphlet directed against the Whigs. After reading about the prosecution in *Galignani's*, Byron had sent the ballad to Murray who showed it to several other friends (Whig and Tory) before Hobhouse.[31] Once again, rapid private circulation leaked into the public domain and Byron's 'New Song' was used by old Whigs, the Tory press and the radicals to ridicule Hobhouse. Understandably, he felt harshly treated:

I have had Courier, Chronicle, Cobbett, Jeffrey, Brougham, Croker, Gifford, Ld. Holland, Wooler, Leigh Hunt (a little), Cartwright, and more Reviews & Magazines, Monthly New and Old, Quarterly, & Weekly than you ever heard of playing off their large & small shot at me for near two years, and your ballad completes a list as extensive and various as ever was arrayed against a public man.[32]

The quarrel reveals a great deal about the fractured state of the liberal reformists, caught between the policies of the 'gentlemen' reformers, Hobhouse and Burdett, and the more radical fringe of 'blackguards' like Henry Hunt and William Cobbett. Hobhouse smartly corrected Byron's view of the Whigs as we shall see in Chapter Six, but he also attempted to rise above his personal hurt to respond to Byron's aesthetic demands. On 21 April 1820 he replied:

I am delighted with your intelligence about Pope. I do recollect the Mira elms & the Lido sands, and wish I was there with you now, that is if you had not written your ballad. (Graham, *Byron's Bulldog*, p, 291)

While Byron was brandishing an array of classical authors to draw Hobhouse away from what he perceived as the influence of political thugs, Hobhouse used a classical defence of Pope to allude to his friend's slipping integrity and to challenge Byron to participate in reform:

No man but you has force & influence enough for such an undertaking – Do not let your purpose cool. You are a fine fellow (damn that ballad though) and have already done wonders, but if you recover Pope will deserve, if possible, more nobly of your country than ever. (Graham, *Byron's Bulldog*, p. 291)

Byron wrote to Hobhouse on 22 April 1820 to extricate himself from the derogatory remarks about Radicals. Again, he appealed to their shared experience of the classics:

I do not think the man who would overthrow all laws – should have the benefit of any, he who plays the Tyler or Cade might find the Walworth or Iden – he who enacts the Clodius – the Milo – and what is there in Bristol Hunt and Cobbett – *so* honest as the former – or *more* patriotic than the latter? – 'Arcades

Ambo' blackguards both. – – Why our classical education alone – should teach us to trample on such unredeemed dirt as the *dis*honest bluntness – the ignorant brutality, the unblushing baseness of these two miscreants; – and all who believe in them. (*BLJ*, VII, p. 81)

In the same letter, Byron defensively asked Hobhouse what 'radical' meant:

Upon reform you have long known my opinion – but *radical* is a new word since my time – it was not in the political vocabulary in 1816 – when I left England – and I don't know what it means – is it uprooting? (*BLJ*, VII, p. 81)

Of course Byron was not so naively out of touch with English politics; his adoption of a tone of mild surprise is designed to win over Hobhouse. The difference between the two men on what used to be shared ground introduces, however, a note of uncertainty in Byron's writing at this time and, as the letters between them show, a gulf had opened up which made them 'both a little formal' with each other.[33]

On 23 April 1820, Byron told Murray that the '*prose* observations in answer to Wilson' were not to be published 'at present' (*BLJ*, VII, p. 83). This may have been because he had decided to forward the battle in verse (his emphasis on the '*prose*' nature of the composition would be in keeping with this). However, it appears that Byron hesitated because of embarrassment about his betrayal of Hobhouse's reformist idealism. Writing to Hobhouse on 11 May 1820, Byron was still trying to clarify his principles:

And pray don't *mistake* me – it is not against the *pure* principle of reform – that I protest, but against low designing dirty levellers who would pioneer their way to a democratical tyranny; < it is against such men > putting these fellows in a parenthesis – I think as I have ever thought – on that point – as it *used* to be defined – but things have changed their sense probably – as they have their names – since my time. (*BLJ*, VII, p. 99)

Byron's awareness of the altered tone of the parenthesis is interesting from a textual point of view, but we can also detect a defensive affectation of distance with regard to contemporary England. The use of the phrase 'since my time', and Byron's sensitivity to changing names shows a newly accentuated anxiety about the distance between poet and audience. On 20 May Byron gave Murray permission to publish the prose 'Edin. Mag. answer':

The prose ... looks better than I thought it would – & *you may publish it* – there will be a row – but I'll fight it out – one way or another. (*BLJ*, VII, p. 102)

The word 'row' was one Byron had been using to describe the political events in Italy and its use here suggests the way he oscillated between literary and political causes. In the *Letter to John Murray Esqre.* (1821), Byron extends the range of his critique of Bowles with the following words:

It is no affair of mine – but having once begun – (certainly not by my own wish but called upon by the frequent recurrence to my name in the pamphlets) I am like an Irishman in a 'row' 'anybody's Customer'. (Byron, *Complete Miscellaneous Prose*, p. 129)

The low Regency connotations of the word 'row' suggest Byron's ready preference for action and linguistic vigour rather than 'shabby genteel' refinement. He was, I think, playing up the idea that his immersion in literary reform was equivalent to active political engagement with the readership.

By 8 June, the politics of publication exerted a different influence and Byron had changed his mind again (ostentatiously) in deferential response to a letter from Hobhouse:

My dear Hobhouse – You are right – the *prose* must not be published – at least the merely *personal part,* – and how the portion on Pope may be divided I do not know. – I wish you would ferret out at Whitton – the 'Hints from Horace'. I think it (the Pope part) might be appended to that Popean poem – for publication or no – as you decide. I care not a damn. (*BLJ*, VII, p. 114)

Byron's submission to his friend's critical judgement is conciliatory, and as an act of confidence he includes a melancholy reflection in which the personal tenor adopted is at least as important as the sentiments expressed:

Surely you agree with me about the real *vacuum* of human pursuits, but one must force an object of attainment – not to rust in the Scabbard altogether. (*BLJ*, VII, p. 116)

Byron's ostentatious disregard for the fate of the poem mixes aristocratic ennui with a more modern anxiety about the worth or reality of anything. His letter offers the 'Popean poem' as an unfixed signifier to which Hobhouse may or may not attach value. The variability of Pope's literary inheritance, like the fluctuating funds which also preoccupied Byron at this time, seem to have intensified his anxiety about his public role as a writer. On 22 June 1820 Byron wrote to Hobhouse and questioned his and Murray's 'continuing silence':

I am aware of the pettiness of such things to a man who is arraigning judges, and preparing constitutions – but trust to a spare moment from debate and legislation to an arrangement with a bookseller on the part of an absent friend – who has written a ballad upon you . . . put the M.S.S. into Longman's hands or in those of any respectable publisher who will undertake them – on their *own* terms . . . of course the *prose* (on Blackwood &c.) is not to be published except that part which refers *to Pope* – & that *not* unless you please – perhaps the best way to do with it – would be to print in some periodical publication as an '*extract* from a letter &c. containing some opinion on the poetry of the day.' (*BLJ*, VII, p. 121)

Under pressure from both Hobhouse and Kinnaird ('For God's sake help us here – do not mix yourself with Italian Politics when your own Country may want you'[34]), Byron stubbornly maintained the relevance of his aesthetic campaign and declined to take an active part in English politics. Although it disappointed his liberal reformist friends, this literary line represented an improvement to Murray who was keen to leave the risky territory of *ottava rima* satire. He advised Byron in a letter of 13 June 1820 that the translation of Pulci

will not be <liked> popular in England – Blackwood is not worth your notice – wch would be sure to raise the reputation of the Magazine . . . All that your Lordships [*sic*] says about Pope – is excellent indeed & I wish you could be induced to enlarge it & I would print it with any thing else in the Shape of Notes that you would make for me in an Edition of Popes Poetical Works wch I am very anxious to rescue from Mr Bowles. (MS., John Murray Archive).

In spite of this encouragement, Byron shelved the possibility of pursuing a battle against the English poetry of the day. He did not mention the Pope/Bowles debate in his letters throughout July and August, being preoccupied with decisions about the Guiccioli marriage, with political turmoil in Italy and his dramatic writing.[35] He continued, however, to write contemptuously of Wordsworth, and in a letter to Murray of 11 September 1820 released a surge of irritation at the state of English literature:

Oh! if ever I *do* come amongst you again I will give you such a 'Baviad and Maeviad' not as *good* as the old – but even *better merited.* – There never was such a *Set* as your ragamuffins – (I mean *not* yours only but every body's) what with the Cockneys and the Lakers – and the *followers* of Scott and Moore and Byron – you are in the very uttermost decline and degradation of Literature. – I can't think of it without all the remorse of a murderer – I wish that Johnson were alive again to crush them. (*BLJ*, VII, p. 175)

This letter suggests that Byron's determination to publish *Hints from Horace* marked a renewed commitment to the cause of literary reform in England. Indeed, as Richard Cronin has suggested, Byron's defence of Pope and return to dramatic unities represents an attempt to 're-establish the cultural barriers that he feels himself to have assisted in demolishing'.[36] Displacing doubts about the '*vacuum* of human pursuits', he wishes for the physical solidity of a Johnson. Johnson's ability to 'crush' would at least make something tangible out of those who appear under the sign of a 'Set' or 'School', or as the disembodied followers of names. The Italian Revolution (one of Byron's reasons for not going home) had lost momentum and Byron discussed the possibility of returning to England with Hobhouse. The latter had finally recovered the *Hints from Horace*, and in a letter of 31 August 1820, he urged Byron to return and to support Queen Caroline:

> come over there's a good fellow – I have looked out your *hints from Horace* – very good, I think, but you will not like to attack friends who are hitched into the rhymes there. (Graham, *Byron's Bulldog*, p. 299)

Very gently, Hobhouse reminded Byron of his shifting personal allegiances. Byron responded in kind to his friend's close intermingling of the personal and the public:

> Here at Ravenna – nobody believes the evidence against the Queen – they say – that for half the money they could have any testimony they please – this is the public talk. – – The 'Hints &c.' are good are they? As to the friends we can change their names unless they rhyme well – in that case they must stand. Except Scott and Jeffrey and Moore – Sir B. Burgess and a few more I know no friends who need be left out of a good poem. (*BLJ*, VII, p. 178)

Here we find Byron's teasing return to ideas about the vacuum of human pursuits and the emptiness of poetic language: satirical targets are interchangeable so names can be changed; only formal effects like rhyme possess any enduring stability. Suddenly energised, however, by the favourable communication from Hobhouse, Byron wrote to Murray on 23 September 1820 and demanded 'a proof (with the Latin) of my Hints from H[orace] &c.':

> I have a notion that with some omissions of names and passages it will do – and I could put my late observations *for* Pope among the notes with the date of 1820, and so on. – As far as the versification goes it is good – and looking back to what I wrote about that period – I am astonished to see how *little* I have trained on – I wrote better then than now – but that comes from my having fallen into the atrocious bad taste of the times – partly. (*BLJ*, VII, p. 179)

Byron's renewed interest in English culture and the exigencies of the dispute with Hobhouse coincided in the desire to work on the *Hints*. The overlap of concerns is suggested by shared terminology: Byron wrote to Hobhouse on 25 September 1820 enclosing 'some hints which may be useful to Queeney – and her orators' (*BLJ*, VII, p. 180). Meanwhile, Murray had claimed that the Queen Caroline affair was one of the factors holding up publication of *Don Juan*. On 8 September 1820 he wrote to reassure Byron that 'Pulci . . . & Don Juan shall also appear & the latter in the way your Lordship desires – as soon as the public are in the humour to read any thing but about the Quean' (MS., John Murray Archive). On 16 October 1820 Murray sent Byron an account of the trial of the Queen ('How it is to terminate the Devil alone who instigated it – can tell') and closed his letter with reflections on the contrasting desirability of revolution in Italy and England:

I confess I joins [*sic*] in all yr regrets that a certain very important Revolution has not taken Place – for never was there more necessity for one – but a Revolution here were madness – it is utterly impossible in the nature of Mankind – that we could create a new one that has baffled ages & is yet the admiration of all Mankind. (MS., John Murray Archive)

This is as close as Murray came to supporting violent political change, but it is crucially only acceptable outside England: the English political system was already perfect for 'all Mankind'. Murray's historical perspective informed his literary critical judgement and we can see how the publisher was desperately keen to pull Byron back into mainstream publication and non-controversial textuality.

The delay in England grew. On 28 September Byron sent a satirical portrait of Rogers to Murray who received it enthusiastically:

As to the Satire it is one of the most superlative things that ever was written – I hastened with it the next morning to Mr. Gifford I put it into his hand without saying a word – and I thought he would have died with extacy – he thinks that if it do not surpass it at least equals anything that you have written & that there is nothing more perfect of its kind in the language – he knew the portrait as readily as if the Person had been before him – This is certainly your natural talent and you should improve it into a Classical standard series of Satires – & be at once Persius – Juvenal – Boileau & our own Pope – it betrays a knowledge of human nature – as well as identity of character that is amazing – If you could do this upon a plan not of selecting individuals but general Character Manners etc you would do a national Service. (24 October 1820: MS., John Murray Archive)[37]

Rogers was, of course, a frequenter of Holland House and we can perhaps detect Byron beginning to turn away from the moderate Whigs who had attempted to undermine Hobhouse. The extravagant praise by Murray and Gifford for this satire and Murray's attempt to steer Byron into 'general Character Manners' give an indication of how keen they were as Tories *not* to publish *Don Juan*. By relishing the satirical sketch of Rogers in private, but urging Byron to avoid particular individuals in public print,

Murray exemplifies the prevailing attitudes to satire in his day, seeking to engage Byron in the discussion of cultural generalities.

For a time, Byron's involvement in the Pope/Bowles controversy appealed to Murray as a conservative literary enterprise. On 27 October he replied to Byron's complaints about the new publications sent out to him:

What you say as to the want of selection in the books which I send you is true – but it has not been occasioned by my bad taste – the Poems are all of them at least Keates [*sic*] Croly &c by a set of fellows who are everlastingly blowing themselves into notoriety & you will find in the last Edinb. Review that Jeffry [*sic*] has allowed some of them to be praised there – <and> the fact is I sent these to you on purpose to provoke your contempt & give you memoranda for a new Baviad wch we very much need to flap away a nest of pretenders – – I have written to Mr Hobhouse for the 'Hints from Horace' which with the novelty which you will probably throw into it will make a very servisable [*sic*] as well as a very interesting poem – There is the English Bards printing over & over again in Dublin & circulating in a way by poor wretches in the Country that prevents the law from stopping it – – I much approve of your intention to preserve in notes to the Hints all that you have so manfully & judiciously said about Pope – It will come a propos for there is a great discussion upon his merits going on now – & Bowles who in his own edition of Pope so shamefully abused him is now furious at an article upon this subject which appeared in the last Quarterly – Gifford is very warmly on your side – by way [*sic*] he a little resembles Pope in character – I wish you may have Bowless edition by you that you may see fairly what he there said & to prevent you from judging merely from his pamphlet to Campbell. (MS., John Murray Archive)[38]

Here we can see how Byron's friends in England loaded *Hints from Horace* with different personal and political inflections. For Murray, the poem offered the potential that Byron would return to the conservative fold of Gifford and the *Quarterly*, while the delay in publishing the *Hints* could be attributed to Hobhouse's ill-advised involvement with radical politics. In a letter of 3 November 1820, Murray told Byron that he had not yet received the *Hints* from Hobhouse (who was 'radicalizing at Battle Abbey'). Hobhouse, on the other hand, associated the *Hints* with a failure on Byron's part to honour old friendships and commit himself to the present reformist cause. On 6 November, Hobhouse wrote again to say that he had located the *Hints from Horace*. He noted immediately that it was out of joint with 'the present state' of Byron's friendships and he even suggested that there might be little point in publishing the poem:

I have looked out the *Hints* – by heavens we must have some 'cutting and slashing' in order to qualify them for the present state of your friendships literary & others – but as I said before the hints are good – good to give though not likely to be taken – Prose & all shall be overhauled. (Graham, *Byron's Bulldog*, p. 302)

Byron continued to ask for the proofs throughout September, October, November and December 1820 when he was involved with the aftermath of the shooting at Ravenna – an incident of peculiar specificity which prompted one of the most famous narrative digressions in *Don Juan*. On 5 January 1821 Murray acknowledged Byron's letter of 14 December including the account of the assassination of the commandant. He advised Byron to avoid any risky entanglement in Italian politics:

Italy is in a Sad State but a foreigner never fares well in foreign troubles & it is a great comfort to your friends here to know that you are too wise to interfere. Every Letter that I receive and every poem that you compose, render [*sic*] your life more valuable to this country, and I trust that you will not put it to uncalled for or thankless hopeless hazard – – It is as you say a strange people – most absurdly & barbarously gouverned [*sic*] – This Nation will take no part on either side –

I have sent your Lordship every Sheet upon which Mr Gifford had made his marks and as your corrections in all the others have been carefully attended to by him, I hope when I receive the last proof sent you back that we may instantly publish. (MS., John Murray Archive).

For Murray, the various stages of retrieving and correcting *Hints from Horace* were marked by a desire to quell Byron's involvement in English or Italian politics. For Byron, the poem offered a chance to inveigh against prevailing codes of social morality and taste. On 11 January 1821 Byron's journal entry records that he had corrected the *Hints from Horace* (just after reading Campbell's defence of Pope (*BLJ*, VIII, p. 21)) and he wrote letters on the same day offering Murray a new preface and informing him that a portion of the *Hints* was still missing:

I . . . have made the few corrections I shall make in what I have seen at least. – I will omit nothing and alter little; – the fact is (as I perceive) – that I wrote a good deal better in 1811 – than I have ever done since. – I care not a sixpence whether the work is popular or not. (*BLJ*, VIII, p. 60)

In a note at the end of the galley proof of *Hints from Horace* (probably dated 11 January (*BLJ*, VIII, p. 61)), Byron protested against 'cutting and slashing' and gave Murray further instructions about appending the prose material on Pope:

– – I will allow none of you to *dock*; except *Gifford*. – – Will you have the goodness also to put all that regards *Pope* (in the prose letter to B[lackwood's] Editor sent last Spring to you) as a *note* under the name of *Pope* [where it?] first occurs in this Essay (which it does [begin?]) as that part of the letter was in fact distinct from the rest of it, it will do as well here. When you talk of altering and omitting you should remember that all the English *refers* to passages in the Latin – and that the merit in this kind of writing consists in the *adaptation* – *now* – to omit or alter much would destroy the closeness of the allusions. (*BLJ*, VIII, p. 61)

Throughout February 1821, Byron sent impatient reminders to Murray about the missing portion of proofs. Meanwhile, the Pope/Bowles controversy which had started in November 1819 was well underway: Byron wrote his *Letter to John Murray Esqre.* on 7 February 1821. On 26 February the Ravenna Journal records that two notes on the Pope/Bowles controversy were dispatched to Murray (*BLJ*, VIII, p. 50). On 1 March 1821 Byron wrote to Murray acknowledging receipt of another proof of the *Hints* but complaining that it was without the Latin and without the note on Pope (though it did contain the passage on Jeffrey which Byron had instructed Murray to remove). On 2 March 1821 Murray wrote to tell Byron that

The Letter about Pope was read yesterday by Mr. Gifford to whom I took it the moment after its arrival – he likes it very much & told me to print it immediately & Mr Gifford will take care to see it carefully through the Press. (MS., John Murray Archive)

Interestingly, in a letter of 20 March, Murray reported that Gifford had recommended the suppression of the note on Lady Montagu, which dealt with Pope in the context of English sexual mores.[39] This letter suggests that Gifford was reluctant to authorise Byron's distinctive particularity of allusion. Indeed, hitherto unpublished letters reveal that Gifford was probably responsible for the non-publication of the *Hints from Horace* during Byron's lifetime.

On 27 March 1821 Murray wrote to tell Byron that the *Letter* on the Pope/Bowles controversy had been well received:

I sent the additions to the Letter, without reading it to the printer for the Letter was advertised for publication this day & was on the point of issuing – It is very gratifying to me to be able to say that Gifford, Scott, Merivale Sotheby, Morritt & other few who have seen it consider it admirably done – Your prose is in the very happiest & most original taste & Style & you have in the most lively & convincing & gentlemanly manner compleatly proved your point – Indeed yr prose is excellent – the Preface to the Doge equally in good taste
 ... I believe I told you that Gifford desired me to tell you how very highly he estimates your Prose – & he always dwells with delight upon the unrivalled purity of the Blank Verse of this Tragedy –
 Gifford does not agree in your estimation of the <English> Hints from Horace – but I will print it – Don Juan 3 – 4 – 5 – in one Vol – & Pulci – Dante – Horace in another – & let the [*sic*] float on the Waters of Public Opinion. (MS., John Murray Archive)

This is the first indication we have that Gifford had reservations about the *Hints from Horace*. Although Murray offered to go ahead with publication regardless of Gifford's view, he must have known that Byron's immense respect for Gifford as an editor and mentor would cause him to hesitate. Murray's brief report of Gifford's negative response to the *Hints* was reinforced in his question to Byron of 24 July: 'Shall I now print the Hints & Pulci anonymously – Gifford does not like the Hints & so let them take their chance.'[40] Gifford's reservations supply a reason for what has been seen as an unaccountably sudden loss of interest in the *Hints* on Byron's part.[41] In September, Byron referred to the *Hints* as an unpublished asset of over 700 lines, but by March 1822, a year after Byron had received the new proofs, the poem remained unpublished. By this time Byron was expressing reservations about the gap between the poem's composition and its appearance. He wrote to Moore on 4 March 1822, listing his unpublished works which included the *Hints* – 'written in 1811, but a great deal, *since*, to be omitted' and 'several prose things, which may, perhaps, as well remain unpublished' (*BLJ*, IX, p. 118).

Delay, uncertainty and crossed purposes had blocked the publication of *Hints from Horace*. The difficulty Byron experienced in recovering the *Hints* from his friend and later from his publisher, and his failure in getting them to support this and the *Don Juan* venture, became part of the fabric of both poems.[42] Horatian irony came to be entangled with the irony of a poet addressing friends who told him he was squandering away his talents. Byron's commitment to the cause of literary taste (which he converted into the cause of political reform) also led him to recast Pope's role in the poem. These pressures on the text constitute the main difference between the 1821 and 1811 versions of *Hints from Horace*.

The first textual emendation of the *Hints* in 1821 occurs in the opening couplet:

> Who would not laugh if Lawrence, hired to grace
> His costly canvass with each flatter'd face.

This was adjusted to remove the mercantile element of both lines and to introduce the concept of the 'classic' work of art:

> Who would not laugh, if Lawrence, skilled to grace
> His classic canvass with each flatter'd face.
>
> (*CPW*, I, p. 289)

The correction shows a shift towards the terms of aesthetic evaluation in Byron's *Letter to John Murray Esqre.* (1821). The second verse emendation was the cancellation of the couplet:

> Satiric rhyme first sprang from selfish spleen.
> You doubt – see Dryden, Pope, St. Patrick's dean.
>
> (114a–b. *CPW* I, p. 293)

In 1811 this had been a digression from the Latin accompanied by a prose note:

MacFlecknoe, and the *Dunciad*, and all Swift's lampooning ballads. Whatever their other works may be, these originated in personal feelings, and angry retort on unworthy rivals; and though the ability of these satires elevates the poetical, their poignancy detracts from the personal character of the writers. (*CPW*, I, p. 432)

This shows the Byron of 1811 falling in with the taste of the times (it is almost exactly Joseph Warton's line on Pope) and the desire to suppress 'personal' attacks in print. The note was cancelled in 1820 for the obvious reason that it detracted from the wholly positive view of Pope Byron now wished to uphold. The different manifestations of 'Pro-' and 'Anti-Augustanism' in the first three decades of the nineteenth century have been traced by Upali Amarasinghe, but the full complexity of Byron's engagement has never been realised.[43]

If Byron's instructions about appending a prose note to *Hints from Horace* on 'all that regards Pope' from the 'Observations' pamphlet had been followed, much of the general satire of the poem would have been redirected against the supporters of Bowles and the Lake School. Only because of the discussions already outlined between Byron, Murray, Hobhouse and Gifford is this note missing from all published versions of the poem.[44] The new prose note would have emphasised the importance of rhyme in Byron's aesthetic hierarchy:

The attorneys' clerks, and other self-educated Genii found it easier to distort themselves to the new Models – than to toil after the symmetry of him who had enchanted their fathers . . . Blank Verse – which unless in the Drama – no one except Milton ever wrote who could rhyme – became the order of the day, or else such rhyme as looked still blanker than the verse without it. (Nicholson, *Complete Miscellaneous Prose*, p. 112)

Byron followed these comments with the startling suggestion that even *Paradise Lost* might have been 'more nobly conveyed to Posterity' in Spenserian stanza form or in *terza rima*. One of the reasons for advocating rhyme appears to be that its difficulty would restore prestige to poetry as formal discipline would retard the publication of work by the 'New School' and 'Mr Southey's Joan of Arc . . . might then have taken up six months instead of weeks in the composition' (p. 112).

Byron's conviction that good verse ought to exemplify 'the fascination of what's difficult' had a number of outcomes: it led to his scathing criticism of John Keats's 'Sleep and Poetry' and it meant that the verse texture of *Don Juan* challenged the critical orthodoxies of the Lake School. We have lost the sense of how deeply unpopular traditional forms of rhyme were becoming to one branch of criticism in the early nineteenth century. Rhyme had been deemed 'unfavourable' to the sublime by such eighteenth-century critics as Hugh Blair and Daniel Webb, and in 1827 William Crowe ruled that the 'quick return of rhyme destroys the gravity and dignity of verse'.[45] The Lake School had popularised blank verse as the vehicle of natural feeling and Wordsworth and Coleridge criticised the 'compulsory juxta-position' and '*antithetical* manner' they associated with Augustan artificiality.[46] In this light, *Hints from Horace* and *Don Juan* may be seen as attempts to counter the lava flow of individual imagination by reintroducing shared (if archaic) forms of discrimination. From one point of view this looks like aristocratic affectation, but from another it may be read as a democratic desire to keep poetry as a communal discourse. At the same time, however, Byron had to recognise that rhyming without readers was a bit like whistling in the dark.

The effect of *Hints from Horace* on *Don Juan* is complex and multi-layered, but we can see that a significant general trait was to implant awareness of readerly fallibility into the texture of the poem. The awareness of the unpredictability of audience reaction gradually alters the texture of Byron's later poetry. Byron's preoccupation with *Hints from Horace* coincided with a directionless stage in the composition of *Don Juan*: he had been dissatisfied with cantos III and IV and pronounced the first draft of III, 'very decent ... and as dull "as the last new Comedy"' (*BLJ*, VII, p. 35). Although McGann states that canto V was written 'in the context of [Byron's] own revived interest in *Hints from Horace* ... which seemed, in late 1820, to reproach him from the past' (*CPW*, v, p. 697), it is worth stressing that Byron had all but completed canto V before the long-awaited proofs of *Hints* arrived in Ravenna. The last addition, stanza 158, was sent to Murray on 1 March 1821, in the same letter in which Byron acknowledged the arrival of the (still imperfect) second instalment of proofs for the *Hints*. So canto V was composed in the anticipation that Horatian and Popean satire should make a difference to the 'very uttermost decline and degradation of Literature' (*BLJ*, VII, p. 175) while cantos VI, VII, and VIII interweave the realisation that a great deal had altered 'since', especially in the poet's relationship with his readers and publisher.

The 1811 *Hints from Horace* assumed that Byron's reader would be able to follow the 'closeness of the allusion' and the deviations from the

Horatian text. The 1821 encounter with the poem introduces a different sort of literary tension in that the poem Byron thought of as an 'Epistle to Hobhouse' attempts to recover a relationship with its addressee while simultaneously alienating itself from Hobhouse and from almost every other English reader as well. The great paradox of *Hints from Horace* is that just as Byron moved towards to the literary values of Murray and Gifford, he broke away from the political culture they represented.

Rising tension between Byron and his readership is legible in the preface to *Marino Faliero* (written between 17–24 August 1820):

I cannot conceive any man of irritable feeling putting himself at the mercies of an audience: – the sneering reader, and the loud critic, and the tart review, are scattered and distant calamities; but the trampling of an intelligent or of an ignorant audience on a production which . . . has been a mental labour to the writer, is a palpable and immediate grievance, heightened by a man's doubt of their competency to judge, and his certainty of his own imprudence in electing them his judges.

Following this 'palpable' sense of rejection, Byron echoes Johnson's verdict on marriage and celibacy:

Were I capable of writing a play which could be deemed stageworthy, success would give me no pleasure, and failure great pain. (*CPW*, IV, p. 305)

When *Marino Faliero* was performed, Kinnaird reported surprise at the responsiveness of the audience: 'It was very affective – The audience felt it too. I could not have believed an English audience so sensible to the beauties of the admirable production.'[47] His low esteem for the bulk of the 'English audience' fosters the creation of a select audience (including Kinnaird) which can appreciate Byron's work. In canto v the reader is also, like Byron the speaker, a victim of the scribbler who, 'spawns his quarto, and demands your praise' (v. 52); and together poet and reader confront the infinite recession of quotation marks which constitutes their poetic tradition:

> 'Not to admire is all the art I know
>   (Plain truth, dear Murray, needs few flowers of speech)
> To make men happy, or to keep them so;
>   (So take it in the very words of Creech).'
> Thus Horace wrote we all know long ago;
>   And thus Pope quotes the precept to re-teach
> From his translation; but had *none admired*,
> Would Pope have sung, or Horace been inspired?
>   (v. 101)[48]

The inclusive 'Thus ... we all know' is an invitation to the reader; its easy
intimacy fosters the community of the poem, and encourages the reader
to enjoy the serendipity of 'dear Murray' as an aside to Byron's publisher.
In a Bloomian sense, it is an example of 'Clinamen' and 'Tessera': Byron
has swerved away from Pope by alternating the lines to fit into *ottava rima;*
he also hijacks the '*Nil admirari*' dictat and antithetically completes it. In
spite of Murray's fears, cantos III, IV and V sold well when they were
published in August 1821. But, between this volume and the subsequent
instalment of *Don Juan,* there was a radical change in the politics of
publication and in the poet's attitude to his readers.

Murray had never been wholly at ease with Byron's 'turn for satire'
(Byron complained that he had 'played the Stepmother to D[on] J[uan] –
throughout'[49]); his firm had lost the copyright to *Cain* and he had to face
a small pamphlet war over its publication. Murray's political allegiances
and the necessity of running a business led to a horrified outburst when
Byron associated with the Hunts ('My company used to be courted for the
pleasure of talking about you – it is totally the reverse now ... we are in
constant alarm but [Augusta] should be deprived of her situation about
Court'[50]). This combination of pressures led him to refuse to publish
cantos VI–VIII of *Don Juan* ('they were so outrageously shocking that
I would not publish them if you were to give me your Estate – Title
and Genius – For Heaven's sake revise them'). Byron then made his
most overt political gesture since his maiden speech, he withdrew from
Murray as a publisher and Murray's 'customers among the Orthodox'
as his readership. The epigraph to cantos VI, VII and VIII intimated this
change of tone:

'Dost thou think, because thou art virtuous, there shall be no more Cakes and
Ale?' – 'Yes, by St. Anne; and Ginger shall be hot i' the mouth too!' –

The motto from *Twelfth Night* constructs Byron's ex-readers and his ex-
publisher as Malvolio, a puritanical hypocrite outside the community
of the poem. This move had been anticipated by the 1821 *Letter to John
Murray Esqre.,* where several reviewers picked up Byron's reference to
England as 'your Country': 'it is by this pronoun that Lord B designated
the country of himself and his fathers'.[51] Byron's flaunted sense of alienation was a response to the erosion of his friends' confidence in *Don Juan*
and was, no doubt, also adopted to rile his critics. Both the epigraph for
the new volume and the prose preface appear in Mary Shelley's fair copy
of the canto dated 1822. It was in this preface to canto VI that Byron
adopted a more judgemental approach towards the opponents of his

poem who (according to Byron) were also the supporters of a discredited ministry and court. The effect of the change of publishers on the reception of the poem was instantaneous. All the Tory and moderate Whig periodicals registered and lamented the significance of Byron's 'falling off' into a 'shilling's worth of dirty brown paper'.[52] Byron's acute awareness of the arbitrary opprobrium which was heaped on Murray, John Hunt and himself became part of the way he addressed his readers.

In 'Some Observations Upon an Article in *Blackwood's Edinburgh Magazine*' (1820), Byron listed the disciples of Pope and added that there were 'others who have not had their full fame . . . because there is a Fortune in Fame as in all other things'.[53] Byron's realisation of the way that names fell in and out of fashion in the literary world informed his view of the way that military fame (like the outcome of the Siege of Ismail) was constructed in the political world. *Hints from Horace* (1811) played with the idiom of Popean satire as a way of advancing Byron's reputation because it was 'the most difficult poem in the language'.[54] By the time that Pope (and that whole 'difficult' tradition) came under attack, Byron himself was experiencing the vagaries of 'the order of the day' in the changed currency of his own name. He was half baffled and half defiant about the forces which made previously unquestioned notions of aesthetic value 'heterodox' and '*unpopular*'.[55]

Byron emphasised the nine years between the original composition of the *Hints* and their second preparation for publication (*BLJ*, VII, p. 179). The appeal of the nine years was that it coincided with Horace's dictum: 'nonumque prematur in annum', but the passage of time haunted Byron in other ways too. In a digression from Horace in the 1811 *Hints*, Byron had attacked the 'Methodistic men' (l. 369) who opposed the theatre on moral grounds, and digressed on the difference between previous generations and 'this nice age, when all aspire to Taste':

> The dirty language, and the noisome jest,
> Which pleased in Swift of yore, we now detest.
>
> (ll. 393–4)

This was exactly the matter which had come to the fore in the reception of *Don Juan*: ''Tis all the same to me; I'm fond of yielding', Byron gibed at Murray and the orthodox families in canto IV, 'And therefore leave them to the purer page/Of Smollet, Prior, Ariosto, Fielding,/Who say strange things for so correct an age' (IV. 98). The most daring cultural revelation in *Cain* was that morality was really a matter of fashion (and that God was as changeable as the English public). This idea resurfaced in Byron's

prose defence of Pope when he referred scathingly to 'this immaculate period, this Moral Millennium of expurgated editions in books, manners –
and royal trials for divorce. – – – – –'.[56] Byron attempted to defend Pope
from Bowles's charge of 'the strange mixture of indecent and sometimes
profane levity which his conduct and language *often* exhibited'.[57] In 1821,
this was as much a defence of Byron's own writing as Pope's, and having referred the reader to the comedies of Congreve and others 'which
naturally attempted to represent the manners & conversation of private
life', Byron attacked

The refinement of latter days – which is perhaps the consequence of Vice
which wishes to mask & soften itself ... The *Delicacy* of the day is exactly in
all it's circumstances like that of this respectable foreigner [a famous French
'Entremetteuse'] – – 'It ensures every '*Succes*' & is not a whit more moral –
than, & not half so honourable – *as* – the coarser candour of our less polished
ancestors. (Byron, *Complete Miscellaneous Prose*, pp. 169–70)

The plethora of quotation marks which appear in the 'Observations
Upon Observations' may provide some explanation of the increased frequency of signalled allusion in *Don Juan* cantos VI, VII and VIII. Innuendo,
legal allegations and journalistic reportage breed quotation marks (or, as
they are suggestively called now, 'scare quotes') and since Byron was ex-
pecting his readership to read him warily, he cultivated his own method
of textual insinuation. By signalling some, but not all, instances of intertextuality he played with the offensive possibility that any allusion might
be 'indelicate'. Henry Crabb Robinson identified in Byron's defence of
Pope a judgement 'given to the world out of spite and affectation'; Lady
Blessington recorded the same impression: 'Byron is so prone to talk for
effect ... and takes pleasure in ... wounding the vanity of the English.'[58]
Their sense of a public performance captures the testing, provocative
style of Byron's relationship with Pope.

   Byron's lack of faith in the taste of his contemporary readers has already been suggested in the discussion of *English Bards and Scotch Reviewers*.
In 1820–1 this became more acute, gathering to a crisis of readership.
Byron's second revision of the *Hints* seems to have prompted an urgent
sense that his readers constituted the main locus of meaning, and that
they could not be relied upon. This suspicion, and Byron's acceptance
of its implications, led to a change of tone in *Don Juan* from canto VI
to the end of the poem. The later cantos of *Don Juan* are increasingly
alert to the relativity governing their reception and they foreground the
relationship between context and literary conventions rather than the
Lake School convention of 'natural' lyrical overflow.

In the 1821 *Letter to John Murray Esqre.*, Byron stressed the role of art, the 'exquisitely artificial' and the 'superartificial'.[59] Bowles's writing on Pope had argued that the 'passions of the human heart which belong to nature in general, are, per se, more adapted to the higher species of Poetry than those which are derived from incidental and transient manners'.[60] Byron rejected this elevation of the general over the particular and the very possibility of 'invariable principles'. In this regard, Byron's prose criticism adumbrates the juxtapositions we have found in his verse texture. Discussing the appeal of Campbell's 'Ship', Byron asks his reader: 'Is the Sea itself – a more attractive – a more moral a more poetical – object with or without a vessel – breaking it's vast but fatiguing monotony?'[61]

The idea of the 'break' admitting a space for human ingenuity appealed to Byron as a way of interrupting the gushing Lake and Cockney Schools. It recalls Henry Fielding's discussion of his 'little spaces' or 'resting-places' between chapters where the reader is advised to pause and take refreshment:

I would not advise him to travel through these pages too fast: for if he doth, he may probably miss the seeing [of] some curious productions of nature which will be observed by the slower and more accurate reader. A volume without any such places of rest resembles the opening of wilds or the seas, which tires the eye and fatigues the spirit when entered upon.[62]

Byron developed this eighteenth-century narrative convention by foregrounding the human activity which creates the 'little spaces' and changes of perspective. One of the most wearisome aspects of the Pope/Bowles controversy was Bowles's insistence that his arguments had been misrepresented by critics who set out to 'pervert' his sentiments.[63] The vast bulk of his writing on the topic was, therefore, a laboured and vain attempt to fix his meaning beyond any doubt with the help of italics, capitalisation and quotation. Byron's reading of Bowles's extensive correspondence on the topic can only have enforced his (already acute) awareness of the relativity of perception and the probability of a text's being misconstrued or reconfigured altogether by its readers. Human craftsmanship in the face of overwhelming odds, therefore, becomes the most significant agency in Byron's recollection of the anchorage off Cape Sigeum:

The Sight of these little scudding vessels darting over the foam in the twilight – now appearing – and now disappearing between the waves in the cloud of night . . . all struck me as something far more 'poetical' than the mere broad – brawling – shipless Sea & the sullen winds could possibly have been without them. (Byron, *Complete Miscellaneous Prose*, pp. 131–2)

In both cases, Byron argues for an intermittent awareness of human design and form.[64] His attraction towards discontinuity in writing may be read fruitfully with Barthes's *The Pleasure of the Text*:

It is intermittence, as psychoanalysis has so rightly stated, which is erotic: the intermittence of skin flashing between two articles of clothing (trousers and sweater), between two edges (the open-necked shirt, the glove and the sleeve); it is this flash itself which seduces, or rather: the staging of an appearance-as-disappearance.[65]

The difference between Barthes and Byron, at this point, would be that Byron is more interested in a disrupted continuum, how one goes on with the rest of the ravelled sleeve or the uncovered skin beneath after interruption. Byron's poem is involved in what Michael Cooke calls 'the universe of the unpredictable'. Barthes, however, is happy to regard the 'flash' as an occurrence which appears among so many other isolated 'stagings'. Byron's insistence that works of human art are worth more than 'inanimate nature' in being 'direct manifestations of the mind' summarises his difference from the Lake and Cockney Schools of poetry and ironically, from the School of Pope. Pope celebrates the human scene as 'A mighty maze! but not without a plan': Byron's poetry repudiates (while his prose rejects outright) 'plan' and 'system'. Instead, he places his trust in what is constructed moment by moment in the formal properties of the poem, while acknowledging that these are, to some extent, contingent on the plan of the reader.[66]

As we have seen, the signals which mark some of Byron's allusions prevent them from being absorbed and assimilated (in a Bloomian way) into the new text. Instead, the uncertain presence of another text is an invitation to the reader to digress. The signalling of allusion offers an intermittent reminder that the reader generates meaning from a verbal texture in which many strands are woven. As we divert from one reading to follow any other of these pathways, we become aware that each reading passes over multiple contiguous threads. This idea of poetic surface comes very close to Sir Joshua Reynolds's image of artistic disaster: 'The detail of particulars', he argued, 'which does not assist the expression of the main characteristick, is worse than useless, it is mischievous, as it dissipates the attention, and draws it from the principal point.'[67] Our flickering awareness of the poem as a surface to be modified by each reader is what makes Byronic digressive intertextuality so different in quality from other Romantic modes of allusion. The difference between them could be read as the difference between Barthes's text of pleasure and the unpredictable text of bliss:

> Text of pleasure: the text that contents, fills, grants euphoria; the text that comes from culture and does not break with it, is linked to a *comfortable* practice of reading. Text of bliss: the text that imposes a state of loss, the text that discomforts (perhaps to the point of a certain boredom), unsettles the reader's historical, cultural, psychological assumptions, the consistency of his tastes, values, memories, brings to a crisis his relation with language.[68]

Having seen how Byron's poetry unsettled his contemporary readers by appearing simultaneously to uphold and to break with English culture, the next chapter examines the ways in which Byron's digressive intertextuality in *Don Juan* historicises high art.

CHAPTER FOUR

Uncertain blisses: Don Juan, *digressive intertextuality and the risks of reception*

In the last three chapters we have seen how Byron disconcerted his first readers, his friends and his publisher by reconfiguring the rich satiric traditions of Churchill, Prior, Sterne and Pope. Their playfulness beckoned to an adventurous and textually experienced class of readers whose own protean potential mirrored the writers' polarities of scurrility and sublimity. But by the early nineteenth century, public manners were changing. In his early career, Byron's peerage offered the alibi of social class for stylistic misdemeanour, but even before he left England his digressive poetics were beginning to place the relationship between poet and reader in jeopardy.

Byron's susceptibility to awkward particulars was especially troubling to the 'middling' readership with its reliance on a conservative, polite concept of the general. The poetics of factual specificity jolted the reader out of neatly consolidated expectations about genre and taste and into sudden encounters with physical minutiae. William Hazlitt described this experience as a form of textual travel sickness the reader shared with the seasick Don Juan, complaining that 'after the lightning and the hurricane, we are introduced to the interior of the cabin and the contents of wash-hand basins'.[1] Shadowing the *ottava rima* verse, the Pope/Bowles controversy was also received as a fall from grace. Thomas Moore recorded in his journal, ' – the whole thing unworthy of him – a Leviathan among small fry – He has had the bad taste to allude to an anecdote which I told him about Bowles's early life, which is even worse than Bowles.'[2] Once again, the personal and the particular are seen to violate the integrity of good taste. From the start of his career, Byron's attention to 'things' made for a peculiarly close, theatrical relationship between him and his readership. Things came to a head with *Don Juan*, and we shall now examine the relationship between poetics and history in this poem to see how the play of digression in Byron's poetry forced his readers to participate in the aesthetic debates of contemporary reviews and pamphlet controversies.

Up to this point, we have focused on the digressive poetics signalled typographically by marks such as brackets or inverted commas.[3] Beyond these devices, however, Byron's *ottava rima* satire invites its readers to change course in a number of other ways such as the intertextual games of the Dedication:

> If fallen in evil days on evil tongues,
>   Milton appeal'd to the Avenger, Time.
> If Time, the avenger, execrates his wrongs,
>   And makes the word '*Miltonic*' mean '*sublime,*'
>   (Dedication, 10)

Here, the allusion to *Paradise Lost* VII, l. 25, is luminously clear, but not separated by quotation marks from the speech of the Dedication. Lucy Newlyn argues that this reference leaves the Milton myth 'intact', but it is recognisably different from Wordsworth's unsignalled use of the same Miltonic moment in 'Tintern Abbey':[4]

>   that neither evil tongues,
> Rash judgments, nor the sneers of selfish men,
> Nor greetings where no kindness is, nor all
> The dreary intercourse of daily life,
> Shall e'er prevail against us.
>   (ll. 128–32)

Wordsworth invokes Miltonic isolation to secure self-sufficiency without inviting the reader to linger on his source. The rolling blank verse cadences of 'Tintern Abbey' glide from paragraph to paragraph, making it less likely that the reader will pause to disinter literary echoes. At this moment of assimilation Wordsworth gathers all that is 'unremembered' and all that is 'unborrowed' into an organic whole: Milton's voice contributes to the harmony, affirms the integrity of the younger poet (changed, no doubt, and yet not utterly) and swells his authority. Never slow to recognise his own genius, Wordsworth praised 'the musical succession [of preconceiv]ed feeling' in the poem.[5] Byron's *ottava rima*, on the other hand, sets up more inquisitive hesitations from line to line and rhyme to rhyme, encouraging readers to be alert to the 'superartificial'.

Don Juan is hospitable to many different voices and wants its readers to be aware that very little is 'unborrowed'. Extensive catalogues of other authors serve to remind readers of the different texts which make up consciousness and identity. This has a very different effect from Wordsworth's account of his undergraduate reading in *The Prelude*:

> Beside the pleasant mills of Trompington
> I laughed with Chaucer; in the hawthorn shade
> Heard him, while birds were warbling, tell his tales
> Of amorous passion. And that gentle bard
> Chosen by the Muses for their Page of State,
> Sweet Spencer, moving through his clouded heaven
> With the moon's beauty and the moon's soft pace.[6]

Wordsworthian blank verse naturalises earlier authors, making them accord to the contours in his mental landscape and form a background of choral support rather than appearing as material texts or re-embodied authors. We find a similar blending of voices when Elizabeth Barrett Browning's Aurora Leigh advocates a loss of identity and difference in reading, 'when / We gloriously forget ourselves and plunge / Soul-forward, headlong, into a book's profound'.[7] Although the 'plunge' is Byronic in its uncompromising speed, Aurora's encounters with earlier authors are part of dutiful family affection:

> I read much. What my father taught before
> From many a volume, Love re-emphasised
> Upon the self same pages: Theophrast
> Grew tender with the memory of his eyes,
> And AElian made mine wet. (I, ll. 710–14).

Barrett Browning's blank verse is more receptive to the art of patchwork than Wordsworth's, but it appears seamless when compared with the discussions of reading in *Don Juan*. Encounters with literary forefathers in Byron's epic belong to a social world of literary commerce, not the hermetically sealed realm of private reading. Specific book titles emerge frequently in *Don Juan* as 'things' with as much – or sometimes more – vitality than the poem's hero:

> Ovid's a rake, as half his verses show him,
>   Anacreon's morals are a still worse sample,
> Catullus scarcely has a decent poem,
>   I don't think Sappho's Ode a good example,
> Although Longinus tells us there is no hymn
>   Where the sublime soars forth on wings more ample;
> But Virgil's songs are pure, except that horrid one
> Beginning with '*Formosum Pastor Corydon.*'
>
>   (I. 42)

In this stanza we can detect the familiar tactics of Byron's allusive textual transmission: the classic authors become exactly what Juan's mother fears – contemporaries one might talk with over dinner or in a tavern. The tone creates a sense of bodily presence as Byron ironically celebrates the local and *risqué*, those awkward moments when the actuality of the classical text disconcerts the code of modern morals.

As McGann's editorial commentaries reveal, there is no established critical vocabulary capable of distinguishing between Byron's multiple forms of intertextuality: indeed, were it available, such a vocabulary might limit the reader's responses to the digressive intertexture of *ottava rima* verse. It is all the more necessary, therefore, to discuss individual instances of digressive play locally to see how their varying effects at the level of the reading experience constitute meaning in the poem. Typographically signalled digressions have the advantage of marked visibility, and as they are among the most distinctive of Byron's compositional practices they provide one of my main measures of digressive frequency. The rest of this chapter focuses on areas of *Don Juan* which display this sort of concentrated digressive activity. Moving away from the first two cantos (which tend to be the main site of previous scholarship on digression and allusion), and looking at digressive intertextuality as local not global phenomena, we shall see how Byron's text asks its readers to relate individual parts to a continually shifting conception of what has gone before. It is evident that, in the course of reading the poem, the reader becomes more receptive to richly accruing layers of meaning and individual readers become part of a process by which meaning is diversified and contingent. Here the notion of poetic allusion is crucial, a concept which in Byron's texts is intricately bound up with an experimental art of digression.

Byron's diverse modes of allusion have presented critics with something of a problem. G. Wilson Knight solved this very skilfully by analysing Byron's repertoire of different Shakespearean characters in prose and verse (namely Hamlet, Falstaff, Richard III, Macbeth and Timon), and by tracing the 'varying, inter-shifting' Shakespearean psychology in *Don Juan* 'as a whole'.[8] More recently scholars have addressed this problem by making broader distinctions, such as Jonathan Bate's detection of 'loud' and 'soft' Shakespearean allusions in *Don Juan*:

The occurrence of two allusions in quick succession, the second usually quieter than the first, is very frequent in *Don Juan*; once the mind is sent to Shakespeare, it dwells there for a moment and picks up a second treasure.[9]

After the focus in the first three chapters on what Bate would call 'loud' allusions, this chapter is concerned with the workings of 'quieter' allusion – the kind of intertextual reference which had been described as 'casual and buried' by Peter Manning (in relation to Byron) and 'maddeningly elusive' by John Hollander (referring to a type of allusion more generally).[10] Having noticed the development of a 'quiet' allusive trope, Jonathan Bate does not dwell on its function in *Don Juan*, but concentrates instead on the ways in which Byron 'proclaims difference, in contrast to the usual Romantic striving for similarity with Shakespeare'.[11] Bate's emphasis on 'Byron's Pose', however, leads to the over-simplified conclusion that in *Don Juan*, the poet achieves an 'untroubled and unself-conscious [relationship] with Shakespeare', and that 'the robust use of quotation in *Don Juan* suits Byron's public persona. His appropriations of Shakespeare are so brazen that they are not problematic.'[12]

By leaning (like Francis Jeffrey rather than Wilson Knight) on a fixed sense of Byron's personality, Bate limits the relationship between Byron and Shakespeare. He focuses on examples of signalled allusion in *Don Juan* because they fit his quasi-Bloomian trajectory as a writer's anxious echoing of a rival. From this viewpoint, Byron's rejection of 'Bardolatry' undercuts both the aesthetic credo of his contemporaries, and the iconographic status of Shakespeare:

> As *Don Juan* as a whole is an accumulative, disparate, unorganic work, so its quotations are not integrated. Byron makes a virtue of the incidental, the momentary, the superficial. Overt quotations and adaptations could also be used to demonstrate the vulnerability of the English classics. Comic, bantering quotations are a form of affectionate mockery that render their subjects human and approachable. Byron is able simultaneously to mock Romantic awe in the face of Shakespeare and to overcome that sense of his own inferiority which was discerned by Goethe.[13]

Bate's paradigm is reductive to the extent that it suggests that signalled quotations are symptoms of a 'disparate, unorganic work'. But, as we shall see, as well as offering surface quotations, each canto of *Don Juan* also uses forms of reference that are more deeply integrated and which rely on the reader to disinter them. Where Bate's paradigm relies on a sense of 'inferiority' as the dynamic of Byron's text, my stress is on ways in which Byron's poem, through a subtler interweaving of reference, raises questions about the nature of the organic itself.

Anne Barton goes much further towards an explanation of the function of different forms of allusion in *Don Juan* and Byron's late dramatic writing:

Quotations from Shakespeare, half-remembered or precise, had always been a feature of Byron's poetry and prose. What emerges, however, in *Don Juan* is a tendency to invoke recognisably Shakespearean situations, without necessarily using their words, in order to complicate or add resonance to relationships or attitudes.[14]

Using Barton's observations as a starting point, we can turn to canto VI which displays a significant rise in the frequency of typographically marked disruptions compared with the preceding two cantos. Different levels of Shakespearean allusion in canto VI suggest that in 1822 the poem becomes more demanding of its readers, and also more open to the risk that they might or might not co-operate in intertextual production.

The horrified reaction of Murray and his advisers to the later cantos of *Don Juan* is today assumed to be part of the public prudishness of the nineteenth century. Twentieth-century critics like McGann and Barton describe canto VI as 'genial' and applaud Byron's 'comic sparkle and *élan*'.[15] Steffan is less enthusiastic, assuming that the seraglio narrative constitutes a deliberate provocation of Murray's 'Synod' but finding the digressions 'excessively diffuse and often flaccid' and 'the improvisation is so free and so trifling that it becomes tedious'.[16] It is interesting that Barton's close attention to allusion produces a positive assessment of canto VI, whereas Steffan's analysis of 'associational license' discloses a 'hodgepodge' moving by 'whimsical and centrifugal jerks'.[17] The term 'hodgepodge' exemplifies that concern for violated canons of correctness which characterised Byron's contemporary critics. If we read intertextually, however, we can begin to look at the ways in which Byron plays with a relationship between the general and the particular, the spoken and the unspoken, with an eye on different groups of readers, and how the poem in Barthes's phrase 'produce[s] its own chiaroscuro'.[18]

Jerome McGann has established that Byron's work on canto VI began as early as January 1822 and extended into April. Anne Barton and G. Wilson Knight remind us that in February, Byron and other members of the Pisan circle began rehearsals for a production of *Othello* which was to be staged in the Great Hall of the Lafranchi Palace.[19] 'Lord Byron was to be Iago', Medwin tells us, 'I shall never forget his reading Iago's part in the handkerchief scene.'[20] As well as influencing *The Deformed Transformed*, as Barton has shown, the dynamics of *Othello* also complicate canto VI in terms of plot and audience relations. Byron uses nuances from the play to address both the private tensions of the Pisan circle and his more public disagreements with the English readership, whose moral superiority he questioned in the *Twelfth Night* epigraph to the new cantos.

A signalled allusion to *Othello* occurs early in the canto at stanza 9:

> I am not like Cassio, 'an arithmetician,'
>> But by 'the bookish theoric' it appears,
> If 'tis summed up with feminine precision,
>> That, adding to the account his Highness' years,
> The fair Sultana erred from inanition.

The quotation of Iago's words turns his disparaging assessment of Cassio's career into a 'feminine' enumeration of grievances. This transfer of speech from a masculine to a feminine sphere of activity is a more interesting form of cross-dressing even than Juan's costume (which tends to be the focus of feminist readings of canto VI).[21] Susan Wolfson defines 'linguistic cross-dressing' in *Don Juan* as 'transfers of verbal property, such as the narrator's calling himself "a male Mrs. Fry" ... or the application of masculine-toned terms to women: the Sultan desires a "handsome paramour"'.[22] If we look at the subtle way *Don Juan* modifies its Shakespearean allusions it is possible to discern a further level on which the poem tests its readers:

> For were the Sultan just to all his dears,
> She could but claim the fifteenth hundred part
> Of what should be monopoly – the heart.
>> (VI. 9)

This emergence of Shakespeare's *Othello* in the texture of canto VI allows us to hear the voice of Iago ('part') and his fascination with literal details of sexuality competing with the voice of Othello – who cannot bear to keep 'a corner in the thing I love' – and his vain attempts to make sexual betrayal into something more dignified. The narrator's sentimental reflection on his boyish devotion uses the all-or-nothing voice of Othello:

> I
> Gave what was worth a world; for worlds could never
> Restore me those pure feelings, gone forever.
>> (VI. 5)

On the verbal level this combines Othello's farewell to his occupation ('O now forever / Farewell the tranquil mind'), his relinquishing of his love for Desdemona (''Tis gone.'), and his estimation of her value ('If heaven would make me such another world / Of one entire and perfect chrysolite, / I'ld not have sold her for it).[23] Three stanzas later, however, we hear the narrator as honest Iago, '[persuading himself] to speak the truth' (II. 3. l. 214) so as to secure Cassio's dismissal:

> I know Gulbeyaz was extremely wrong;
>   I own it, I deplore it, I condemn it;
> But I detest all fiction even in song,
>   And so must tell the truth, howe'er you blame it.
>
> (VI. 8)

The narrator's reluctance to impart details of reprehensible behaviour incites the reader, Othello-like, to supply those very details. The poem discloses each reader as a potential hypocrite, a technique which duplicates Iago's repertoire of hints and tonal traps. But Byron will not allow identities of characters from the play to settle for long on characters of his poem. Stanza 14 offers Iago's sexual experience as the basis for knowledge:

> Now here we should distinguish; for howe'er
>   Kisses, sweet words, embraces, and all that,
> May look like what is – neither here nor there,
>   They are put on as easily as a hat,
> Or rather bonnet, which the fair sex wear,
>   Trimmed either heads or hearts to decorate,
> Which form an ornament, but no more part
> Of heads, than their caresses of the heart.
>
> (VI. 14)

This warning about women is closely patterned after the terms in which Iago alerts us to his selfish scheming in the opening scene of the play:

> others there are,
> Who, trimm'd in forms, and visages of duty,
> Keep yet their hearts attending on themselves.
>
> (I. I. ll. 49–51)

And the knowing tone once again recalls the way in which Iago instructs Othello in female duplicity during the central temptation scene: 'I know our country disposition well; / In Venice they do let God see the pranks / They dare not show their husbands: their best conscience / Is not to leave undone, but keep unknown' (III. 3. ll. 205–8). The next stanza picks up Iago's words, both in the narrator's observation that 'feminine delight' is 'resigned / Rather to hide what pleases most unknown' (VI. 15) and in the choice of 'tokens' of love. The contiguity between the narrator of *Don Juan* and Iago is disturbing because it hints at how the reader's responses are being directed, like Othello's, towards the handkerchief. We too are being led by the nose and encouraged to assemble evidence from insinuations. This dramatises the way in which the reader's imagination works over fragments, and can draw a pattern out of personal interest. The narrator comments on this process directly in stanza 18 as he points up the exigencies of metrical composition:

> I own no prosody can ever rate it
> As a rule, but *Truth* may, if you translate it.
>
> (VI. 18)

The draft variants for this couplet demonstrate Byron's insistence on the conditional nature of experience: he corrected 'but Truth will' to 'but Truth may', opening the stanza to philosophical uncertainty just after battling to 'close the octave's chime' (*CPW*, v, p. 304). The digressions forced by prosody are foregrounded as a set of rules which classically educated readers used to agree on, whereas in contrast, the shifting codes of what society 'requires' create an invisible 'whole' which repeatedly collides with the parts of *Don Juan*. However, after the Pope/Bowles controversy and the rise of the Lake School, the 'trash of Keats' and the Cockneys, the rules of English prosody could also be seen as open to the risk of becoming historically specific, subject to the whims of fashion, caprice and the partiality of an untrustworthy public.

A link between sexual mutability and the unreliability of language prompts Byron's use of innuendo in the same way that Iago cleverly plants unfinished ideas for Othello to complete:

OTH.   What hath he said?
IAGO. Faith, that he did ... I know not what he did.
OTH. But what?
IAGO. Lie.
OTH. With her?
IAGO. With her, on her, what you will.
OTH. Lie with her, lie on her? – We say lie on her, when they belie her, – lie with her, zounds, that's fulsome! (IV. I. ll. 31–6)

This favourite Shakespearean pun recurs when Byron the narrator shifts from discussion of Gulbeyaz's overacted welcome for the Sultan to a more general admission of dishonesty in sexual relationships:

> If fair Gulbeyaz overdid her part,
>   I know not – it succeeded, and success
> Is much in most things, not less in the heart
>   Than other articles of female dress.
> Self-love in man too beats all female art;
>   They lie, we lie, all lie, but love no less.
>
> (VI. 19)

The misogyny of describing the heart as another article of female dress is here averted by reflecting on a hidden whole (loving no less) which underlies all the different lying 'parts'. Repeatedly throughout canto VI, the reader is led to construct a whole meaning from specific trifles light as air. An interest in the different grounds for 'ocular proof' flickers between the texts of *Othello* and *Don Juan*. Medwin remembered that after reading Iago's part in the handkerchief scene, Byron remarked:

'Shakespeare was right ... in making Othello's jealousy turn upon that circumstance. The handkerchief is the strongest proof of love, not only among the Moors, but all Eastern nations: and yet they say that the plot of "Marino Faliero" hangs upon too slight a cause.'[24]

As usual, Byron's response to a literary text is bound up with an awareness of his own relationship with an audience and what 'they say'. In this case, Byron's response to *Othello* is also caught in the recent scandal of Queen Caroline's trial (for which, as we have seen, he offered 'some hints' to Hobhouse). In 1820 the ministry of George IV had attempted to discredit Caroline by producing 'ocular demonstration' of her infidelity. The narrator of *Don Juan*, in his preoccupation with beds and sheets 'white as what bards call "driven / Snow"'(VI. 25), juxtaposes the voices of Iago and Othello with the contemporary divorce trial of Queen Caroline during which bundles of her bed linen were presented as evidence of adultery.[25] The comparison between Caroline's sheets and 'driven snow' had been made by journalists who supported the Queen, but the issue of dirty linen also takes us to the lust-stained bed which Othello is determined to see, and which Byron's contemporary readers searched for in *Don Juan*. Threads of allusion are enmeshed in historical circumstance as Byron's digressive performance of a play within a play draws his readers to reflect on their participation in the public construction of good taste. The production and reproduction of art in *Don Juan* is always historically specific and draws attention to the reader's discrimination and judgement of textual inter-relationships.

When Juan finds himself in the harem, the reader's combination of fear and curiosity is shared by Gulbeyaz (as another interested party), and Byron's ambiguous presentation of the Sultan's wife derives much of its poignancy from the stanza which relates her sleepless, suspicion-racked night:

> Oh the heavy night!
> When wicked wives who love some bachelor
> Lie down in dudgeon to sigh for the light

...
> To toss, to tumble, doze, revive, and quake
> Lest their too lawful bed-fellow should wake.
>
> (VI. 24)

Recalling Othello's lament 'O heavy hour!' (v. 2. l. 99), together with one of the scenes which prompt it – Iago's fictitious account of his disturbed night sharing Cassio's bed ('... and sigh'd, and kiss'd, and then / Cried "Cursed fate, that gave thee to the Moor!"'(III. 3. ll. 431–2)) – the poem advertises its turn to the episode of the harem at night. Intertextual echoes create a confusion of tragedy and comedy as the reader is caught between the perspectives of Iago and Othello. Byron's allusive play destabilises our generic frame of reference while distant echoes from Shakespeare's tragedy unsettle the 'genial' mood of the seraglio narrative. When we are told that the office of '"the Mother of the Maids"' was 'to keep aloof or smother / All bad propensies' (VI. 30–1), we receive a flickering apprehension of Desdemona's fate. But having used the rhythms of *Othello* to prepare the reader for a decisive outcome once Juan enters the harem, Byron suddenly puts the tragedy into reverse and reintroduces the earlier (potentially comic) material of obstacles to marriage. The scrutiny of Juan casts him as a stranger,

> Though differing in stature and degree,
> And clime and time, and country and complexion;
> They all alike admired their new connexion.
>
> (VI. 40)

This description of the concubines uses Iago's hints about Desdemona's wilfulness, drawn from the central temptation scene of Act III. Here Othello's wonder at Desdemona's love is turned to disbelief:

> Not to affect many proposed matches,
> Of her own clime, complexion, and degree,
> Whereto we see in all things nature tends;
> Fie, we may smell in such a will most rank,
> Foul disproportion; thoughts unnatural.
>
> (III. 3. ll. 233–7)

In a similar way the reader of *Don Juan* is drawn into an ironic perspective on the 'Magnetism, or Devilism' (VI. 38) of sexual attraction, and a consciousness of seeing 'with Christian eyes or Heathen' (VI. 37). The episode may also involve the gentle teasing of certain members of the Pisan circle, for in February 1822, Edward Trelawny was recently arrived

on the scene, and Mary Shelley in particular had received him as a kind
of Othello figure, noting his 'Moorish' appearance and his ability to tell
strange stories.[26] We are drawn further backwards into the plot of Othello
with the description of Dudù:

> she sighed,
> As if she pitied her for being there,
> A pretty stranger without friend or guide,
> And all abashed too at the general stare
> Which welcomes hapless strangers in all places,
> With kind remarks upon their mien and faces.
>
> (VI. 45)

This stanza conflates the dominant moments of the early scenes of *Othello*,
especially Othello's portrait of Desdemona's response to him:

> She gave me for my pains a world of sighs;
> She swore i' faith 'twas strange, 'twas passing strange;
> 'Twas pitiful, 'twas wondrous pitiful.
>
> (I. 3. ll. 159–61)

The way is softened for a lovers' encounter. After this introduction, however, the poem suddenly projects the reader forward into the final scenes
of *Othello*, as Byron juxtaposes the perilous comedy of Juan and Dudù
with the setting of Desdemona's death. The comic potential of the scene
is unsettled by hints of tragedy: 'each lovely limb / Of the fair occu-
pants' reminds us of Desdemona seeming 'lovely fair' to Othello; the
woman 'slightly stirring in her snowy shroud' (VI. 66) takes us back to
Desdemona's request for her wedding sheets to be her shroud. In a similar
way, the simile of one maiden who,

> as the fruit
> Nods from the tree, was slumbering with soft breath
> And lips apart, which showed the pearls beneath.
>
> (VI. 65)

refigures Desdemona's last moments as Othello kisses her: 'I'll smell it
on the tree, / A balmy breath ...' (V. 2. ll. 15–16).

The effect of using tragedy to haunt comedy in this way is complex.
Shakespearean drama is famous for mixing tragic and comic modes, but
it rarely provides the simultaneous 'scorching and drenching' that we
find in Byron's *ottava rima* verse. What we might call an experience of textual simultaneity emerges from Byron's poetics of conflicting particulars

(now estranged from the clearly-defined satiric universe of Pope, Swift and Sterne). In eighteenth-century satire, juxtapositions created a chaos indicative of repeated failures of taste: in *Don Juan* the reader is involved in the recreation of chaos at the level not simply of image, but also of po-etic texture. The process of digressive allusion initiated in footnotes and eighteenth-century satire, and later censored as an unfortunate 'part' of Churchill's verse, has in *Don Juan* taken over the poetic texture as a whole.

Carmela Perri's work on the poetics of allusion reminds us that iden-tification of the source of an allusion is not enough: the reader needs to be able to negotiate with the context of the source in order to complete the allusive process. 'The only freedom left to the reader', Perri claims, 'is the certainty that the task is unfinished': the meaning of allusion is not in its content, but in the reader's perception of a form.[27] This readerly responsibility is emphasised by the off-hand self-referentiality of Byron's narrative:

> – or what you will; –
> My similes are gathered in a heap,
> So pick and chuse – perhaps you'll be content.
> (vi. 68)

'What you will' is a fleeting reminder of the source of the canto's epigraph in Shakespeare's *Twelfth Night*; but it also alerts us to a wry awareness that the subtitle can represent an appeal either to personal choice or mere whimsicality. Byron's 'perhaps you'll be content' has its uneasy shadow in Iago's advice to Othello as he watches Othello's certainty disintegrate ' – Pray be content' (iii. 3. l. 458). As the reader recognises the voice of Shakespearean tragedy and co-produces its modulation into sexual comedy, the act of reading becomes a shared performance that modifies the usual Romantic preference for Shakespeare in the head.

The 'general commotion' caused by Dudù's scream abruptly inter-rupts the mood of the bedchamber scene and sends the reader back to Iago's stage-management of Cassio's disgrace. Byron reworks 'the clamour', transposing the action from a dispute between soldiers to a sexual skirmish amongst women – again teasing the Pisan circle for the cluster of jealousy and suspicion around Jane Williams and Percy Shelley. The temporal setting of the scene at the moment 'ere the middle watch was hardly over' (vi. 70) echoes the timing of the Shakespearean precedent ('here's a goodly watch indeed' (ii. 3. l. 151)), and the aural commotion of Shakespeare's scene ('Who's that that rings the bell?' ... 'Silence that dreadful bell, it frights the isle' (ii. 3. ll. 152; 166)) is refigured as Juanna's description of the harem:

> And here Juanna kindly interposed,
>   And said she felt herself extremely well
> Where she then was, as her sound sleep disclosed
>   When all around rang like a tocsin bell.
>
> (VI. 84)

The response to Dudù's scream, 'that upstarted all / The Oda' (VI. 71), translates the scene of Cassio's brawl into feminine eclât and the 'strict investigation' (VI. 74), replays Othello's demands for an explanation: 'give me to know/How this foul rout began' (II. 3. ll. 200–1). Cassio's mortification, 'I pray you pardon me, I cannot speak' (II. 3. l. 180), is mirrored in Dudù's embarrassment:

> Dudù had never passed for wanting sense,
>   But being 'no orator as Brutus is,'
> Could not at first expound what was amiss.
>
> (VI. 74)

This illustrates the way in which Byron's poetic texture always presents more than one thread of allusion at a time. The reference to *Julius Caesar* juxtaposes a masculine, public, frame of reference with a more intimate, feminine realm of experience: the topic of Antony's speech, male honour and Roman virtue, is reapplied to a sexual encounter. Throughout the scene, Byron plays down his own responsibility for the narrative:

> I can't tell why she blushed, nor can expound
>   The mystery of this rupture of their rest;
> All that I know is, that the facts I state
> Are true as truth has ever been of late.
>
> (VI. 85)

This deploys the earnest ('honest') puzzlement of Iago: 'More of this matter can I not report' (II. 3. l. 231), as the burden of interpretation is passed to the reader:

> And that's the moral of this composition,
>   If people would but see its real drift; –
> But *that* they will not do without suspicion,
>   Because all gentle readers have the gift
> Of closing 'gainst the light their orbs of vision;
>   While gentle writers also love to lift
> Their voices 'gainst each other, which is natural,
> The numbers are too great for them to flatter all.
>
> (VI. 88)

As Byron never tired of pointing out, his readers had to construct the innuendoes to which they took exception. The mention of 'numbers' in the last couplet and the unpicking of 'natural' with 'flatter all' highlights the fact that market pressures tended to compromise aesthetics and morality. Canto VI plays with the ways in which suspicious perception can shape the reader's response. As if to drive this home, parenthetical asides continually stress the 'honesty' and 'modesty' of the narrator as opposed, we understand, to the designs of the reader:

(as I said) (VI. 12)
(to a modest mind) (VI. 15)
(I think) (VI. 16)
– how / Could you ask such a question? but we will / Continue. (VI. 33)

Scenes of interrogation and critical scrutiny recur throughout the canto as the shifts in the narrative necessitate a reappraisal of expectations. We are invited to share the misery of Gulbeyaz's jealousy to the extent that her 'catechism of questions' (VI. 100) and her 'convulsion' (stanzas 106–11) invoke a memory of Othello, while Baba's behaviour offers a further reflection of Iago's temptation:

> But there seemed something that he wished to hide,
> *Which* hesitation more betrayed than masqued.
>
> (VI. 100)

By the time we reach this refiguration of *Othello*, however, we realise that Gulbeyaz's enquiries about 'where and how/ [Juan] had passed the night' (VI. 99) reflect the reader's own curiosity. The narrative process figures not only Gulbeyaz, but also Byron's contemporary audience as creatures of 'sensual phantasy' (V. 126). A self-torturing desire to have the worst suspicions confirmed applies not only to Gulbeyaz, but also to Byron's feminine 'arbiters of taste' in 'moral England, where the thing's a tax' (VI. 29). Once again, the particularity of 'the thing' is designed to discomfort systematised morality.

    Queen Caroline's trial for divorce showed how a salacious appetite for sexual misdemeanour went to the heart of the English Establishment – Castlereagh spent six years gathering sheets and rehearsing witnesses.[28] The political scandal is advertised as part of the fabric of canto VI when Byron invokes '"A strange coincidence," to use a phrase / By which such things are settled now-a-days' (VI. 78).[29] This intrusion of contemporary factual material disturbs the texture of Dudù's dream explanation, and the signalled quotation to the Caroline trial reminds readers how strange it is that they allow themselves to be shocked by every trace of sexual nuance in *Don Juan*. Like Iago, the English Tories at the Caroline trial had gloated over the possibility of female lust and, like Othello, they were threatened by signs that they themselves were induced to discover in *Don Juan*.[30]

Although public reaction to his poem took the form of perpetual affront, Byron insistently pointed out that his precursors had not provoked similar moral outrage:

> I say no more than has been said in Dante's
> Verse, and by Solomon and by Cervantes;
>
> By Swift, by Machiavel, by Rochefoucault,
>   By Fenelon, by Luther, and by Plato;
> By Tillotson, and Wesley, and Rousseau,
>   Who knew this life was not worth a potato.
>
>   (VII. 3–4)

Byron's use of Shakespeare in canto VI of *Don Juan* allowed distant readers in England, as well as readers in the intimate Pisan circle, to participate in 'things the turning of a hair or feather / May settle'. Once Juan and Dudù stand before Gulbeyaz, Byron leaves the reader to guess their fate: 'far be't from me', the narrator claims, 'to anticipate / In what way feminine Caprice may dissipate' (VI. 119). It has been argued that by the time he was writing canto VI, Byron no longer expected English women to be among his readers. But this may be an overstatement. In 1822 the production of *Othello* by the Pisan circle was 'laid aside' as Edward Williams put it. Medwin was more explicit: 'All at once a difficulty arose about a Desdemona, and the Guiccioli put her Veto on our theatricals.'[31] Byron had obtained permission from his Dictatress to continue *Don Juan*; but the risks of 'feminine Caprice' offer greater not lesser influence as Byron's epic digresses towards home.

In the siege cantos, the notion of risk itself is not merely a wayward particular but becomes a part of the poem's fabric. In these cantos, the vagaries of chance double as the texture of reading. The reader of *Don Juan* will recognise Shakespearean allusions as one of the poem's most frequent invitations to digress; there are, however, other trails of intertextuality which run parallel with (or sometimes cross) every trace we elect to follow. Canto VIII, for example, contains signalled allusions to Wordsworth,

the prayer book burial service, popular song, military jargon, the Book
of Psalms, Shakespeare, Cowper and the Book of Daniel. It also sustains
a running dialogue with Castelnau. Whether the reader follows some or
all of this shadowy trail is open to chance and it is to the poem's configurations of chance and contingency that we turn in the next section of
this chapter.

It is unsurprising that Byron should have a more enhanced awareness
of the dynamics of risk than any other poet in the period. The work of
social and economic historians such as Anthony Giddens in our own
time has proposed that conscious engagement with risk is one of the determining characteristics of modernity.[32] Whereas William Wordsworth
deplored the accelerating unpredictabilities of the industrial age, and
looked for stability in timeless figures of endurance like pedlars, shep-
herds or leech gatherers (mainly divested of the troublesome particularity of merchandise, sheep or leeches), Byron inscribed the uncertainty of
the modern world and its fatalistic implications for authorship into the
texture of his poems.

On 16 July 1819 John Murray began a letter to Byron:

My Lord
La Sort est jetté – Don Juan was published yesterday, and having fired the
Bomb – here I am out of the way of its explosion – its publication has excited
a very great degree of interest – public <opinion be> expectation having risen
up like the surrounding boats on the Thames when a first rate is struck from its
Stocks – as yet my Scouts and dispatches afford little idea to public opinion – it
certainly does not appear to be what they had chosen to anticipate. (MS., John
Murray Archive)

In its early days, Murray and Byron continually referred to the publication of *Don Juan* in terms of a shared military campaign against public
opinion: Murray is here using a French version of 'the die is cast' – words
Plutarch attributes to Caesar on crossing the Rubicon. The roll of the
dice and meditations on 'Chance, Providence, or Fate' (VII. 76) seem to
have preoccupied Byron during a period of fraught financial dealing in
1820. Between April and July 1820, Murray delayed the publication of
cantos III and IV unsure of how they would affect his reputation.[33] Meanwhile, Byron was preoccupied with mortgage funds and insurance and
was subject to conflicting advice from Kinnaird and Hanson:

> Between the devil and deep Sea,
> Between the Lawyer and Trustee? –

... I am at my wits' end betwixt your contrary opinions ... I prefer higher Interest for my Money (like everyone else I believe) and shall be glad to make as much as I can at the least risk possible. (*BLJ*, VII, p. 69)

In a subsequent piece of correspondence on the same financial dilemma, Byron substituted for his epigram on indecision a quotation from Gay's *Beggar's Opera*:

> 'Or this way, or that way, or which way I will –
> Whate'er I decide, t'other bride will take ill. –'.
>
> (*BLJ*, VII, p. 72)

Byron's finances were bound up in a marriage settlement with Lady Byron, so it is perhaps unsurprising that the fluctuations of funds and rates of interest slide into references to sexual mutability. In June Byron decided that he would 'make no further limitation about the price of Stocks – and must take [his] chance' (*BLJ*, VII, p. 116), and these financial arrangements ran into those for the official separation of Teresa Guiccioli from her husband ('committing [herself], forever'(*BLJ*, VII, p. 110)). The mixed scenario of financial and sexual uncertainty with the accompanying dynamics of risk and return, can be traced in Byron's writing during these months. In *Marino Faliero*, the Doge recurrently links his fortune with the roll of the dice.

> DOGE. The die is cast. (I. 2. l. 564)

> DOGE.   I have set my little left
> Of life upon this cast: the die was thrown.
>
> (III. 1. ll. 54–5)

> DOGE. The die is thrown ...
> I am settled and bound up, and being so,
> The very effort which it cost me to
> Resolve to cleanse this commonwealth with fire,
> Now leaves my mind more steady.
>
> (IV. 2. ll. 32; 73–6)

Part of the material included by Byron in his appendix for *Marino Faliero* dealt with the history of casinos in Venice:

It was a strange sight to see persons of either sex masked, or grave in their magisterial robes, round a table, invoking chance, and giving way at one instant to the agonies of despair, at the next to the illusion of hope, and that without uttering a single word. (*CPW*, IV, ll. 541–2)

The dramatic potential of such a scene is evident, but it would also have appealed to Byron as an exploration of the contingencies which

shaped his own career and which were particularly pressing at this moment. *Marino Faliero* was written during a period of suspension in the
composition of *Don Juan* since Murray was delaying over publication of
cantos III and IV. Canto V was written between October and December
1820 and, as we have seen, 1822 has been established as a turning-point
in the history of *Don Juan*. In cantos VII and VIII we can see a heightened
frequency of images of risk and financial calculation as Byron counted
the cost of an impending divorce from his publisher and from a portion
of his readership.

Augmented images of gaming and hazard work along with an increased frequency of marked parenthesis and allusion, to expose the
poem still further to the chanciness of readerly participation. If we examine the relationship between the signalled allusions and the fainter
echoes, we become more aware of the intricate unreliability of literature itself. As Peter Cochran has shown , Byron's free use of Castelnau,
his 'instinct to depart from his authenticating source whenever artistic
whim dictates', suggests that *Don Juan*'s concern with 'facts' is inextricably
bound up with an acceptance of the risk that truth may be 'translate[d]'.[34]
Whereas in the war cantos this perception becomes the basis for baiting
Byron's English readers, the English cantos, as we shall see, explore the
possibility of a shared experience of the arbitrary.

Canto VII is framed by evocations of uncertainty: in stanza I Byron
invokes 'Love' and 'Glory':

> we lift on high
> Our eyes in search of either lovely light.

And in the final stanza 87, we pass through a critical moment, 'that
awful pause, dividing life from death', when we are alerted to 'the shouts
of either faith / Hurrah! and Allah!' The use of the word 'either' with
its hint of arbitrary human circumstances, the literary duplication of a
physical shrug, is continued in the image of Suwarrow as a 'dancing
Light, / Which all who saw it followed, wrong or right' (VII. 46).[35] The
narration at this point refuses to endorse any single course of action, and
its digressions persistently draw attention to the risks and liabilities of
warfare. The text weaves the stock phrases of Homeric battle with the
vocabulary of gaming and financial dealing, so that the 'heroic action'
at Ismail is inextricably bound up with the speculative economic base of
Regency England:

> The second object was to profit by
> The moment of the general consternation,

> To attack the Turk's flotilla, which lay nigh
>   Extremely tranquil, anchored at its station:
> But a third motive was as probably
>   To frighten them into capitulation;
> A phantasy which sometimes seizes warriors,
> Unless they are game as Bull-dogs and Fox-terriers.
>
> (VII. 24)

The first line was suggested by Castelnau's ' Le second objet était de profiter', but Byron emphasised the chanciness of gaming by using 'probably' for 'le plus plausible' and by introducing the image of the gaming ring. Byron's insertion of a market frame of reference around the battle scene suggests a double sense of 'heavy losses'. The phrase 'A sad miscalculation' (VII. 28) uses a politely professional register to account for a huge military blunder in the same way that the phrase 'collateral damage' became notorious in the 1990s as shorthand for expendable civilian casualties. By intermittently picking up the thread of sporting or gaming vocabulary, Byron maximises the reader's sense of incongruity and also alerts us to different ways of counting the cost. Suwarrow, we are told, 'calculated life as so much dross' (VII. 77) and he is ordered to take Ismail '"at whatever price"' (VII. 40). The auctioneering and sporting echoes can suggest the insouciance of the officer class (whose insolent behaviour was a source of great irritation and several speeches in the House of Lords by Byron's friend, the Earl of Essex):

> Whether it was their engineer's stupidity,
>   Their haste, or waste, I neither know nor care,
> Or some contractor's personal cupidity,
>   Saving his soul by cheating in the ware
> Of homicide, but there was no solidity
>   In the new batteries erected there;
> They either missed, or they were never missed,
> And added greatly to the missing list.
>
> (VII. 27)

In Hell, as W.H. Auden tells us, 'inhabitants are identified not by name but by number. They do not *have* numbers, they *are* numbers.'[36] The word-play on 'missed / missing' mixes the luck of a shoot with the idea of being shot at. The casino of institutional finance recurs in stanza 29 when Byron describes a cannonade 'which was returned with interest'; Suwarrow, we are told, 'could afford to squander / His time' (VII. 52). This frequency of allusion to the hit-or-miss of market forces suggests that as well as investing the war cantos with literary reference, Byron has inscribed his narration with those fluctuating funds whose

degrees of risk so preoccupied him in 1820. By drawing attention to
the economic basis for fighting or writing, *Don Juan* insists on the link
between systems of combat, commerce and the consumer-led literary
market:

> The statesman, hero, harlot, lawyer – ward
>   Off each attack, when people are in quest
> Of their designs, by saying they *meant well*;
> 'Tis pity 'that such meaning should pave Hell.'
>
> I almost lately have begun to doubt
>   Whether Hell's pavement – if it be *so paved* –
> Must not have latterly been quite worn out,
>   Not by the numbers Good Intent hath saved,
> But by the mass who go below without
>   Those ancient good intentions, which once shaved
> And smoothed the brimstone of that street of Hell
> Which bears the greatest likeness to Pall Mall.
>
> (VIII. 25–6)

As McGann points out, 'hell', is slang for a gambling club; Byron had
already used this term in *Hints from Horace* (l. 239; *CPW*, v, p. 733) and
throughout July 1822 *Galignani's Messenger*, the newspaper he read while
in Italy, reported that 'prodigious sums have been lost in the H-lls'.[37] In
the stanza immediately following the ones on 'Hell' we encounter the
'strange chance' of Juan's being separated from the rest of his side. Byron
alluded to an accident from his own career when he likened this to 'one
of those odd turns of Fortune's tides' such as the division of 'chastest
wives from constant husbands' sides / Just at the close of the first bridal
year' (VIII. 27), an allusion which hazards personal involvement.

  The narrator's own interest in the workings of 'Chance, Providence,
or Fate' (VII. 76) is foregrounded in his discussion of the unpredictable
'roll of Fame' (VII. 32):

> Renown's all hit or miss;
> There's Fortune even in fame, we must allow.
>
> (VII. 33)

As we have seen in his revisions of *Hints from Horace*, Byron's sense of writing against the odds led him to use similar motifs in his defence of Pope.
In 'Some Observations Upon an Article in *Blackwood's Edinburgh Magazine*' (1820) he discussed writers 'who have not had their full fame', and
observed, 'there is a Fortune in Fame as in all other things' (Byron. *Complete Miscellaneous Prose*, p. 117). The 'artillery's hits or misses' at Ismail
reconfigure the random chances of survival and success which, as

Byron was keenly aware, applied to the literary world and to his own reception.

As is well known, Byron detested the way that Wellington had been credited with military success: '"It was the exaggerated praises of the people in England ... that indisposed me to the Duke of Wellington"', he is supposed to have told Lady Blessington.[38] In terms of the 'Fortune in fame', Wellington's career was the inverse of Byron's. *Don Juan*, however, makes the most of the idea of fortune not only as a plot device (as in the lots which are made from Julia's letter, or the 'gaming' (XIV. 18) of the London marriage market), but as a process in which the reader takes part in the haphazardness of digressive poetics:

> And then with tears, and sighs, and some slight kisses,
>   They parted for the present, these to await,
> According to the artillery's hits or misses,
>   What Sages call Chance, Providence, or Fate –
> Uncertainty is one of many blisses,
>   A mortgage on Humanity's estate –
> While their beloved friends began to arm,
> To burn a town which never did them harm.
>
> (VII. 76)

The choice of 'blisses' is predictable in terms of the rhyme, but unexpected in its location of heightened delight, even sexual pleasure (with its echo of 'kisses') in 'uncertainty'. The disturbing proximity of the 'mortgage' metaphor cannot cancel the teasing openness to chance which we sense in the third rhyme. Through this stanza we can hear Byron undercutting a universal acceptance of 'Chance, Providence, or Fate', while embracing, on the level of the individual, a small scale unpredictability – the 'beloved' sexual irresponsibility of Juan and Dudù. This instance of (unsafe) sexual waywardness seems to offer resistance to the large scale (wholesale) chance of arming so as 'to burn a town which never did them harm'.[39]

Byron also used the idea of uncertainty as a pleasure in *Sardanapalus*:

> SARDANAPALUS. There's something sweet in my uncertainty
>   I would not change for your Chaldean lore.
>
> (II. I. ll. 263–4)

It is interesting that this positive sense of 'uncertainty' is not found in Byron's verse before 1821. In his 'Detached Thoughts' from that year, Byron wrote a meditation on the excitement of gambling:

I have a notion that Gamblers are as happy as most people – being always *excited*; – women – wine – fame – the table – even Ambition – *sate* now & then – but every turn of the card – & cast of the dice keeps the Gambler alive – besides one can Game ten times longer than one can do anything else. – I was very fond of it when young – that is to say of 'Hazard' for I hate all *Card* Games even Faro . . . I loved and missed the *rattle* and *dash* of the box & dice – and the glorious uncertainty not only of good luck or bad luck – but of *any luck at all* – as one had sometimes to throw *often* to decide at all . . . it was the *delight* of the thing that pleased me. (*BLJ*, IX, p. 23)

The thing again. This meditation locates pleasure in the suddenness of change which so disconcerted Cohen's reading of the opening cantos of *Don Juan*. It is not until Byron returned to *Don Juan* and left Murray in 1822, however, that variability could be fully inscribed as texture, teasing the reader with the possibility of different sorts of digressive intertextuality. Byron's games with allusion are games with predictability and chance because the reader's response is an unknown quantity. Bernard Beatty has observed that a characteristically Byronic technique is to offer a mode, subvert it, but then endorse it in unexpected fashion. Beatty, however, does not elaborate on the crucial role of the reader in fashioning such unexpectedness.[40] We can sample the multiple layers of allusion in Byron's use of Shakespeare in cantos VII and VIII: our gaze is prefigured by the 'two poor girls', transported from the harem to the field of Ismail, who 'with swimming eyes, / Looked on as if in doubt if they could trust' (VII. 73). Their uncertainty, delicately rendered by the two 'ifs', offers an image for the way we see the surface of the poem 'swimming' at this point. Byron's digressive allusions may lead us to a more covert reference, or they may draw a blank: sometimes the trail of other texts will offer an extensive digressive labyrinth, whilst at other times an allusion will offer little or no return.

In the siege cantos we might have expected the frequency of signalled allusion to decrease in line with the more serious subject matter, but instead we are presented with copious overt allusions to Shakespearean drama and other literary texts. The penultimate stanza of canto VII, for example, is a compound of Shakespearean and Miltonic intimations of conflict:

> Hark! through the silence of the cold, dull night,
>   The hum of armies gathering rank on rank!
> Lo! dusky masses steal in dubious sight
>   Along the leaguered wall and bristling bank
> Of the armed river, while with straggling light
>   The stars peep through the vapours dim and dank,
> Which curl in curious wreaths – How soon the smoke
> Of Hell shall pall them in a deeper cloak.

(VII. 86)

McGann picks up the echo of *Macbeth* (I. 5. ll. 50–3), but we can also hear the chorus of *Henry V* describe the 'hum of either army' before Agincourt in the prologue to Act IV. The 'dusky masses' with 'vapours dim and dank' might remind us of the description of 'smoke and dusky vapours of the night' in 1 *Henry VI* (II. 2. l. 27) and the 'straggling light' provides a flickering glimpse of the 'poor straggling soldiers' of *Timon of Athens* (v. I. ll. 6–7). Human battle in *Don Juan* creates a 'Hell' and, with Shakespeare, Byron merges a Miltonic account of mischief in waiting. The 'dusky masses [stealing]' and the 'vapours . . . which curl in curious wreaths' also invoke Milton's Satan as he moves towards Eden and Eve in *Paradise Lost* ('Aloft, incumbent on the dusky air' (I. l. 226); 'In dusky wreaths, reluctant flames, the sign / Of wrath awaked' (VI. ll. 58–9)). It is important that none of these echoes constitutes a direct, signalled or 'loud' allusion. Instead, Milton and Shakespeare form a compound memory of epic warfare which allows the poet and reader to touch familiar material before that texture is disrupted.

In canto VIII Shakespearean contexts figure both as familiar background and as estranged moments of foreground. *Othello* resurfaces as a source of military images. In stanza 8, 'the roar / Of War's most mortal engines' draws on Othello's willed departure from his occupation:

> ye mortal engines, whose wide throats
> The immortal Jove's great clamour counterfeit;
> Farewell.
>
> (III. 3. ll. 361–3)

and Othello's chaos haunts the evocation of military chaos in stanza 82:

> the heat
> Of Carnage, like the Nile's sun-sodden Slime,
> Engendered monstrous shapes of every Crime.
>
> (VIII. 82)

McGann's commentary refers the reader to Cuvier at this point, but it seems more likely that Byron is mixing Iago's destructive designs –

> I ha't, it is engender'd; Hell and night
> Must bring this monstrous birth to the world's light.
>
> (I. 3. ll. 401–2)

– together with the sexual revels of Antony and Cleopatra ('By the fire / That quickens Nilus' slime' (I. 3. ll. 68–9)). Mingled in this fluid allusive texture is Alexander Pope's creation of the vapourish confusion of the underworld in canto IV of *The Rape of the Lock*. The muddiness of *The*

Dunciad throughout provides a disturbing model for textual miscegenation.[41] In Pope's satire, the restless sliding mass offers an image of cultural confusion from which the poet stands aloof, but for Byron the nightmarish fantasies of Ismail are dangerously close to the meandering process of his own poem. Contemporary readerly judgement condemned the poetics of *Don Juan* as grotesque debauchery while revering the antics of the warriors in battle as 'glory'. By bringing the two together, Byron confronts his readers with their responsibility for the assemblage of contexts which shapes meaning.

Byron's ability to find momentary excitement even within the wider horror of carnage at Ismail is evident in his presentation of Juan 'Flung here by fate or Circumstance . . . / Dashed on like a spurred blood-horse in a race' (VIII. 54). It reminds us of Byron's warning self-comparison in a letter to Murray of 1820: 'You must not treat a blood horse as you do your hacks otherwise he'll bolt out of the course.'[42] Juan's battle against the odds (and sometimes on the wrong side) reconfigures the ironies and accidents of *Don Juan*'s 'intellectual war'.

The effect of this mixture is that *Don Juan* redefines the epic tradition not only at the level of panorama (as in 'A panorama view of hell's in training' (I. 200)), but also at the level of the line and even the word. A single syllable is enough to deflect the reader into another scene, to adjust the perspective and let the light fall in a different way. McGann identifies an 'echo' of *Hamlet* ('Let the galled jade wince, our withers are unwrung' (III. 2. ll. 245–6)) when Byron turns to consider the people or 'Mob' under Wellington's 'heavy' pensions:

> The veriest jade will wince whose harness wrings
> So much into the raw as quite to wrong her
> Beyond the rules of posting, – and the Mob
> At last fall sick of imitating Job.
>
> (VIII. 50)

There is, however, another Shakespearean source which carries the sense of 'the people' starting to stir to a recognition of injustice. At the beginning of Act II in I *Henry IV*, two carriers and an ostler converse in an inn yard:

FIRST CARRIER. I prithee, Tom, beat Cut's saddle, put a few flocks in the point; poor jade is wrung in the withers out of all cess.

SECOND CARRIER. Peas and beans are as dank here as a dog, and that is the next way to give poor jades the bots: this house is turned upside down since Robin Ostler died. (II. I. ll. 5–10)

Although the line from *Hamlet* holds a closer linguistic echo, it has almost certainly been compounded with the sense of mistreatment ('Beyond the rules of posting') from the scene in *Henry IV.* This allows us to see how Byron responded to Shakespeare's particularity: the wording from *Hamlet* flares up as a verbal oddity, but the emotional dynamic of the stanza comes from a specific dramatic incident. The effect of such digressive allusions is to challenge the expectation of epic unity with a divided allegiance to parts which perplex the whole. Divided allegiance is, of course, the political threat which destabilises Wellington's self-presentation as hero:

> The Briton must be bold who really durst
> > Put to such trial John Bull's partial patience,
> As say that Wellington at Waterloo
> Was beaten, – though the Prussians say so too; –
>
> > (VI. 48)

Byron's affront to the prevailing view of Wellington follows his 'heterodox' defence of Pope. These stands are made not just for the sake of opposing the popular view, but because a view which is received rather than realised entails smoothing over vital particulars.

More of the Shakespearean matrix of canto VIII can be seen in stanza 43, where the reader is teased with the possibility of multiple allusions, and of the widely differing tones of the digressive process:

> They fell as thick as harvests beneath hail,
> > Grass before scythes, or corn below the sickle,
> Proving that trite old truth, that life's as frail
> > As any other boon for which men stickle.
> The Turkish batteries thrashed them like a flail
> > Or a good boxer, into a sad pickle,
> Putting the very bravest, who were knocked
> Upon the head, before their guns were cocked.
>
> > (VIII. 43)

McGann's commentary informs the reader that the first two lines of this stanza are Biblical (*CPW*, v, p. 733). It would be in keeping with the process of *Don Juan* to refer to the Old Testament as 'trite old truth', but it is also one of Byron's characteristic ways of crediting Shakespeare:

> I think one Shakespeare puts the same thought in
> The mouth of some one in his plays so doating,
> Which many people pass for wits by quoting.
>
> > (VII. 21)

The elegiac image of collapsing troops is undercut by a coarser register of haggling ('As any other boon for which men stickle'). Byron also disturbs the harvest simile by introducing the physical labour of agriculture ('thrashed them like a flail'), and then by slipping into the slang of prize fights and eating ('pickle' in *OED* carries the meanings of preserved food, a sorry plight, and a single grain of wheat or oats). The battle-as-harvest occurs several times in Shakespearean drama, most notably in *Henry V*, with Henry's speech before Harfleur:

> If I begin the batt'ry once again
> ... the flesh'd soldier, rough and hard of heart,
> In liberty of bloody hand shall range
> With conscience wide as hell, mowing like grass
> Your fresh-fair virgins and your flow'ring infants.
> (III. 3. ll. 7–14)

This moment from the history plays may be filtered through an account of Macbeth's military achievements:

> As thick as hail,
> Came post with post; and every one did bear
> Thy praises
> (I. 3. ll. 97–9),

and Byron's stanza may also be drawing on Shelley's *Hellas* (with its own disconcerting reference to food):

> the batteries blazed
> Kneading them down with fire and iron rain:
> Yet none approached till like a field of corn
> Under the hook of the swart sickleman
> The band, intrenched in mounds of Turkish dead,
> Grew weak.
> (ll. 380–85)[43]

In stanza 43 we might be aware of several juxtaposed contexts: 'as thick as ... hail' from *Macbeth*, the image of about-to-be mown grass from *Henry V*, and the sense of the imminent scything from *Hellas*. It appears here as elsewhere in *Don Juan* that Byron is using a network of other texts to create a claustrophobically dense literary texture of warfare. As the reader considers how to respond to these verbal oddities and anomalies, digressive minutiae counter the generalising tendency of epic.

Rather than proclaiming 'difference from' Shakespeare, as Bate suggests, *Don Juan* finds unfamiliarity within Shakespeare as well known quotations are realised in unexpected ways. Byron highlights the subversive questioning of national military purpose which is contained within Shakespeare's *Henry V* where three soldiers meet the disguised King before Agincourt and put the cause to trial:

But if the cause be not good, the king himself hath a heavy reckoning to make; when all those legs and arms and heads, chopped off in a battle, shall join together at the latter day, and cry all, 'We died at such a place'; some swearing, some crying for a surgeon, some upon their wives left poor behind them, some upon the debt they owe, some upon their children rawly left. I am afeard there are few die well that die in a battle; for how can they charitably dispose of any thing when blood is their argument? (IV. I. ll. 135–46).

Willliams's speech tests the raw edges of individual things against the abstract notion of a cause. In the play his points are answered and subsumed, but Byron's digressive use of Shakespeare brilliantly keeps the general overview of leader and leader writers under interrogation by the 'particular endings of his soldiers' (IV. I. l. 160). The awkwardness and grotesqueries of the siege cantos (such as the cruel jokes about rape and the gratuitous anecdote about dismemberment '(but they lie) 'tis said / To the live leg still clung the severed head' (VIII. 84)), are all part of this unsettling texture. In the same way, the rescue of Leila (with its curious echoes of Keats) is calculated to be '"quite refreshing"' because 'to quote / Too much of one sort would be soporific' (VIII. 90; 89). As the *Scots Magazine* complained: 'The episode of the little child . . . would have been extremely touching, had it not been bedevilled by that accursed mockery which the poet *will* indulge upon every event, and every subject' (*RR*, B: V, p. 2215).

Over and over again, the reader comes up against moments where it is necessary to share responsibility for being witty and rhyming 'like Nero, o'er a burning city' (VIII. 134). We find our way by faint traces of previous texts, sometimes following routes that no one else will have found through the poem. This is directed in part by the surface of the poem which leads us to digress with signalled allusion but also leaves us to digress with fainter echoes. We cannot predict exactly what will occur; our reading of a stanza can turn in several different ways, and when we watch what happens on a small scale we may modify our broader view. When Byron incorporates a signalled allusion there is a strong probability that the reader will recognise it while being uncertain about what the new configuration will be.

'Odd' is a word which recurs throughout canto VIII: 'some odd angle' (VIII. 20), 'one of those odd turns of Fortune's tides' (VIII. 27), 'that odd impulse' (VIII. 38), 'Some odd mistakes too happened in the dark'

(VIII. 130). It is a word which signals unpredictability or irregularity: the odd one is the surplus or the remainder, 'the third man ... who gives the casting vote' (*OED*). The 'odds' represent 'chances' or 'balances of probability in favour of something happening or being the case' (*OED*). The recurrence of this word at this point in the poem works as a double for the reader's uncertainty when confronted by the poetic texture of literary and cultural echoes.

Throughout cantos VII and VIII signalled allusion functions to question received patterns of language:

> 'Ashes to ashes' – why not lead to lead?
>   (VIII. 10)

Byron's insistence on a literal reading of quotation assists this process:

> 'God save the king!' and kings!
> For if *he* don't, I doubt if *men* will longer.
>   (VIII. 50)

This little gibe recreates the patterns of reformist Whig toasts in which the establishment slogans were ironically qualified ('The King and Constitution – and a speedy recovery to both'; 'Trial by Jury – and may its suspensions be suspended'[44]). The digressive interruptions of *Don Juan* are, however, open to a wider audience than the participants of an exclusive political club. In the siege cantos, in particular, Byron commends to all readers of newspapers the way in which digressive allusions fragment journalistic rendering of fact. To this end, emphatic use is made of the parenthetical aside, offering the reader the experience of a parallel universe which juxtaposes official report and uncensored horror. In canto VIII, parentheses can function as a temporal space in or during which someone is killed:

> He climbed to where the parapet appears;
> But there his project reached its utmost pitch,
>   ('Mongst other deaths the General Ribaupierre's
> Was much regretted) for the Moslem Men
> Threw them all down into the ditch again.
>   (VIII. 71)

The parenthesis here holds a fragment of military dispatch, but its digressiveness alters the value it would have had in a different context. Its effect eerily anticipates Virginia Woolf's detached reporting of the deaths of Mrs Ramsay, Prue Ramsay and Andrew Ramsay in the 'Time Passes' section of *To the Lighthouse*.[45] This graphic interruption of mortality recurs three stanzas later as authorial digression indulges a minor correction:

> The Kozacks, or if so you please, Cossacques –
>   (I don't much pique myself upon orthography,
> So that I do not grossly err in facts,
>   Statistics, tactics, politics and geography) –
> Having been used to serve on horses' backs,
>   And no great dilettanti in topography
> Of fortresses, but fighting where it pleases
> Their chiefs to order, – were all cut to pieces.
>
> (VIII. 74)

The parenthesis here makes an incursion on the territory of the footnote but in the time it takes to suggest pedantic attention to the proper name for 'Cossacques', their existence has been cancelled out anyway.

Digressive allusion may be seen as a vehicle of individual uncertainty which stands against (rather than reflects) the massive uncertainties of Ismail. From a humanist perspective, the digressions of the Siege of Ismail affirm the ability of Juan, the narrator and (crucially) the reader to behave unpredictably in an environment where the scale of 'Fate, or Circumstance' threatens to cancel out the living particular.[46] When Shakespearean or other texts are overtly signalled, therefore, it is important that they are not easy guarantees of success or artistic 'independence'. By signalling the 'oddness' of allusion, and by not signalling it consistently, Byron demands that the reader makes his or her 'casting vote'. To recognise oddness, however, the reader has also to assist in the construction of continuity. What Byron achieves in cantos VI, VII and VIII is the creation of a Shakespearean texture in which Shakespearean text can still turn up as a 'trump card' (VIII. 25). In order to examine these literary digressive allusions it has been necessary to neglect the variety of Byronic intertextuality that invites the reader to come to terms with everyday texts as well as the literary landmarks of national genius. The next chapter turns to *Don Juan*'s play with history through the public communication of newspapers.

CHAPTER FIVE

'The worst of sinning': Don Juan, moral England and feminine caprice

This chapter traces a new instance of the poem's intertextural weaving of history and form. Here the effects of *Don Juan*'s various literary intertexts are complicated by material drawn from the less highly wrought source of contemporary newspapers. Digressive allusions disclose journalistic details in the fabric of the poem, opening its literary texture to chance daily 'events'. Disconcerting the prevailing view that 'accident' should never impinge on the work of art, Byron's texts insist that the reader is fully aware of and implicated in the construction of what is accidental. After investigation of *Don Juan*'s play with the gazettes, the issue of contingency will focus on a great source of nineteenth-century journalistic scandal, 'feminine Caprice'. This form of transgression is thematised in the poem's plot, but it is also closely linked with the digressive mode of the narrator, especially in the English cantos where the reader is drawn into the dynamics of an intricately constructed plot and the complex allusive play that colours it.

As we have seen, Byron's references to other texts are bound up with his awareness of audience relations. In the multi-volume publication of *Don Juan* the recurrence of a particular allusion can test how the poem's relationship with the reader might have changed since the last usage. When we recognise the same intertextual moment in a different context within the poem, we also experience the precariousness of allusion itself; we are involved in the risk of audience reception. In cantos x and xi, for example, a well-known scene from *Macbeth* is reused and modified as the narrator watches

> all my gentler dreams
> Of what I *then dreamt*, clothed in their own pall,
>   Like Banquo's offspring; – floating past me seems
> My childhood in this childishness of mine:
> I care not – 'tis a glimpse of 'Auld Lang Syne.'
>
> (x. 18)

The connection between *Macbeth* as a Scottish play, and Byron's exaggerated nostalgia for a former life is reaffirmed in canto XI as Juan negotiates
the English social round 'without any "flaws or starts," ' (XI. 47), and is
admitted to literary coteries where

> as in Banquo's glass,
> At great assemblies or in parties small,
> He saw ten thousand living authors pass.
>
> (XI. 54)

These *Macbeth* allusions filter our consciousness of *Don Juan*'s public loss of
'honour love, obedience, troops of friends'. In the play, Macbeth's vision
is of a future he dreads, but Byron the narrator gives us a prophecy that
looks backwards to 'gentler dreams / Of what I *then dreamt*'. The allusion
directs the reader to Byron's inaugurating statement, 'I want a hero', and
his subsequent list of people who have

> fill'd their sign-posts then, like Wellesley now;
> Each in their turn like Banquo's monarchs stalk,
> Followers of fame, 'nine farrow' of that sow.
>
> (I. 2)

If by the time we reach canto XI we can still recall Byron's assertive
opening, the return of Banquo's line of descendants now juxtaposes the
fame of Wellington with Byron's wry view of his own absence in the
future. The presence of another text is a vehicle for our awareness of
historical change: interrupted literary contexts generate the poem's acute
consciousness of the passing of time and the mutability of literary fame.
   Like Byron's critique of British foreign and economic policy, his picture
of contemporary London and English society is intermingled with and
mediated by literary allusion. Despite the sentimental pose of the exiled
Scot, *Don Juan*'s mix of literary, historical and journalistic texts interpo-
lates layers of artifice between narrator, reader and the ostensible objects
of the poem. The high frequency of digressive allusion in the English
cantos offers a continual check to the medium of communication, qualifying nostalgia by impeding the construction of an ideal and unified
past. By drawing attention to the complex texture of narrative, Byron
alienated nineteenth-century Britain from its own self-presentation, inviting the reader to read 'home' and 'nation' as a series of fragmented
and misbegotten texts. The incorporation of newspaper reports along
with literary allusion is one of the poem's most brilliant and challenging
innovations.

In the preface to cantos VI, VII and VIII Byron announced his quarrel with what is 'read in the gazettes'. He pointed out that Castlereagh's suicide had received a privileged literary treatment: in contrast to the savage newspaper responses to Shelley's drowning, the minister made 'a sentimental Suicide', and became by virtue of the press 'the Werther of Politics' (*CPW*, v, p. 296).[1] Byron's way of objecting to the sentiment was to allow a parenthetical literary allusion to comment on journalistic reportage.[2]

He merely cut the 'carotid artery' (blessings on their learning) and lo! the Pageant, and the Abbey! and the 'Syllables of Dolour yelled forth' by the Newspapers – and the harangue of the Coroner in an eulogy over the bleeding body of the deceased – (an Anthony worthy of such a Caesar). (*CPW*, v, p. 296)

Byron's source for the notorious detail of the 'carotid artery' was almost certainly the newspaper *Galignani's Messenger* (motto: 'Bona Collegit, Inania Spernit') which was published daily Monday to Saturday from Paris and to which Byron subscribed while he was living in Italy.[3] Its coverage of British news was drawn from a wide variety of sources including British national and regional papers, and it had a Westminster correspondent. The final page included a section titled 'News from France' which dealt with European affairs not covered in the British papers. The paper concluded with advertisements. Each Sunday, *Galignani's Weekly Repertory, or Literary Gazette* reprinted a selection 'from the most esteemed English Reviews and Magazines' on every subject connected with 'Polite Literature, Scientific Discoveries and Improvements, Philosophical Researches, Rural Economy etc. etc. etc.'. Both publications offered 'Original Anecdotes, Letters, Poetry'. Byron referred to the newspaper as Murray's 'Holy Ally', and in the years 1821–3 the *Messenger*'s selection of material leant more towards Tory papers and journals than others.[4] In the Sunday *Literary Gazette*, however, the *Examiner* was occasionally represented and in the *Messenger*, editorial debate between the Tory *Courier* and the Whig *Chronicle* featured regularly. Although he objected to the paper's inaccurate reporting of the death of Shelley, Byron was still subscribing to *Galignani's* in April 1823 when he forwarded his copies to Lord and Lady Blessington.[5]

It was this newspaper which carried the scrupulously precise and simultaneously evasive account of Castlereagh's death from the *Herald*:[6]

On coming out of his room this morning (Monday), and going into his dressing-room, Dr. Bankhead followed him; and just as they got in, the Marquis said, 'It is of no use,' and immediately fell into the Doctor's arms, and was a corpse in a moment. It was discovered that he had cut the carotid artery, which leads to the brain, with a small penknife, with the point turned the reverse way to what they usually are, which he had taken out of his writing desk.

... Lady Londonderry's sufferings, and the lamentations of the domestics, present a scene of the most heart-rending affliction. (*GM*, no. 2327, 16 August 1822)

Byron's allusion to the event is likely to have been prompted by the literary texture of this report – even the penknife comes out of a writing desk – and the 'scene of the most heart-rending affliction' stages Castlereagh's suicide as popular theatre. The 'harangue of the Coroner' was reported in *Galignani*'s from the *Courier* which again emphasised the dramatic qualities of the scene:

The Coroner addressed the Jury in a speech of much feeling, in which he commented on the excellent qualities of the deceased Marquis in private life. (*GM*, no. 2328, 17 August 1822)

Byron engaged directly with this report in the preface to cantos vi, vii and viii:

That he was an amiable man in *private* life, may or may not be true; but with this the Public have nothing to do. (*CPW*, v, p. 295)

The preface shows us that although Byron's information was mediated by Galignani's editorial policy as well as the particular political outlooks of his letter-writing friends he was closely aware of events in England. This awareness has generally been played down by Byron himself, his friends and his critics, who have all accepted the view of a Byron as Regency dandy out of touch with English society.[7] Curiously, in spite of his protestations that things had changed 'since [his] time', Byron's reading provided him with a broader survey of public discourse in England than would have been available to most of his contemporaries. His vehicles of information, however, meant that whilst he was in full possession of many relevant facts, transposition of detail proved to be a defamiliarising process. Byron referred to the Sunday paper as 'Galignani's pic-nic sort of Gazette' (*BLJ*, x, p. 40), and, as Elizabeth French Boyd has suggested in connection with periodicals like the *Edinburgh Review*, the eclecticism of both publications may be seen as a source for some of *Don Juan*'s reflections on English society in particular.[8] Byron's use of very topical pieces of news out of context was received by his contemporaries as writing from a dislocated social position rather than as a reflection of the fragmented culture the author and his readers shared.[9]

The newspaper's juxtaposition of political outlooks, for example, offers an interesting context for Byron's fluctuating use of the words 'people' and 'mob'. The significance of these changes has been discussed by Malcolm Kelsall who maintains that Byron's use of 'the people' and 'mobs' in the same stanza (IX. 25) 'totters with insecurity'.[10] Alternatively, we can read this stanza as a collage of literary and journalistic voices in which the instability reflects competing discourses of nationhood in contemporary Britain. In *Galignani's Messenger* for 26 August 1822, a piece from *The Times* discussed how the press had reported the transportation of Castlereagh's remains to Westminster Abbey. Several Tory papers had expressed horror at the 'coarse exultation of the populace', but *The Times* was more cautious:

Let not the name of 'rabble' be foolishly applied to this unsophisticated class of our fellow subjects. What the rabble feel strongly, it is certain that many of those who are not rabble think. (*GM*, no. 2334)

This report shows that the naming of political factions is as self-conscious in 1822 as it was in 1812 when Byron drew attention to the different agendas behind the appellations of 'People' and 'Mob' in his parliamentary speech in support of the frame-breakers. The debate is about how parts are to be related to a concept of the whole nation: could dissonant voices be read as mere 'accidentals' or as a synecdochal representation of the collective view? By assembling opposed editorial perspectives and by the fluidity of its manner of reference (sometimes suppressing and sometimes highlighting the contextual frames), *Don Juan* fragments conservative complacency about a unified Britain.

In canto VII, the scathing account of John Bull's 'hallucination' –

> Debt he calls wealth, and taxes, Paradise;
>   And Famine, with her gaunt and bony growth,
> Which stare him in the face, he won't examine,
> Or swears that Ceres hath begotten Famine.
>   (VII. 45)

– sounds like an *ottava rima* recasting of a satirical poem which appeared in *Galignani's Messenger* no. 1920 (19 April 1821):

> The Wonderful Era
> Tho' miracles, ceasing, are now seen by no man
> In the rest of the globe, still in England they're common.
> Ask why there is nothing but starving redundant?
> You're told 'tis because of our *harvests abundant*!

Why the country's finances are running so taper?
You're answered because we have gold, and *not* paper!
And why poverty reigns, when our armaments cease?
'Tis all through transition from warfare to *peace*!
What then places the land in a 'flourishing' station?
'Why our *debt*,' replied Van, 'is *the wealth* of the nation'
And this being true, without food, without breeches,
No country like England for *rolling in riches*!
Such miracles blessing, no perils dare brave us –
And *only another* is wanting to save us!

Byron was composing canto VII in 1822 when the news on England's financial situation was much the same as the year before. In one sense, it is this unchanging condition of the country which lies behind the frustration of 'he won't examine'. Part of the point of Byron's repetition is that because of the British Establishment's ability to put a self-congratulatory gloss over other evidence, political satire has an unusually long shelf life. Material features of the text of *Don Juan* draw attention to particulars which interrupt the smooth presentation of national propaganda. That same materiality, however, recognises that readers will only notice what they have chosen to see.

Throughout cantos VII–XI, Byron interrupted his narrative with snatches of the current newspaper debate. By mentioning bishops 'taken by the tail' (VIII. 76), 'taxes, Castlereagh, and debt', 'Ireland's present story' (VIII. 125), ' "Gentlemen Farmers" ', and the falling price of oats (IX. 32), Byron returned to England the news which he had received out of it.[11] The precision of his reference is clear in the parting shot of canto X:

Teach them the decencies of good threescore;
   Cure them of tours, Hussar and Highland dresses;
Tell them that youth once gone returns no more;
   That hired huzzas redeem no land's distresses;
Tell them Sir W[i]ll[ia]m C[ur]t[i]s is a bore,
   Too dull even for the dullest of excesses –
The witless Falstaff of a hoary Hal,
A fool whose bells have ceased to ring at all.

(X. 86)

Mary Shelley appreciated the joke, calling it 'the most severe satire I ever read – what is Falstaff without his wit but a thing an old play must give a name to – and Hal without his youth but an unpardonable rake', but she didn't appreciate how nicely the image refracted a patriotic outlook.[12] Byron's stanza is a direct answer to a report from Edinburgh on the

King's visit (staged by Walter Scott) to Scotland, reprinted in *Galignani's Messenger* on 26 August 1822:

His Majesty appeared at the levee on Saturday in a full Highland uniform, of what is called the Stuart tartan. It is a dress which requires a tall and robust figure to produce advantageous display, and the general opinion of the levee was, that this martial and picturesque dress was never worn to more advantage: he wore the Highland broad sword, pistols and phileberg, and had quite a martial air. Next appeared in a similar garb Sir Wm. Curtis; but the worthy Baronet's figure was anything but that of the hardy, swarthy Highlander; what it wanted, however, in the air of the soldier, was abundantly supplied in the comfortable and jolly expression of the citizen. The worthy Baronet laughed heartily himself at the merriment his presence excited among the Highland Chieftains, who, for the first time, had to rank such a figure among their clans. Sir Wm., however, makes a better soldier than Falstaff, while he rivals him in the better part of his other gay qualifications. (*GM*, no. 2334)

We can see how Byron has punctuated the excited report of the Royal Tour ('Highland dresses', 'merriment', 'Sir Wm. Curtis' as 'Falstaff') with an alternative point of view. Byron burlesques the newspaper's patriotic Falstaff allusion by casting him as an exhibit of senility: Falstaff becomes 'witless' and (sexually) impotent, 'A fool whose bells have ceased to ring at all'.

Two stanzas earlier, Byron warns his 'gentle countrymen' that he is about to 'renew / Our old acquaintance'. The juxtaposition of 'new' and 'old' in these lines duplicates the mixture of material characteristic of the English cantos. By intermingling reminiscence and contemporary journalism, Byron unsettles the tone of nostalgia. To some extent, the Tory reviewers' insistence that Byron was out of touch carries a tacit recognition that he was indeed striking home: indeed, the narrator of the English cantos must have appeared as a sort of Banquo's ghost, a disruptive presence at a feast, showing how the present is predicated upon the past:

> Oh, pardon me digression – or at least
> Peruse! 'Tis always with a moral end
> That I dissert, like Grace before a feast.
> (XII. 39)

The picture conveyed through the English cantos in *Don Juan* has usually been ascribed to Byron's remembered experience of Regency London; but the city which Juan encounters is much closer than has been recognised to the view of London propagated by the Tory press in 1822–3 while Byron was composing these cantos.

Juan's encounter with the highway robber at the beginning of canto XI has been likened by Elizabeth French Boyd to an incident in Hope's *Anastasius*, but the emphasis on the robber's peculiar vocabulary makes it likely that Byron's reading of newspaper reports also contributed to the episode.[13] *Galignani's Messenger* carried a regular column of crime stories from Bow Street, and on 6 January 1821 it offered a lengthy report of the 'Mysterious Death' of a man found shot dead. His killer came forward and gave an account of an attempted highway robbery which had been foiled by the intended victim drawing and firing on his assailant. Two details in particular may have caught Byron's attention: the highwayman's melodramatic exclamation 'Oh! I am killed!' (Tom calls out, ' "Oh Jack! I'm floored" '(XI. 13)), and the reported sentiments of the man who shot him:

The very peculiar and conflicting feelings of the moment – gratitude for my own providential escape – and sorrow for the victim of his own attempted crime, operated powerfully on my mind. (*GM*, no. 1834)

Juan also 'wished he had been less hasty with his flint' (XI. 14) and went swiftly through the process of the coroner's inquest (a formality which *Galignani's Messenger* always observed). On 10 April 1822 its Bow Street criminal column reported 'the disgraceful scene' of a fight between two women, one of whom was called 'Sall'. This may be the source of the name for 'Sal' who never receives Tom's blood-stained cravat.

The Bow Street column specialised in reproducing the individual dialects of people hauled before magistrates. Most of them, when groping for explanations, would refer to 'something of that 'ere sort' (rather as Tom gestures to ' "that 'ere bloody Frenchman" ') and the reports also emphasised the communication difficulties between law-enforcers and transgressors, as in their account of a 'Ball and Rout Extraordinary' on 19 April 1821:[14]

Mr C. 'I merely went in for a *lark*'
Magistrate '... I must say I do not understand your language'
Mr C. 'Well, Sir, I suppose you have been a young man yourself, sometime or other, and everybody, now-a-days, knows what a *lark* means.'
The magistrate declared himself perfectly unaware of the meaning of the word, and made some severe remarks upon the Rev. Gentleman's manner, but eventually, he was discharged. (*GM*, no. 1920)

In this way, contemporary slang was reproduced in italics, or underlined, or placed in inverted commas, thus providing a rich contemporary source for Byron's 'flash' vocabulary.[15] The activities of 'diddling', 'flooring', 'smashing', 'catching flats' and 'flash capers' were related, translated and to some degree sentimentalised for the *Messenger*'s readers. Byron's use of the highway robbery, therefore, details not just the corrupt British economy, but the way in which this corruption is negotiated in public discourse. Language comes under particular scrutiny in the English cantos because it is the medium which realises the relation between individual parts and the party-political or national whole.

The *Messenger* employed a different register for its court and social columns. Here, hyperbolic catalogues advertised the sumptuousness of each occasion. An account of a 'Ball and Supper at Chandos House' in the issue of 19 April 1821, for example, shows how the splendour of the Regency era was sustained into the 1820s:

It would be difficult to describe, adequately, the brilliancy of the scene – the whole interior of the mansion literally blazed with light; costly *or-molu*, and crystal *candelabra*, meeting the eye in every direction. The great saloon, or principal drawing room, was beautifully chalked for the dance. In the noble rooms adjoining, six tables (of twelve each) were laid with services of massive plate for the *élite* of the brilliant circle. (*GM*, no. 1920)

This description shows that Byron's picture of London society in canto XI is not merely a distant memory of his 'years of fame':

> Then dress, then dinner, then awakes the world!
> Then glare the lamps, then whirl the wheels, then roar
> Through street and square fast flashing chariots, hurled
> Like harnessed meteors; then along the floor
> Chalk mimics painting; then festoons are twirled;
> Then roll the brazen thunders of the door,
> Which opens to the thousand happy few
> An earthly Paradise of 'Or Molu.'
>
> (XI. 67)[16]

The stanza reverses the newspaper's tendency to make the 'happy few' stand for the whole nation, moving instead from the wider 'world' to minute details of interior decoration. An interesting feature of the *Messenger*'s account of the ball is the emphasis on the lighting: it suggests that Byron's lines on the 'joy' which met London's 'grand illumination' in canto VII and the remarks on London's lights in canto XI. 26–8 are as much a response to immediate circumstances as a memory of past extravagance. Indeed, lighting was still worthy of comment on 15 November 1822 when the paper reported a 'Banquet in Guildhall':

The hall was splendidly illuminated with gas-lights, which poured their effulgent beams from immensely large lustres suspended from the centre of the Hall ... From the top of the Gothic pillars, festoons of gas lights were also suspended, which greatly added to the brilliant *coup d'oeil*. (*GM*, no. 2404)

This extract illustrates the way that certain words in journalistic prose are marked as bearers of special significance. By giving details of social occasions in this way, the newspapers heightened the effect of the fragility and transience that surrounded them. The nostalgia, in other words, isn't all Byron's – instead we may see *Don Juan* as an inscription of wider social and cultural dislocation. *Galignani's Messenger* reprinted British newspaper editorial debate about whether Britain had deteriorated as a world economic power and whether the social scene of London was as vibrant as it used to be. In this debate, Tory papers tended to assert unchanging prosperity whilst the opposition papers took a more pessimistic line.

One standard Tory argument in 1822 was that nothing at all had declined over the last ten years:

It is strange to see how foreigners mistake our national character; and indeed how we mistake it ourselves. A dull and plodding people – a despairing and ruined nation! Why, let any man look at the columns of any of our Morning Papers, and they will find them filled with dinners and balls, sumptuous entertainments, quadrilles and cotillons – our fashionables flying from one scene to another with the quickness of magic; seen at every public place the same night – a trip at Almack's, and a squeeze at the Opera. To be sure, we sometimes wish that a little more novelty were given to the scene, for the personages we saw ten years ago we see still. (*GM*, no. 2303, 19 July 1822, reprinted from the *Courier*)

Galignani's Messenger reprinted the highlights of London society news, and Byron would have been aware that his portrait of the Amundevilles leaving town fully lived up to the *Courier's* expectations:

Another feature in our character is the delight we take in having every movement, every act, of our lives known; to figure among the arrivals or departures – to have it published not only where we dance or dine, but whither we go, or when we return 'Captain A. goes from London to Kew,' 'Mr and Mrs T. repair from Pall Mall to Hounslow,' – the whole fashionable world must know it. (*GM*, no. 2303, 19 July 1822)

We can compare this Tory applause for the 'gaieties ... of our capital' with Byron's coverage of the transience of fashion:

> A paragraph in every paper told
>   Of their departure: such is modern fame:
> 'Tis pity that it takes no further hold
>   Than an advertisement, or much the same;
> When, ere the ink be dry, the sound grows cold.
>   The Morning Post was foremost to proclaim –
> 'Departure, for his country seat, to-day,
> Lord H. Amundeville and Lady A.'
>
> (XIII. 51)

Byron's *ubi sunt* intonation in part voices a national anxiety which seeps out of reports like that in the *Courier* quoted above. To describe the English cantos as Jerome McGann does, as 'grounded in Byron's nostalgia for a world he had left behind with equal bitterness and regret', and to claim that 'they are his *Remembrance of Things Past'* (*CPW*, v, p. 742) is to seal the poem off from history. By recovering newspaper intertexts, we can see how Byron was writing of things present, but threatened by transition.

One focus of change was the Congress of Verona and its effect on the stock market (as well as the stock market's effect on the Congress). This is one point at which *Don Juan* overlaps with *The Age of Bronze*:

> Who hold the balance of the world? Who reign
>   O'er Congress, whether royalist or liberal?
> Who rouse the shirtless patriots of Spain?
>   (That make old Europe's journals squeak and gibber all.)
> Who keep the world, both old and new, in pain
>   Or pleasure? Who make politics run glibber all?
> The shade of Bonaparte's noble daring? –
> Jew Rothschild, and his fellow Christian Baring.
>
> Those, and the truly liberal Lafitte,
>   Are the true lords of Europe. Every loan
> Is not a merely speculative hit,
>   But seats a nation or upsets a throne.
> Republics also get involved a bit;
>   Columbia's stock hath holders not unknown
> On 'Change; and even thy silver soil, Peru,
> Must get itself discounted by a Jew.
>
> (xii. 5–6)

These stanzas juxtapose a sense of chance or change ('pain / Or pleasure', 'seats a nation or upsets a throne', ''Change' for 'Exchange') with the imperatives of those 'merely' speculating. By calling the financial control of Europe 'The shade of Bonaparte's noble daring', Byron foregrounds a sense of loss:

> I have seen Napoleon, who seemed quite a Jupiter,
>   Shrink to a Saturn
>
> I have seen a Congress doing all that's mean.
>
> (xi. 83–84)

But the loss is not experienced as nostalgia for something located in the past; it is an experience of movement, or the instant of change. In *The Age of Bronze*, it can be felt as satirical dynamic when Byron considers the transformation of Marie Louise:

> She comes! – the Andromache (but not Racine's,
> Nor Homer's) Lo! on Pyrrhus' arm she leans!
> Yes! the right arm, yet red from Waterloo,
> Which cut her lord's half shattered sceptre through,
> Is offered and accepted! Could a slave
> Do more? or less? – and *he* in his new grave!
> Her eye, her cheek, betray no inward strife,
> And the *Ex*-Empress grows as *Ex* a wife!
>
> (ll. 757–64)[17]

The present tense commentary of this passage alerts us to its newspaper origin.[18] What Byron sees is a scene described in *Galignani's Messenger* on 3 December 1822:

– on her arrival, the Duke of Wellington was in waiting to receive her Imperial Highness, and he led her leaning on his arm to the Grand Salon. What must have been her sensations at that moment! What must she have felt while thus taking the arm that had hurled both her husband and herself from the greatest Throne in the universe. Apparently, however, she betrayed not the slightest emotion. (*GM*, no. 2419)

Byron has supplanted the rhetorical questions with digressive allusion: by digressing to point out that this Andromache was 'not Racine's, / Nor Homer's', he introduces the extreme emotion of high culture in order to negate it. Byron does not locate Waterloo in the distant past – by pointing to 'the right arm, yet red', he seems to bring Waterloo into the present while the reference to Napoleon, 'and *he* in his new grave' has all the scandalised emphasis of a very recent piece of gossip. What the reader is given is a compound scene of (cancelled) classical agony, amputated limbs at Waterloo, the burial of Napoleon, a soirée at Verona and, in place of fortune, the fickleness of women. This matrix leads us to a consideration of the woman's place within Byron's mode of digressive allusion.

Throughout *Don Juan*, remarks about Byron's female readers, those whom Cohen called 'the supreme arbiters of the destiny and reputation of the new poetry', sustain these links we have traced between digression and transgression.[19] Juan, we are told,

> had good looks; – that point was carried
> *Nem. con.* amongst the women, which I grieve
> To say leads oft to *crim. con.* with the married –
> A case which to the Juries we may leave,
> Since with digressions we too long have tarried.
>
> (xv. 84)

Digressions in this stanza comprehend both verbal deviations shared by
reader and narrator, and sexual diversions in the plot.[20] The seductive
potential of *Don Juan* was legendary before the first cantos were published.
According to a letter printed in the *Examiner* on 10 November 1822, the
reputation of the poem was such that 'all ladies of character *blush* at its
very mention'. As we saw in the first chapter, reviewers presented it as
a work which could prompt 'palpable' ill effect. As a poem which could
'captivate and corrupt' it was officially out of bounds for most women
readers although several male reviewers shared the fear of the *Literary
Chronicle* that *Don Juan* was 'abjured by married men and read in secret
by their wives'. By focusing on the element of sexual transgression latent
in digression, we can briefly re-examine the repeated allusions to the
myth of the Fall which have been seen by many critics as a determining
pattern in *Don Juan*.[21] References to Eve's fall and the lost Eden occur
throughout the poem, but there is a concentration of allusions in canto
xiv when the narrator considers the 'real sufferings of their she condition'
and introduces Adeline's plans to intervene in the ' *"tracasserie"* ' between
Juan and Fitz-Fulke (xiv. 41).

The frequency of Miltonic allusion at this point in the poem invites
us to compare the marriage of Adeline and Lord Henry with Milton's
picture of the relationship between Adam and Eve ('At eighteen . . . /She
had consented to create again / That Adam, called "the Happiest of
Men"'(xiv. 55)). Although Bernard Beatty argues that the reader should
be prepared to see Aurora as an ideal Edenic figure in the last cantos
of the poem, I would suggest that the reader is equally prepared to see
Adeline as an about-to-fall Eve, ready to move out of mythical stasis and
into the flux of history. Just as *Paradise Lost* moves forward firstly with
Satan's and then Eve's desire, *Don Juan* places its plot in the hands of
a woman. Milton's Eve and Byron's Adeline generate the digressions
which are both the matter and the dynamic of their respective poems.
Milton's Eve famously prefers digression to any other narrative mode:

> Her husband the relater she preferred
> Before the angel, and of him to ask
> Chose rather; he, she knew would intermix
> Grateful digressions, and solve high dispute
> With conjugal caresses, from his lip
> Not words alone pleased her.
>
> (*Paradise Lost*, viii. ll. 52–7)

The physical intimacy of Milton's couple before the Fall contrasts with
the 'conjugal, but cold' relationship between Henry and Adeline whose

interview in canto XIV is closed, not intermixed, with kisses. Lord Henry, we are told, 'Had still preserved his perpendicular' (XIV. 71), but the narrator feels, 'Still there was something wanting' (XIV. 72). That something, it is tempting to assume, is a form of digression. In canto XI a variant for stanza 44 shows Byron returning from his asides to the reader to reflect that a 'poem's progress should be perpendicular' (*CPW*, v, p. 478). Lord Henry displays the linear purpose which the poem itself eschews. Like Eve's, Adeline's act of digression might be or will be 'fatal', but the poem's attention to feminine sexual misdemeanour is remarkable for the way in which it realises a liberating movement in the fall from social grace.

Perhaps our first intimation of the poem's receptivity to digression as a feminine tendency comes as the narrator describes his own Eve-like enjoyment of instruction:

> 'Tis pleasing to be school'd in a strange tongue
>   By female lips and eyes – that is, I mean,
> When both the teacher and the taught are young,
>   As was the case, at least, where I have been;
> They smile so when one's right, and when one's wrong
>   They smile still more, and then there intervene
> Pressure of hands, perhaps even a chaste kiss; –
> I learn'd the little that I know by this.
>
> (II. 164)

The hesitation at the end of the second line duplicates someone stumbling 'in a strange tongue' and the verb 'intervene' hangs on the end of the line allowing the reader to pause on the brink of the couplet. In this way, the interventions which the poem celebrates are wrought in the texture of the verse. An often repeated half-truth about Byron's use of the Don Juan myth is that, unlike the legend, he makes women prey on a man. With the exception of Catherine and possibly Fitz-Fulke, however, taking the sexual initiative repeatedly or over the long term is not possible for Juan's women: English women, in particular, may experience only one plunge of sexual recklessness. This is why feminine acts of digression occur as accidental and unique demonstrations of the liberating valency enjoyed throughout by the narrator.

The libertinism of digression has been discussed in Peter Conrad's study, *Shandyism: The Character of Romantic Irony*. In his study of virtuoso performances, Conrad finds that 'for Byron the picaresque is the promiscuous: Juan's malleable eagerness to slide into any erotic attachment which presents itself answers to Byron's own gleeful irresponsibility with narrative and style'.[22] For Conrad it is the narrator rather than Juan

who performs as libertine, displaying 'a random, opportunistic willing-
ness to take pleasure wherever he finds it'. This is demonstrated in the
way Byron handles his *ottava rima*, 'as unscrupulous in his manipulation
of a ductile stanza form, as his hero is meant to be with women'.[23] But
Byron actually treats his stanza form with respect: the rhymes of *ottava
rima* are audacious, but the challenge is levelled at the reader, not the
language. 'Palpable' disruption was experienced by readers struggling
to distort their pronunciation and to set visual anticipation against aural
expectation of the rhyme.

Performing another version of the Romantic ironist as hero, Conrad
offers what could be described as a phallo-centric view of the process of
Don Juan which does not do justice to the way the poem feminises digressive activity. Similarly, Bernard Beatty's study of *Don Juan* detects
a 'likeness between poetic and erotic procedures', firstly in 'the co-
operation of accident and significance' in the rhyme scheme and then in
the 'outrageous gaps' between episodes in the poem which challenge the
reader to 'see a connection between them'.[24] This completion, according to Beatty, hints at an affinity between love-making and the writing of
poetry:

> It is in the gaps and jumps of the narrator's artfully mirrored consciousness that
> we come into closest contact with Lord George Gordon Byron himself for he
> does not know, yet makes available, the sources on which he relies. He gives
> himself away ... The flow of sexual life, when it is not interrupted and self-
> regarding, involves a similar intensification yet yielding of consciousness and
> selfhood. (Beatty, *Byron*'s Don Juan, p. 122)

For Beatty, the reader's experience of *Don Juan* offers an erotics of conversation. Yet Beatty does not consider how the reader is to give him- or
herself away in response to Byron's generosity. Indeed, towards the end
of his discussion of 'The Amorous Sphere', Beatty seems to withdraw
the process of the poem from both narrator and reader:

> it is the circumstances themselves, in all their unforeseen contingency, which
> must carry some natural tendency to produce those kinds of proximity which
> provoke and promote the glow of conscious union. The forward movement of
> the poem itself is clearly analogous to this. (pp. 127–8)

Here, juxtaposition is held to be responsible for erotic tension, calling into
question Beatty's earlier emphasis on synthesis. His belief that discontinuity affirms the 'glowing' presence of continuity overlooks the reader's part
in interruption and deviation. There is an affirmative value in narrative
intermission which is different from the effect of subsuming all contingencies into 'some natural tendency'. Put another way, Byron offers a

fuller appreciation of the artifice and intricacy of different sexual roles evident in Pope's 'Epistle to a Lady': 'Woman's at best a Contradiction still' (l. 270).

Throughout *Don Juan* we can see Byron experimenting with the idea that women are unique indicators of movement, whether by offering an internal geography to be mapped, or, as happens later in the English cantos, by their own capacity for liberating movement. The similarity which many critics have detected between Adeline's 'mobility' and the narrative style of *Don Juan* is not an isolated point of contact, but part of the texture of the poem.[25] It may be argued that the plot only moves forward as Juan's love affairs are interrupted by other men, but masculine activity is interrupted, in turn, by the narrator's digressions. Lambro's return to his home, for example, is delayed by a series of reflections, one of which juxtaposes the masculine activity of tour, exploration or Odyssean quest with feminine travel in the domestic sphere:

> The approach of home to husbands and to sires,
>   After long travelling by land or water,
> Most naturally some small doubt inspires –
>   A female family's a serious matter;
> (None trusts the sex more, or so much admires –
>   But they hate flattery, so I never flatter;)
> Wives in their husbands' absences grow subtler,
> And daughters sometimes run off with the butler.
>   (III. 22)[26]

By placing his 'trust' in parenthesis alongside 'flattery', the narrator suggests that trust in women, as much as flattery of them, is an ornamental embellishment. This digression offers another space in which to hint at feminine deviation for as we emerge from the parenthetical attention on 'the sex' we discover that wives and daughters have slipped away in the interim. By locating this sort of female errant activity in the context of 'husbands' absences', however, Byron qualifies the cliché of 'the Inconstancy of Woman' with the suggestion that feminine digression may only be a different route of escape from the home repeatedly left by men for 'long travelling by land or water'.[27]

Connecting his own style with the erring of his characters, the narrator mockingly characterises digression as a form of romantic isolation:

> But let me to my story: I must own,
>   If I have any fault, it is digression;
> Leaving my people to proceed alone,
>   While I soliloquize beyond expression.
>   (III. 96)

This translates the process of the poem into a shared journey in which Byron lags behind the main party. A variant for the stanza has the narrator 'chattering' instead of soliloquising and it could be argued that by trailing behind and talking, leaving others to push the expedition forwards, Byron is adopting a feminised subject position. Jane Austen, for example, makes use of digressive walking parties in *Pride and Prejudice* and *Persuasion* where potential lovers linger behind or walk on 'without knowing in what direction'.[28]

As we proceed through the poem, connections between digression and women proliferate. Gulbeyaz is first seen as the framed subject of a painting ('As Venus rose ... from the wave' (v. 96)); through digressive allusion, however, she surmounts the restrictions placed on her and rebels like a masculine hero:

> Her form had all the softness of her sex,
> >   Her features all the sweetness of the devil,
> When he put on the cherub to perplex
> >   Eve, and paved (God knows how) the road to evil;
> The sun himself was scarce more free from specks
> >   Than she from aught at which the eye could cavil;
> Yet, somehow, there was something somewhere wanting
> As if she rather *order'd* than was *granting*.
>
>   (v. 109)

In his commentary on canto v, McGann sees this as an amalgam of proverbial wisdom, *Hamlet*, and the conventions of early church painting.[29] There is evidence to suggest, however, that Byron is alluding in a deliberately casual manner to *Paradise Lost*. Gulbeyaz embodies Satan's trajectory as he alights as a spot on the sun, disguises himself as 'a stripling cherub' (III. 636), and opens the way for Sin and Death to pave a route 'by wondrous art' (x. 311) between Hell and the world. These hints of *Paradise Lost* enlarge our conception of Gulbeyaz by supplying her with the sublime inner space which we associate with the Miltonic abyss, and the swift changes of Satan's movement across the universe. Byron addresses her changeability three stanzas further on:

> Judge, then, if her caprices e'er stood still;
> Had she but been a Christian, I've a notion
> We should have found out the 'perpetual motion.'
>   (v. 112)[30]

In the variants for the next stanza, we can see Byron experimenting with more Miltonic allusion:

<Besides forbidden fruits, for She neer paused / nor would have paused> ...
<Her thirst / Had Paradise itself to her been shown> / <She would have cut
the tree of knowledge down> (*CPW*, v, p. 277)

These images of Eden did not appear in the published version of canto v,
but they show us the way in which Byron associates Eve's and subsequent
female digressiveness with an impulse towards liberation. As well as being
'the latest of her whims' (v. 114), Juan is a way for Gulbeyaz to '[err]
from inanition' (vi. 9).

This association between erring women, whim, and inconstancy fits
into a familiar pattern of misogynistic humour – 'constant you are, / But
yet a woman' (1 *Henry IV*, ii. 3. ll. 109–10). When Byron resumed work
on *Don Juan* in 1822, he began with the 'affairs of woman':

> Not all the reveries of Jacob Behman
>   With its strange whirls and eddies can compare: –
> Men with their heads reflect on this and that –
> But women with their hearts or heaven knows what!
>   (vi. 2)

In the manuscript, the concluding couplet was followed by 'or' and then
two other possible couplet endings. Mary Shelley, who was working as
the fair copyist, was left to choose which ever couplet she wanted.[31]
It is, therefore, difficult to discriminate between feminine 'whirls and
eddies' and the 'non-descript and ever varying rhyme' (vii. 2) that carries
Don Juan forward. We might suppose that whereas Byron presents his
'ever varying' procedure as a mode of detachment, 'feminine Caprice'
is depicted as physical or emotional instability. This, however, does not
explain the moments when Byron the narrator also portrays himself as
emotionally volatile:

> all my fancies whirling like a mill;
> Which is a signal to my nerves and brain,
> To take a quiet ride in some green lane.
>   (ix. 85)

Jerome McGann observes that 'when Byron "contradicts" himself, he
is not changing his mind but revealing its ability to see an idea or event in
several different ways at nearly the same time'. McGann compares this
process with the way that 'nearly all [Byron's] characters exhibit a similar complexity of thought or response at some time' (*Don Juan in Context*,
pp. 104–5), specifically aligning Julia with Byron: 'Like Byron, she is a
mass of contradictions and of course a very epitome of "inconstancy"'

(p. 105). Initially, Byron may have envisaged a difference between 'feminine Caprice' (VI. 119) and his 'old Lunes', but as the poem progresses, it is tempting to see Byron and the poem embracing a feminine prerogative of change. This does not alter the fact that *Don Juan* is a poem packed with misogynistic jokes but it does complicate our response to them. The digressive texture of the poem should lead us to question the conclusions of Moyra Haslett and others who succumb to the lure of the general and describe the poem as part of 'masculinist ideology'.

One of the most familiar anti-feminist tropes of the poem is the way that, as Caroline Franklin has expressed, 'heroines are encountered as types, representative of their countries – foreign exotic lands which must be explored, and which constitute a testing-ground for the male protagonist'.[32] In canto IX, however, the exploitable landscape of the female body is also a threatening marker of age and time for the male narrator:

> Oh, thou 'teterrima Causa' of all 'belli' –
>   Thou gate of Life and Death – thou nondescript!
> Whence is our exit and our entrance, – well I
>   May pause in pondering how all Souls are dipt
> In thy perennial fountain: – how man *fell,* I
>   Know not, since Knowledge saw her branches stript
> Of her first fruit, but how he falls and rises
> *Since, thou* hast settled beyond all surmises.
>
>   (IX. 55)

The crucial word omitted from the allusion which several editors have needed to supply is 'cunnus', but Byron's reference to it as 'nondescript' is of key importance. According to the *OED*, 'nondescript' was employed in the early nineteenth century mainly in writing on natural history, for example, *Memoirs of Mammoth Bones, of Incognita or Nondescript Animals* (1806). The word was therefore used in accounts of travels and voyages which presented newly discovered species as 'nondescript', or not hitherto described. As well as playing on his own omission, Byron's joke is that his missing word is a 'perennial' cause rather than a new discovery. Fascinatingly, however, 'nondescript' is also the word he had chosen earlier in the poem to characterise his own narration: 'A non-descript and ever varying rhyme' (VII. 2). The word is not used anywhere else in Byron's poetry and the echo here suggests that there is indeed a link between female sexuality and the process of the poem.

The idea of sexual experience as a journey, 'From thee we come, to thee we go' (X. 56), is not new, but by echoing the prayer-book service of the burial of the dead, Byron materialises sexual destination as a plot of earth. This place can be an Eden in prospect or the grave in retrospect. Unlike Shelley's poetry, *Don Juan* does not present human sexual encounter as a way of approaching the transcendent, but inscribes its connection with 'clay' and 'human dust' (IX. 75; 77). The process of coming and going is rendered in physical terms, and aligned with the quotidian nouns of travel:

> Love, that great opener of the heart and all
> The ways that lead there, be they near or far,
> Above, below, by turnpikes great or small.
>
> (IX. 80)

Byron's memory of tolls is not far from this metaphor and, as well as hinting at the divers routes of sexual gratification, the exhaustive mapping of experience suggests a tediously well-trodden path. And yet the turnpike itself, when Juan travels across England, is more than a mundane experience of passage:

> Now there is nothing gives a man such spirits,
>   Leavening his blood as Cayenne doth a curry,
> As going at full speed – no matter where its
>   Direction be, so 'tis but in a hurry,
> And merely for the sake of its own merits:
>   For the less cause there is for all this flurry,
> The greater is the pleasure in arriving
> At the great *end* of travel – which is driving.
>
> (X. 72)[33]

The sensation of movement is exalted six stanzas further on as Byron invokes (and outdoes) nature, classical mythology and Horace to celebrate the technology of road-construction:

> What a delightful thing's a turnpike road!
>   So smooth, so level, such a mode of shaving
> The earth, as scarce the eagle in the broad
>   Air can accomplish, with his wide wings waving.
> Had such been cut in Phaeton's time, the God
>   Had told his son to satisfy his craving
> With the York mail; – but onward as we roll,
> 'Surgit amari aliquid' – the toll!
>
> (X. 78)

The speed and lightness of these two stanzas reveal the difference between travelling 'for the sake of its own merits', and travel which has as its 'great end' the 'languid rout' of sensation. Although both can be construed as digressive activity, they involve crucially different attitudes to time. Women in *Don Juan* mark time as they offer physical space to be traversed and temporal space to be passed. In prospect, the landscape is worth a detour, and in retrospect, the time is wasted. This anti-feminine perspective, however, may be counterbalanced by the ways in which women figure in the poem as travellers as well as fertile soil or dangerous oceans. If Byron reflects his society's anti-feminine prejudices, he is also able to identify with the victims of its social codes.

The potential shared by all the women of *Don Juan* (except Catherine and possibly Fitz-Fulke) is an ability to intuit that the 'end' of their digression will be death, incarceration, or humiliated exposure in a red cloak. Byron defends the pregnant country girl in canto XVI by digressing to turn her male accuser ('Scout, the parish guardian of the frail'(XVI. 67)) into Dryden's monster of dullness. As Scout dishes out 'A mighty mug of *moral* double ale', the italics remind the reader of the coronation in *Mac Flecknoe*: 'In his sinister hand, instead of Ball, / He plac'd a mighty Mug of potent Ale' (ll. 120–1).[34] The texture of the verse encourages us to identify and renounce the dark forces of moral litigation and pulls the reader into complicity with a feminine capacity to risk everything by committing itself to err:

> 'Ye Gods, I grow a talker!' Let us prate.
>   The next of perils, though I place it *stern*est,
> Is when, without regard to 'Church or State,'
>   A wife makes or takes love in upright earnest.
> Abroad, such things decide few women's fate –
>   (Such, early traveller! is the truth thou learnest) –
> But in Old England when a young bride errs,
> Poor thing! Eve's was a trifling case to hers.
>
> (XII. 64)

'Poor' is the compassionate adjective offered to keep the country girl company in the great hall (XVI. 67). The stanza is interrupted by two signalled allusions, a parenthetical aside, and the innuendo of 'upright earnest'. McGann traces the first allusion to *The Merchant of Venice* – where Antonio bids farewell to the loquacious Gratiano and Lorenzo, 'Fare you well, I'll grow a talker for this gear' (I. 1. l. 110) but it seems much more likely that the poem is compounding memories of different plays, and in this case that the disruptive effect of the allusion is to invite sympathy with 'their she condition' (XIV. 24). Coriolanus greets his mother with the words, 'You gods! I prate, / And the most noble mother of the world / Leave unsaluted' (v. 3. ll. 48–50). The context of this quotation makes Byron's use of it provocative as he turns to pay homage to women who defy ' "Church or State" ', whereas Volumina is an embodiment of both those values. The women in *Don Juan* who '[make] or [take] love' show the same commitment to digressive action (dismaying public countenance) as the narrator to verbal digression.

Don Juan's contemplation of the figure of the erring bride revisits late eighteenth-century and early nineteenth-century conduct literature, juxtaposing traditional words of warning with imaginative sympathy for the subject. In Maria Edgeworth's *Letters for Literary Ladies*, for example, the dutiful Caroline writes to advise Julia 'upon her intended separation from her husband':

You say that it is easier to *break* a chain than to *stretch* it; but remember that when broken, your part of the chain, Julia, will remain with you, and fetter and disgrace you through life. Why should a woman be so circumspect in her choice? Is it not because when once made she must abide by it? "She sets her life upon the cast, and she must stand the hazard of the die." From domestic uneasiness a man has a thousand resources: in middling life, the tavern, in high life, the gaming table, suspends the anxiety of thought ... But what resource has a woman? ... In higher life ... the wife who has hazarded least, suffers the most by the dissolution of the partnership ... She loses her home, her rank in society. She loses both the repellant and the attractive power of a mistress of a family. "Her occupation is gone." She becomes a wanderer.[35]

Edgeworth's allusions to *Richard III* and *Othello* open the possibility that the erring bride might be a figure of tragic stature. Byron, I believe, invites his readers to realise this possibility by tracing the different strands of Miltonic, Shakespearean and earlier Byronic texts in the poem.

Building on eighteenth-century associations of the tour with sexual experience, Byron's responses to feminine sexual digression are inextricably linked with the poem's discussion of travel. The parenthesis '(Such, early traveller! is the truth thou learnest)' creates an island in the stanza for the reader to discover that truth is different 'Abroad'; the parenthesis affords both temporal and geographical space from which the reader, too, emerges into 'Old England'. The return to England in Byron's process of digression is complicated by the suggestion that sexual mores are stranger at home than they are abroad.[36] This reverses the usual tendency of travel literature to highlight social oddity abroad in order to endorse English codes of behaviour. England's moral climate is made to antedate Eden in terms of its punitive treatment of erring women: 'Eve's was a trifling case to hers.' By referring to Eve's 'case', Byron inserts Biblical and Miltonic history into the context of a contemporary 'law-suit' (XII. 65). The effect of this is to suggest that contemporary English social codes are hopelessly out of date and out of proportion – modern women, the poem suggests, are still being held responsible for original sin. The detached register of travelogue is, however, interrupted by the interjection, 'Poor thing!' with its sudden openness to tender compassion and disturbance of legal and clerical authority.

As the narrator of *Childe Harold's Pilgrimage* (*CHP*), Byron celebrated masculine 'strength to bear what time cannot abate' (*CHP*, III. 7), but in the English cantos of *Don Juan*, we are presented with a feminine perspective on 'what crimes it costs to be a moment free' (*CHP*, IV. 85). The 'lands and scenes romantic' of Juan's travels are associated with affairs 'Where lives not law-suits must be risked for Passion' (XII. 68), but Juan's intimation of greater physical risk for love abroad is gradually questioned by the narrator's transference of earlier images of travel to the limited social circle of the English cantos.

At the simplest level, extensive geographical space is suggested by the use of different languages: Byron manages to convey the distances that can be travelled in a social sphere by importing French terminology and the codes of other societies:

> The reason's obvious: if there's an eclât,
>   They lose their caste at once, as do the Parias;
> And when the delicacies of the law
>   Have filled their papers with their comments various,
> Society, that china without flaw,
>   (The hypocrite!) will banish them like Marius,
> To sit amidst the ruins of their guilt:
> For Fame's a Carthage not so soon rebuilt.
>
> (XII. 78)

In this stanza Byron unpicks Pope's mockery of a feminine world view which equates the breaking of 'frail *China*' and '*Diana*'s Law'.[37] By juxtaposing the demand for flawlessness and the parenthetical indictment of hypocrisy, Byron complicates the superior overview which enables Pope's satire. The feminine experience of social transgression is enlarged spatially by the use of foreign words and references, and temporally by inviting the reader to remember Marius and Dido. Caroline Franklin's research, in particular, has shown the extent to which Byron's texts are embedded in a philosophical context of patriarchalism. His sympathetic image of female isolation in this case, however, was probably inspired by Madame de Staël's reflections on women of superior abilities in

De La Littérature. The intelligent woman, De Staël argues,

> is left to the strength of her own mind, to struggle as she can with her afflictions. The interest usually inspired by females, the power of which is the safeguard of men, all fail her at once: she drags on her isolated existence like the Parias of India, amongst all those distinct classes into none of which she can ever be admitted, and who consider her as fit only to live by herself, as an object of curiosity, perhaps of envy, although, in fact, deserving of the utmost commiseration.[38]

Recognition of specific echoes and allusions such as this one allows the reader to resist the absolutism of masculinist ideology. Byron's use of 'the law' in this stanza has all the Lacanian resonance of the name of the Father, inscribed in the 'comments various' of the newspapers. This symbolic authority, like all the other quoted texts in *Don Juan*, is scrutinised and brought into question by its inclusion in quotation marks. Feminine digression is finally realised as a romantic ruin and the reference to 'Fame' as a 'Carthage' suddenly identifies the figure of the fallen woman with Byron himself.

The place which Byron actualises as a ruined name is both a landscape and a measure of time. The narrator's momentary reflection on the 'glorious Gothic scenes' (x. 61) of Juan's passage along the Rhine describes the imaginative movement which is a romantic response to ruins:

> A grey wall, a green ruin, rusty pike,
>   Make my soul pass the equinoctial line
> Between the present and past worlds, and hover
> Upon their airy confine, half-seas-over.
>
>   (x. 61)

An image of the equinoctial line is used by the narrator to describe the approaching threshold of middle age and to describe the calm indifference of Adeline's poise, 'Which ne'er can pass the equinoctial line / Of anything which Nature would express' (xiii. 34).[39] All the narrator's hints lead us to believe that eventually Adeline will cross the equinox of 'Patrician polish' and that like the journeys of Juan's other women, it will be a digression permitting no return: the potential undoing of the 'splendid mansion' which is Adeline's heart is likened to 'an Earthquake's ruin' (xiv. 85). As with the satanic abyss located earlier in Gulbeyaz, this inner geography is more fraught with risk than the external distance toured by Juan. The distance traversed by women who love 'without regard to "Church or State"' (xii. 64) discovers a kinship between the travelling, quoting, cavilling narrator who has wandered from the British world of fashion and the women who wander within it.

Byron's depiction of English society as another world is in keeping with a satirical perspective, but it also works to recreate a perspective of exile:

> Then there was God knows what 'à l'Allemande,'[40]
> 'A l'Espagnole,' 'timballe,' and 'Salpicon' –
> With things I can't withstand or understand,
> Though swallow'd with much zest upon the whole;
>
> (xv. 66)

> Don Juan sat next an 'à l'Espagnole' –
> No damsel, but a dish, as hath been said;
> But so far like a lady, that 'twas drest
> Superbly, and contained a world of zest.
>
> (xv. 74)

The geography of dinner contributes to the exploration of domestic space. By producing an atlas out of the banqueting table, Byron builds up an alternative tour which will depend on the contingency of Adeline rather than accidents at sea or the fortunes of war. The image of 'a world of zest' in a woman is saved from bathos because it is involved in a shift of scale. The first extract presents people swallowing parts of the world 'with much zest upon the whole', but in the second extract, the experience of 'zest' has become a world itself. Our experience of global distance is modified between the two images and this process is intensified in the presentation of Adeline.

Canto XII contains an extensive discussion on the comparative attractions of 'foreign dames' and 'fair Britons'. The survey leads the narrator to conclude that 'the whole matter rests upon eye-sight' (XII. 71), and he applies three images to English women which align them with other landscapes of desire in the poem. They are compared to 'Polar summers, *all* sun, and some ice' (XII. 72), to land which 'though the soil may give you time and trouble, / Well cultivated, it will render double' (XII. 76), and their one ' "*grande passion*" to a 'Tornado' (XII. 77). On the face of it, this makes Byron's depiction of English women indistinguishable from, for example, the 'genial soil' or 'Typhoon' which characterised Gulbeyaz, whilst the image of the Polar summers equates women at home with yet another new found land. The picture of English women as a landscape to be explored is, however, qualified by meditations on what happens to them if they do the exploring:

> Abroad, though doubtless they do much amiss,
> An erring woman finds an opener door.
>
> (XII. 79)

Typically in the next stanza, the narrator '[leaves] the matter where [he] find[s] it' and refuses to impose a moral absolute. In English public morality, we are told people 'care but for discoveries and not deeds' (XII. 80). The narrator hints that the poem will disclose the Fall of the House of Amundeville, but the allusive texture of the poem alerts us to how arbitrary the process of discovery is:

> Here the twelfth Canto of our introduction
>   Ends. When the body of the book's begun,
> You'll find it of a different construction
>   From what some people say 'twill be when done:
> The plan at present's simply in concoction.
>   I can't oblige you, reader! to read on;
> That's your affair, not mine.
>
> (XII. 87)

Caroline Franklin sees Adeline as an archetypal Northern 'self-repressed' woman, but the element of allusive play in the English cantos allows the reader to see and hear much more.[41] From the start, the marriage between Adeline and Lord Henry is placed on difficult terrain:

> She loved her lord, or thought so; but *that* love
>   Cost her an effort, which is a sad toil,
> The stone of Sysiphus, if once we move
>   Our feelings 'gainst the nature of the soil.
>
> (XIV. 86)

This introduction to Adeline's emotional life echoes one of the stations of *Childe Harold's Pilgrimage*. In canto IV the poet ponders the tomb of Metella:

> Was she as those who love their lords, or they
>   Who love the lords of others?
>
> (*CHP* IV. 101)

His detached conjectures on her 'lovely form' change, however, into an admission that her inner life is a mystery:

> Yet could I seat me by this ivied stone
> Till I had bodied forth the heated mind
> Forms from the floating wreck which Ruin leaves behind.
>
> (IV. 104)[42]

The approach to Adeline follows through the desire to '[body] forth the heated mind', but attributes to a feminine mind what had been the prerogative of a masculine poet. Following the Sysiphus image, Byron returns to the territory of *Childe Harold's Pilgrimage* to realise the marriage

between Adeline and Lord Henry as the Alpine landscape which in 1816
had reflected the masculine hero's unique suffering:

> They moved like stars united in their spheres,
>   Or like the Rhone by Leman's waters wash'd,
> Where mingled and yet separate appears
>   The river from the lake, all bluely dash'd
> Through the serene and placid glassy deep,
> Which fain would lull its river-child to sleep.
>
> (XIV. 87)

Coleridge, Steffan and McGann note the overlap with the third canto
of *Childe Harold's Pilgrimage*:

> Is it not better, then, to be alone,
> And love the Earth only for its earthly sake?
> By the blue rushing of the arrowy Rhone,
> Or the pure bosom of its nursing lake,
> Which feeds it as a mother who doth make
> A fair but froward infant her own care,
> Kissing its cries away as these awake; –
> Is it not better thus our lives to wear,
> Than join the crushing crowd, doom'd to inflict or bear.
>
> (III. 71)

Although the *Don Juan* analogy does not allocate parts to Henry and
Adeline, we associate the blue movement of the Rhône with 'the dashing
and proud air of Adeline' (XV. 56), and the 'imperturbable' Henry with
the 'placid' lake. This hint is confirmed in stanza 88 when we are told
that Adeline's 'intense intentions . . . run like growing water / Upon her
mind' (XIV. 88).[43] Whereas in *Childe Harold*, Byron used the image of river
meeting lake to turn from 'the crushing crowd', in *Don Juan* the scene is
a threshold before entrance into this social world. Adeline will be likened
to the sparkle of gems and the foam of champagne as *Don Juan* turns
from the natural images of *Childe Harold* to a celebration of human society.
The distance travelled by Byron in *Childe Harold's Pilgrimage* canto III is
translated firstly to characterise English gothic architecture and then to
realise an English marriage.

For the reader who remembers Byron's isolation on the shores of Lake
Leman, the recognition of the same scene offers a moment of familiarity,
but also strangeness as we have to transfer the experience of *Childe Harold*'s
voyaging to the internal journey of a woman. In the earlier poem, the
act of speculation by the lake is resolved in that it supplies a form for
consolation. With Adeline, however, speculation is deflected by other

matter. Don Juan wonders 'how much of Adeline was *real*' (XVI. 96), and the narrative then runs into the discussion of 'mobility', and from there on to 'The Sinking Fund's unfathomable sea' (XVI. 99). As with so many other allusions in *Don Juan*, the return of *Childe Harold* is feminised. When Adeline is likened to the steep cascade and the blue dash of the Rhône, she assumes what was a masculine role in the earlier poem – 'the swift Rhone cleaves his way between / Heights which appear as lovers who have parted' (III. 94). The lake, in both pieces of writing, is presented as a mother, and in *Childe Harold* it is also associated with 'a sister's voice' (III. 85). In both cases, the active spirits of *Childe Harold*'s narrator and of Adeline are 'reproved' in the moment of contact with the 'placid, glassy deep'.

Adeline, therefore, is as close to Byron the narrator as her appreciation of Pope implies. By depicting her in terms of movement and cascade, Byron anticipates her fall (which does not happen in the poem and may not happen), suggesting that the social distance she will traverse will be a version of his own fall, of the romantic questing of Harold, and of the epic voyaging of Juan. Byron's presentation of Adeline as a fellow-traveller emerges in the echoes of *Childe Harold*, traces of the past which haunt the Norman abbey in *Don Juan* before the ghost appears. Byron lends to the terrain of Adeline's marriage the indeterminacy which was presented as a sublime natural experience in *Childe Harold's Pilgrimage*. The reader also experiences juxtapositions of post-war politics with sublime landscape. Just as the narrator of *Childe Harold* was unable to see the awe-inspiring whole of the Alps without interpolating particular details of contemporary political strife,

> While Waterloo with Cannae's carnage vies,
> Morat and Marathon twin names shall stand.
>
> (III. 64)

so the Rhône and Leman, whose relationship forms a simile for the Amundeville marriage, provoke a reference to Waterloo:

> Had Bonaparte won at Waterloo,
>   It had been firmness; now 'tis pertinacity:
> Must the event decide between the two?
>   I leave it to your people of sagacity
> To draw the line between the false and true,
>   If such can e'er be drawn by man's capacity:
> My business is with Lady Adeline,
> Who in her way too was a heroine.
>
> (XIV. 90)

Once again, the shadow of what might happen to Adeline prompts Byron's questioning of absolute moral judgements. A figurative link between the decisive actions of a sexually disgraced woman, Byron's hero at Waterloo and Byron himself creates a territory in the poem where people are allowed their own 'way', leaving it for the community outside the poem to 'draw the line'.

By announcing that Adeline 'in her way too was a heroine', Byron re-defines generic conventions more quietly than in his earlier challenge, 'I want a hero.' In Adeline's sphere, the reworking of prior convention includes Byron's revision of his earlier work. Some of the echoes of Harold's quest are inevitable overlaps (for example, Juan's journey along the Rhine), but other memories are more disturbing. The changing events of the eve of Waterloo are traced in the countenances of the ladies, with

> cheeks all pale, which but an hour ago
> Blush'd at the praise of their own loveliness.
>
> (*CHP* III. 24)

Byron redeploys the observation in the morning assembly at the Norman Abbey, where the ladies

> – some rouged, some a little pale –
> Met the morn as they might.
>
> (XIII. 104)

In other words, they are all pale. The second image is starker because it describes a quotidian occurrence: for the party in the abbey, facing each day represents the ordeal of battle. The 'blush' of *Childe Harold* is replaced by the 'rouge' of the English cantos. Whereas the fading colour of the skin in *Childe Harold* is a response to the sublime, in *Don Juan*, early morning pallor reveals encroaching age and, in the case of Juan and Fitz-Fulke, an account of incidents the night before.

The social circle of the Amundevilles epitomises the 'contentious world' which both Harold and Byron sought 'to fly from'. In *Don Juan*, however, Byron recasts the isolation of Harold and the narrator so that it is experienced by a woman from the very middle of the 'coil' and 'wretched interchange'. Adeline's soul-betraying look of 'weariness or scorn' is given in a parenthesis and it allows us to meet her as a feminine Childe Harold. The connection between Byron's first hero and one of his last heroines is their capacity for swift digressive action. In *Childe Harold*, the narrator recoils from human society because:

> There, in a moment, we may plunge our years
> In fatal penitence, and in the blight
> Of our own soul, turn all our blood to tears,
> And colour things to come with hues of Night:
> The race of life becomes a hopeless flight
> To those that walk in darkness: on the sea,
> The boldest steer but where their ports invite,
> But there are wanderers o'er Eternity
> Whose bark drives on, and anchored ne'er shall be.
>
> (*CHP* III. 70)

The main intertext of this stanza is Byron's biography – there was nothing conditional about his own 'plunge'. Reflecting this discovery, the fatal 'moment' or 'turn' in the English cantos is provided by feminine sexual deviation:

> They warm into a scrape, but keep of course,
> As a reserve, a plunge into remorse.
>
> (XII. 73)

This 'plunge' is the equivalent of a parenthetical afterthought and is designed to counter digressive behaviour, but the very suddenness of the change recalls the reflexes of thought in *Childe Harold*. Movement in *Don Juan* is realised in physical terms (the 'plunge into remorse' derives from the simile 'Like Russians rushing from hot baths to snows'), and here it offers a multi-layered revision of Byron's earlier writing: from abstract meditation to tangible action, and from masculine quest to feminine experience.

Perhaps the most obvious marker of change between *Childe Harold* and *Don Juan* is the image of the unanchored bark. This was one of the figures used by Walter Scott to characterise Byron in his famous review of the third canto of *Childe Harold* in the *Quarterly Review* in which he counselled Byron to heed the advice of his critics, observing that 'the roughest fisherman is an useful pilot when a gallant vessel is near the breakers' (*RR*, B: II, p. 2046). Byron returned to this image in *Childe Harold* canto IV, in his wish to build

> from the planks, far shattered o'er the rocks
> ... a little bark of hope, once more
> To battle with the ocean and the shocks
> Of the loud breakers.
>
> (*CHP* IV. 105)

In the text of *Childe Harold* and in Scott's review of it, the solitary pilots
and fishermen are men. In *Don Juan*, Byron recalls the image in talking
about himself:

> But at the least I have shunned the common shore,
>   And leaving land far out of sight, would skim
> The Ocean of Eternity: the roar
>   Of breakers has not daunted my slight, trim
> But *still* sea-worthy skiff; and she may float
> Where ships have foundered, as doth many a boat.
>
>   (x. 4)[44]

Coleridge, Pratt and McGann note the echo of *Adonais* (with its source in
Childe Harold canto IV), but none of them traces the link between Byron's
allusion to himself and his depiction of feminine questing later in the
English cantos:

> A something all-sufficient for the *heart*
>   Is that for which the Sex are always seeking;
> But how to fill up that same vacant part?
>   There lies the rub – and this they are but weak in.[45]
> Frail mariners afloat without a chart,
>   They run before the wind through high seas breaking;
> And when they have made the shore through ev'ry shock,
> 'Tis odd, or odds, it may turn out a rock.
>
>   (XIV. 74)

This image of women as pilgrims of eternity, hazarding their lives, takes
its cue from the sympathetic view of 'something wanting' in Adeline's
marriage. Although *Don Juan* provides many images of the containment
of feminine experience, its digressive mixture of reactionary and eman-
cipated voices unsettles the complacencies of the 'cruizing' language and
instead leads the reader to participate in the 'odds' which shape morality
and culture.

To conclude the discussion of feminised digression in the English
cantos of *Don Juan* I shall explore the ways in which a particular moment of intertextuality might seek a response in its reader. The passage
I wish to examine is the vintage metaphor Byron supplies to counter the
'common place' description of Adeline in canto XIII:

> I'll have another figure in a trice: –
>   What say you to a bottle of champagne?
> Frozen into a very vinous ice,
>   Which leaves few drops of that immortal rain,

Yet in the very centre, past all price,
  About a liquid glassful will remain;
And this is stronger than the strongest grape
Could e'er express in its expanded shape:

'Tis the whole spirit brought to a quintessence;
  And thus the chilliest aspects may concentre
A hidden nectar under a cold presence.
  And such are many – though I only meant her,
From whom I now deduce these moral lessons,
  On which the Muse has always sought to enter: –
And your cold people are beyond all price,
When once you have broken their confounded ice.

(XIII. 37–38)

Byron's digression on the merits of the frozen champagne image to express Adeline's 'hidden nectar under a cold presence' has been traced by several scholars to Walter Scott's review of *Childe Harold's Pilgrimage*, canto IV, in the *Quarterly Review* for April 1818.[46] The well-known layer of intertextuality may be further extended by considering another possible source for Byron's image of distillation. This new context allows us to see how the forms of *Don Juan* are always shaped by historical contexts. Once we realise the very particular implications of Byron's choice of image, the meaning of the local episode changes and our awareness of the process of reading changes as well. Beside the pleasure of contact with the richness of the text, we are also aware that the link might not have been made; we might have missed the turn and another route would have provided a different experience. This is why source hunting is not adequate to the texture of *Don Juan*: a catalogue of references cannot tell us what actually happens when digressive intertextuality encounters different readers or the same reader in a different reading.

An additional intertext for the frozen champagne image appears in *Galignani's Messenger*. The section of the *Messenger* which drew most comment from Byron was the reporting of political debate in which Hobhouse carried on a high profile campaign against the Tories, and, in particular, George Canning, MP for Liverpool, who had been a senior member of Lord Liverpool's repressive government.[47] On 20 May 1821 Byron wrote to congratulate Hobhouse for his 'pretty ... piece of invective' against Canning which 'Galignani gave with great accuracy' (*BLJ*, VIII, p. 121). Notwithstanding this conflict, Byron admired Canning more than other Tory politicians, and praised him as 'an orator, a wit, a poet, a statesman' in a note to the preface to cantos VI, VII, and VIII of *Don Juan*.

Galignani's Messenger for Thursday 5 September 1822 (no. 2343) carried a report of a dinner given by the Canning Club in Liverpool to Canning himself prior to his expected departure for India. In the aftermath of Castlereagh's suicide, Canning was seen as a national asset who ought to stay in England. The speeches made on that occasion were reported at length and Canning's thanks to the assembled Club included the following remarks on their conservation of constitutional principles:

In northern climes, the essence of a generous vintage is often preserved in a small liquid nucleus, which remains unfrozen amidst the surrounding congelation; that nucleus, when the time of thaw comes, diffuses itself through the whole, and communicates to the mass its spirit and its flavour. So, I trust, that in all times – even in times such as the worst that we have seen, and such as, I hope, we are not likely soon to see again – in this club will be constantly preserved the spirit of loyalty and constitutional freedom, to be diffused, when the occasion shall arise, amongst the community with which you are surrounded.

We can compare this with Scott's comments on Byron:

there was the heart ardent at the call of freedom or of generous feeling, and belying every moment the frozen shrine in which false philosophy had incased it, glowing like the intense and concentrated alcohol, which remains one single but burning drop in the centre of the ice which its more watery particles have formed.[48]

If we examine verbal echoes, the *Galignani* passage is closer to *Don Juan* canto XIII. 37–8 than Scott's review in three instances; Canning's speech supplies the words 'essence', 'liquid' and 'spirit': Scott's review, however, contains 'frozen', 'ice', and 'concentrated' (not in *GM*). Linguistic echoes allow Canning's and Scott's uses of the frozen vintage metaphor equally compelling claims to be Byron's source and this extends to the matter of context as well.

Stephenson and Gilroy have discussed the way in which Scott's review extols the value of originality – a quality which Byron self-consciously advertises in the run up to his offering 'another figure in a trice' (XIII. 37). *Galignani's Messenger*, however, provides material for the stanzas which follow the frozen champagne image.

> And your cold people are beyond all price,
> When once you have broken their confounded ice.

> But after all they are a North-West Passage
>   Unto the glowing India of the soul;
> And as the good ships sent upon that message
>   Have not exactly ascertained the Pole

(Though Parry's efforts look a lucky presage)
  Thus gentlemen may run upon a shoal;
For if the Pole's not open, but all frost,
(A chance still) 'tis a voyage or vessel lost.

(XIII. 38–9)

Not only were the newspapers of autumn 1822 full of debate about Canning's imminent departure to take up the governor-generalship of India, but also about the fate of the most recent British expedition led by William Parry to find the north-west passage. Parry's ships, the *Fury* and the *Hecla*, were in a strait blocked by ice throughout the summers of 1822–3, but *Galignani's Messenger* carried optimistic speculative reports about their progress and the chances that a change in weather 'would serve to break up the ice' (*GM*, no. 2380).

Canto XIII was written in February 1823 which is, of course, much nearer in time to the *Galignani's Messenger* material than Scott's review of 1818.[49] As Stephenson's discussion of the Scott source makes clear, 'Byron was intensely interested in the critical reception of his works' and it is more than likely that he would recall Scott's image from 1818 – in which case the report of the Canning Club dinner might have served as an associative trigger.[50] Indeed, there is a possibility that Canning used this rhetorical figure as a private tribute to his friend Scott who was supposed to be at the farewell dinner. In a letter to J.B.S. Morritt of 7 September 1822 Scott wrote: 'I had intended for Liverpool to hear Canning's farewell speech, and had my place taken, etc. when lo! I was particularly commanded to Dalkeith, which I could not gracefully disobey.'[51] But there is a more particular reason why Canning's speech, once recovered, becomes an audible murmur in *Don Juan*'s metaphoric fluency.

The scene of Canning's farewell dinner befits 'that calm Patrician polish in the address' with which Byron characterises Adeline. Entertaining Lord Henry's political allies around the dinner table is the main theatre for Adeline's display of poise. Beyond thematic proximity, however, we can sense Byron's translation of Canning's politics of thawing. The hints that Adeline's ice will be broken by an affair with Juan are in place in canto XIII. 12 where we are told that she was 'The fair most fatal Juan ever met':

> Although she was not evil, nor meant ill;
> But Destiny and Passion spread the net.

Following this in stanzas 25–6, Byron used a newspaper convention of replacing names with 'blanks' to disguise the location of Lord Henry's mansion because:

> there is scarce a single season
> Which doth not shake some very splendid house
> With some slight heart-quake of domestic treason –
> A topic Scandal doth delight to rouse.

As well as the narrator's innuendo, the *bona fide* manifestation of the family ghost to Juan augments our expectation that the release of Adeline's 'high spirit' (XIII. 31) will result in the ruin of the house of Amundeville.

We are aware in the English cantos that our role in the poem is in part governed by our relationship with its plot: it is less certain, however, whether the plot at this point is being shaped by Byron, the narrator or by Adeline. The promise of access, therefore, to Adeline's liquid 'very centre' (XIII. 37), translates Canning's figure of patriarchal moral values diffusing to sustain the community, into a much more dangerous dissolution. Whereas Harold Bloom's discussion of the champagne metaphor freezes the possibility of intertextual play ('severity and courtliness fuse here into definitive judgment, and bring the spirit of this female archetype to a quintessence') the unfreezing which Byron anticipates depends on feminine passion rather than manly virtue in a 'northern clime' and signals sexual, rather than 'constitutional' freedom.[52] It is also predicated on his readers' ability to recognise and respond to this disruption. Canning's clubbable image of the spirit of loyalty is infiltrated by Byron's emphasis on the instability of what the law calls 'domestic treason' and what the poem questions by its disruption of complacent social and political surfaces.

A key word which appears in both the Scott review and the Canning speech, but not at this moment in *Don Juan*, is 'generous'. Scott refers to 'the call of freedom, or of generous feeling', and Canning speaks of 'the essence of a generous vintage'. The word connects the sources outside the poem, completing a triangle of textual relationships so that for just a moment, the reader epitomises that generosity, and holds all three together. Scott's review of Byron and Canning's farewell to England combine to enrich our reading of Adeline by suggesting the explosive potential and the exquisite artifice of her physical, 'fatal' generosity without solidifying these possibilities into absolutes. Awareness of this complex texture also complicates our reading of our own role in the poem. *Don Juan* invites receptions which take up digressive allusion with varying degrees of commitment, or none at all. Sometimes we are rewarded by completing the triangle of textual relationships as I have outlined above. Elsewhere, minutiae in the texture of the poem elude our grasp, but not our touch. Byron teases the reader about his or her uncertain role:

> And, gentle reader! when you gather meaning.
> You may be Boaz, and I – modest Ruth.
>
> (XIII. 96)

These lines hold hints of the delicacy of touch required ('gentle', 'gather', 'may be', 'modest') and it is the uncertainty of these digressive ventures which sustains a relationship between poet and reader against the odds of generality, closure and absolutism in 'this vile age' (XIII. 97).

CHAPTER SIX

'Between carelessness and trouble': Byron's last digressions

All the untidy activity continues,
awful but cheerful.
Elizabeth Bishop, 'The Bight'

Why did Byron suddenly return to Pope at the end of 1822 in the middle of the English cantos of *Don Juan*? And what does this tell us about digressive poetics at the end of his career? Byron completed the first draft of canto XII in early December 1822, but before resuming work on canto XIII in February he wrote two poems in heroic couplets: *The Age of Bronze* and *The Island*.[1] He also worked fitfully on *The Deformed Transformed*, the irregular blank verse drama which had been started in January 1822, and like *Don Juan*, remained unfinished at his death.[2] The break in *ottava rima* composition was not unprecedented – he had left *Don Juan* once before in 1820–21 to revise *Hints from Horace* and experiment with historical drama. At that time, the interruption of his epic could be seen as Byron forsaking the licentious Italian *ottava rima* for neo-classical closed couplets and dramatic unities, mainly in order to teach a lesson in aesthetic discipline to Bowles, the Lakers and all those who, in Gifford's terms, 'require[d] checking'.

When we read Byron's later poems in the context of their composition and his reception during 1822–3, the shift between *Don Juan* and *The Age of Bronze*, *The Island* and *The Deformed Transformed* appears not simply as a continuation of neo-classical rigour. This time, from the start, Byron was recasting Popean poetics for a readership that he knew had changed, and he experimented now with a much more radical and offensive Pope than the figure praised by Warton as one who, unlike Dryden, does not 'disgust ... with unexpected inequalities and absurd improprieties'.[3] Frederick Beaty sees *The Age of Bronze* as reflecting Byron's 'determination to return to his earlier adaptations of serious, if not tragic, Juvenalian satire'.[4] This is certainly true, but the poem is as much a deviation as a return. Its aesthetic choices are negotiations of the politics of reading and represent Byron's search for a new political identity at a time when, as Leigh Hunt pointed out, 'Your Lordship and your Bardship sometimes get mightily at variance.'[5]

Byron announced his new work to Leigh Hunt in January 1823: 'it is calculated for the reading part of the Million – being all on politics &c. &c. &c. and a review of the day in general – in my early English Bards style'.[6] The choice of form was significant and Byron referred to it again at the end of the letter: 'It is in the heroic couplet measure – which is "an old friend with a new face["].' The heroic couplet was indeed an old friend for Hunt and Byron. As long ago as 1815 they had together discussed the criticism of Pope in Wordsworth's 'Essay, Supplementary to the Preface' (1815). What was at issue then was the eighteenth-century poet's ability to produce natural description. Wordsworth had disputed the power of 'the celebrated moonlight scene' in Pope's *Iliad*.[7] Writing on this topic to Hunt, Byron described Wordsworth's comments as a 'pretension to accurate observation':

By the way – both he & you go too far against Pope's "so when the Moon &c." it is no translation I know – but it is not such *false* description as asserted – I have read it on the spot – there is a burst – and a lightness – and a glow – about the night in the Troad – which makes the "planets vivid" – & the "pole glowing" the moon is – at least the sky is clearness itself – and I know no more appropriate expression for the expansion of such a heaven. (*BLJ*, IV, p. 325)

Hunt replied to Byron: 'I was apprehensive that you might come upon me with some objections on the score of Wordsworth.' He conceded that Wordsworth's criticism of the Homeric landscape was wrong ('You have Wordsworth completely on the score of Greece, & on all the false geographical representation which he attributes to the passage in Pope'), but Hunt upheld the objection to Pope's style:

my charge against the passage goes no further than poor versification & a 'gorgeous misrepresentation of <u>Homer</u>.' It unquestionably wants his simplicity, the last couplet in particular; but it is not without beauties of its' own, & it is curious to find that it is really so like a Grecian landscape. (MS., John Murray Archive)

Their discussion about Pope coincided with Hunt's composition of *The Story of Rimini* and with Byron's sending to Hunt his own copy of *English Bards and Scotch Reviewers*, together with an account of how Rogers had advised its suppression so as to spare the sensibilities of Lord and Lady Holland. The heroic couplet had therefore been bound up from the start with poetical and political allegiances, with Hunt tending to defer to Wordsworth, and Byron keeping in with Holland House. During the winter of 1822–3, these 'old friends' are revisited, but not quite on the same terms.

Reflecting on some effects of the versification of *The Story of Rimini*, Hunt observed that 'all the reigning poets, without exception, [broke] up their own heroic couplets into freer modulation'.[8] Hunt's 'freer modulation' inevitably contested the poise and balance of Pope, Byron's 'most beautiful of poets'.[9] On the face of it, it seems strange that in 1815 Byron had remained on such good terms with Hunt while rounding on many of Pope's other detractors. What Byron did criticise at the time was Hunt's faith in 'system': 'When a man talks of his *System* – it is like a woman's talking of her *Virtue* – – – I let them talk on.'[10] Perhaps Hunt had dodged Byron's condemnation by maintaining – as he would later in his *Autobiography* – that Pope was at one time his 'closest poetical acquaintance'.[11] Still, throughout his career Hunt remained ambivalent about Pope's merits. His preference for 'superfluity' in the couplets of *Rimini* (and what Byron called the poem's 'originality – & Italianism') over Popean canons of correctness provides a fruitful context for understanding Byron's return to the heroic couplet in December 1822.[12] Violent critical reactions to *The Liberal* at this time led both Hunt and Byron to scrutinise the construction of cultural authority and to reflect on the satirical resources at their disposal. For each poet, Pope's heroic couplets were bound up with a trial of identity and reputation.

The characterisation of Pope as smooth, French and feminine was common among critics as diverse as William Hazlitt, Leigh Hunt and Francis Jeffrey.[13] Hazlitt wrote that Dr Johnson and Pope would have 'converted [Milton's] vaulting Pegasus into a rocking-horse',[14] an image which Keats extended in 'Sleep and Poetry': 'with a puling infant's force / They swayed upon a rocking horse / And thought it Pegasus' (ll. 185–7). As Upali Amarasinghe notes, the image of the bard astride a rocking horse may have been inspired by Byron in the first place. After Leigh Hunt was released from prison in 1815 he was visited by Byron who used to ride 'with a childish glee' on the rocking-horse belonging to Hunt's children.[15]

Keats's dislike of the poet who 'cuts a figure – but . . . is not figurative' accords with the limitations of the rocking-horse (rather than the mobile hobby-horse). Heroic couplets lacked the Miltonic reach which Keats found in the 'dark passages' of 'Tintern Abbey' and which he sought to emulate in the *Hyperion* poems.[16] Reviewing 'Sleep and Poetry', Leigh

Hunt concurred with the general disparagement of what he termed 'the late French school of criticism and monotony which has held poetry chained for long enough'. In the same article, however, he referred to Pope as 'a great poet' who 'was thrown into the society of the world, and thus had to get what he could out of an artificial sphere'. This was a small qualification, but it left space for a later reassessment.[17]

Led by Hunt, the Cockney School's initial absorption of the Wordsworthian epigraph to *Lyrical Ballads* (1805), '*Quam nihil ad genium, Papiniane, tuum*', hindered the perception of Pope as an anti-governmental voice. Embowered at Twickenham with Bolingbroke after the latter's return from exile, Pope's 'Patriot Whig' opposition to Walpole offered a pattern for poetic national integrity not dissimilar to the line Hunt and Keats traced back to Chaucer.[18] Both Joseph Warton's edition and Johnson's account of Pope in *Lives of the Poets* depoliticised the poet, and his oppositional potential was overshadowed by perceptions of style. A more virile and combative Pope, however, was given voice in Hunt's motto to his journal, the *Examiner*: 'Party is the madness of the many for the gain of a few' (ironically this quotation was attributed to Swift throughout the first seven years of the journal).[19]

During Hunt's collaboration with Byron in Italy, his preface to *The Liberal* (1822) identified Pope as a writer of integrity along with Chaucer, Milton and Marvell, distinguished from the alternative crew of 'slaves and sycophants ... bed-chamber lords ... or turncoats'.[20] The advertisement to the second volume of *The Liberal* drew extensively on *The Dunciad* to describe the outcry raised against the journal; but Hunt's essay on rhyme, 'The Book of Beginnings', returned to a view of Pope's versification as cautious, minute and ladylike ('like a miniature-painter'; 'Pope seems to fear every stepping-stone in his way') with none of the 'manly' strength of Dryden.[21] Hunt presented a contradictory view: Popean aesthetics were the symptom of an enervated artificial society, but Pope himself was its energetic scourge.

In 1820–1 while defending Pope, Byron almost unwittingly endorsed the feminisation of 'the greatest moral poet of any age'.[22] He sprang in a chivalrous way to 'poor Pope's' defence, defending his 'pure moral', asserting that he was 'the only poet that never shocks', and arguing that as Pope was 'less robust' than Lady Mary Wortley Montagu, it was impossible for him to have committed the alleged rape upon her.[23] Even Byron's names for Pope up to this time were emphatically feminine sobriquets such as the 'little Queen Anne's man' and 'the "little Nightingale" of Twickenham'.[24] In 1822–3, however, Byron seems to have followed Pope's own aggressive masculinisation of his poetic persona as he took on the satiric role not of Tiresias, but Thersites.[25]

The 1823 correspondence between Byron and Hunt suggests that Pope was once more a topic of discussion. On 16 January Byron wrote to Hunt praising his parody and adding, 'I send you Pope – and Warton's essay also – it is perhaps better as more condensed than his Notes to the formal Edition.'[26] This most likely referred to Byron's copies of Warton's nine-volume edition of Pope's works and the second edition of volume one of Warton's *Essay on Pope* (1762), referred to as 'much damaged' in the sale catalogue of 1827 (perhaps a sign that Hunt had used it thoroughly). The exchange of books suggests that having mentally cast John Murray as one of the odious booksellers of *The Dunciad* ('I had hoped that the race of Curl and Osborne was extinct') Byron was re-educating Hunt to instil a fuller appreciation of Pope.[27]

Once again style had become (as it always was) a political issue. Byron wrote to Hunt: 'You think higher of readers than I do – but I will bet you a flask of Falernum that the most *stilted* parts of the political "Age of Bronze" – and the most *pamby* portions of the <South Sea> Toobani Islanders – will be the most agreeable to the enlightened Public; though I shall sprinkle some *uncommon* place here and there nevertheless.'[28] This cynical wager suggests how knowingly Byron invoked form, and how aesthetic choices were part of his politicised relationship with the reading public. Byron's last couplet poems used both Juvenalian declamatory heroics and 'namby-pamby' or 'Rimini-Pimini' rhymes to test different authorial voices and also different readerships. Hunt's comments on *The Island* criticised Byron's use of the heroic couplet as 'very rhymey and conventional' (suggesting that he missed the very point of Byron's bet).[29] His comment tells us, however, that they were both alert to formal effects in relation to the contemporary audience.

Back in England John Hunt kept his brother and Byron regularly informed about the details of print runs, modes of advertising, public response and sales. Along with Douglas Kinnaird, John Hunt was pre-occupied with the question of whether or not to put Byron's name to the last cantos of *Don Juan* and his other new poems. In 1820 Kinnaird had begged Byron to 'come & take some part in Politics – Your <u>name</u> were a powerful charm', but in 1823 he was less sure: 'Is your name to be prefixed to the Island? Of course not to the Juans – It is to be recollected that if the Juans be voted improper for the female part of the public, you lose a large sale – .'[30] *The Age of Bronze* was published anonymously 'by way of experiment', as Kinnaird put it '& we shall have a chance of framing some notion of the result of publishing on your own account'.[31] The correspondence of later 1822 and early 1823 marks a new phase in Byron's publishing career in which everyone involved was cautious about Byron's reputation. John Hunt wrote to reassure Byron that the risks of publishing *The Age of Bronze* had been kept to a minimum:

As the <u>Age of Bronze</u> will all be in type at once, I shall order the copies to be struck off as they are called for – so that no over-printing, – as in the case of the <u>Liberal</u>, – shall operate as a drawback upon the profits – which will be accounted for to be [*sic*] Kinnaird. (21 March 1823: MS., John Murray Archive)

The poem was an experiment as well, in that it knowingly revisited and revised the allegiances of Byron's early career.

Closed Augustan couplets were, as William Keach has pointed out, 'something of a cultural fetish' for the Tory traditionalists.[32] We looked earlier at the way in which *English Bards and Scotch Reviewers* employed the Juvenalian force of Gifford's anti-Jacobin diatribes. Carl Woodring sees this first satire as Pittite in its cultural allegiance and suggests that between the two periods of composing *Childe Harold*, Byron began 'to align satiric couplets ... with the duty of conserving the best in a given heritage ... The satiric couplet became a tool to be picked up whenever Byron had an impulse to preserve old furniture'.[33] This conservatism is apparent in the coincidence of Byron's view on Keats's 'Sleep and Poetry' with that of *Blackwood's*, and in Byron's long-standing regard for William Gifford. After Byron's break with Murray and his 'government connections' in 1822, however, this inbred sympathy with the traditionalists came under pressure and Byron had to confront the distance between his old heroic style and the current reception of his work.[34]

The fabric of Byron's poetry, as we have seen, always interweaves traditional craftsmanship with historical contingency and the circumstances of reception. *English Bards and Scotch Reviewers* had been a splenetic rejection of the world of publishing (interspersed with its attacks on political figures); *The Age of Bronze* was a more carefully targeted repudiation of the cultural and political systems that his English friends wanted him to rejoin. Byron never broke away from Gifford's cultural tutelage, but he veered off far enough for Murray and Kinnaird to suspect him of writing *Ultra-Crepidarius* (Leigh Hunt's satire) against Gifford in 1823. Byron replied from Missolonghi:

It is not true that I ever *did – will – would – could* or *should* write a *satire* against Gifford – or a hair of his head – ... I have always considered Gifford as my *literary* father – and myself as his '*prodigal* Son.' (*BLJ*, XI, p. 117)

Byron was aware that by associating with Leigh and John Hunt, his 'prodigality' would be much in evidence to English readers. Although heroic couplets had long been the tool of established and even entrenched political views, Byron's return to Pope's form represents an effort to locate an effective position as a newly independent and increasingly radical voice.

The idea of such 'independence' is not methodically worked out by Byron, but it is a word which recurs in his letters and conversations at this time and I would like to use its recurrence to question Malcolm Kelsall's view that the rejection of 'all parties' in *Don Juan* was a pointless gesture.[35] In this as well, Kelsall aligns Byron's position with that of Pope:

the evasions and ambivalences of Pope's and Byron's nicely poised ironies ultimately proved unsustainable. There was no alternative position to which to evolve, no 'emergent ideology' to replace the 'residual'. On the contrary, what we see happening in Pope's and Byron's key works, *The Dunciad* and *Don Juan* is a disintegration of language. Style (and thus ideology) falls apart.[36]

But style doesn't fall apart in *Don Juan*. Because he doesn't look at the interplay of different forms at the end of Byron's career, Kelsall underestimates the dynamic testing and renewal of form which goes on up to and beyond Byron's journey to Greece. These formal experiments were a critical way of testing the alternative position, or road not taken. Kelsall is right about the messiness of the Whig cause after Napoleon and Peterloo and Caroline, but Byron's aesthetics comprehend that mess rather than being confined by it. *Don Juan* doesn't fizzle out into a series of redundant Whig checks and balances; it gathers itself, adjusts to the changing politics of readership, and recreates itself. Nor is it simply a work of 'nicely poised ironies'. The turn to the heroic couplet in *The Age of Bronze* employed 'an old friend with a new face' in order to explore the consciousness of that change. Meanwhile, the couplets in *The Island* set out (according to Byron) 'to avoid . . . running foul of my old "Corsair" and style'.[37]

As Peter Manning has demonstrated, *The Corsair* was firmly associated with aristocratic Whig politics through its publication with 'To a Lady Weeping'.[38] In her ground-breaking reassessment of Byron's artistry, Susan Wolfson finds that the 'energies of freedom and eruption are set against the demands of constraint and conservatism' in his use of form. Focusing on the case of *The Corsair* she argues that 'heroic couplets are one way that Byron restores the aristocratic codes of order', and traces the way in which 'shifting alliances of form and subject are forecast by contradictions in Byron's dedicatory preface to Moore'.[39] Discussing

Byron's later career, Richard Cronin argues that Byron's defence of Pope and revival of classical drama in 1820–1 were of a piece with his horrified response to the Cato Street Conspiracy and represent an attempt to reimpose the social barrier of a classical education.[40] All these readings accord with the established view that Lord Byron could only engage with revolutionary politics outside England because he remained, at heart, an English peer. In his last poems using heroic couplets, however, classical allusions and digressive couplets are detached (and yet not utterly) from their aristocratic milieu and take on a shifting alliance with the radicalism of Leigh Hunt and Douglas Kinnaird.

Although in his *Letter to John Murray Esqre.* Byron had criticised the '"shabby genteel"' Cockneys, he excluded Hunt from most of the attack, aiming instead for Hunt's 'disciples' or 'little chorus' ('Of my friend Hunt – I have already said that he is anything but vulgar in his manners'[41]). As a product of the rigorous classical tradition at Christ's Hospital, Hunt could not be accused of being one of the 'Lempriere dictionary quotation Gentleman'.[42] On 29 October 1822 he wrote to tell Byron he should 'translate Catullus's address to the female booksellers of antiquity' in order to shame Murray into handing over unpublished poems. Hunt then supplied his own 'Improvvisatore-ship' of the poem with a transcription of the Latin in case Byron didn't have a copy of Catullus in his library.[43] In the same month, Hunt wrote to tell Byron that he was 'translating a trampling satire of Alfieri's upon trade and money-getting'.[44] This anticipates the matter of *The Age of Bronze*, although Hunt's influence on this poem has hitherto been overlooked. The partnership between Byron and the Hunts worried both Hobhouse and Moore (as though the Hunts embodied the most monstrous bits of *Don Juan*[45]), but Douglas Kinnaird, who approved of *Don Juan*, also approved of John Hunt ('I continue to think highly of his integrity – & I see no reason to think you will have cause to repent having made him your Publisher'[46]). After a cooling of friendship with first Hobhouse and then Murray, Byron in 1822 turned to Hunt (briefly) then increasingly to Kinnaird as his most appreciative English readers.

If the second *Hints from Horace* had been a Popean poem addressed to a somewhat distanced Hobhouse, a worried Murray, a sceptical Gifford and a vanishing readership, *The Age of Bronze* was aware that Byron's alliance with the moderate Whig cause had slipped still further. As we saw in Chapter One, reviewers responded strongly to the rupture of class boundaries in *The Liberal*, and even after its demise they continued to identify Byron with radical politics. *Blackwood's* ironically suggested that

The Age of Bronze was written by the Cockneys and had been attributed
to Byron as a joke:

the 'Age of Bronze', begotten by a Cockney, on the body of a muse, name
unknown, is laid upon the steps before his Lordship's door. The noble Childe,
careless about such matters, tells his valet to give the bantling to any woman
in the house who chances to be nursing; and thus the ricketty wretch passes
for the work of one whose real progeny always shew blood and bone, and glory
in the sin of their sire. (*RR*, B: i, p. 202)

Their heavy-handed mockery suggests that *Blackwood's* wished to defuse
the poem's satiric potency (it showed 'carelessness' and a 'superfi-
cial knowledge of various matters ... gleaned from the Opposition
newspapers, and the talk of inferior Whigs').

Superior Whigs like Lady Holland did not relish the appearance of the
poem either: 'Ld Byron's *Age of Bronze* makes little or no sensation. What it
does, is not favourable: I have not read it. He writes too much', she wrote
in April 1823.[47] Her lack of warmth is significant, given that Holland
House was a bastion of neo-classical standards, and that she and Lord
Holland had given explicit approval to the tragedy, *Marino Faliero*. For
the Hollands, as Leslie Mitchell has observed, 'Dryden, Swift and Pope
remained unrivalled.'[48] Byron's return to Pope in 1822–3 was, however,
less than welcome. By objecting to Byron's productiveness, Lady Holland
identified a threat to the 'scarcity principle' of aristocratic elitism. This
was not quite the same as the stylistic 'vulgarity' Byron identified in the
Cockneys in 1821, but it suggests that his later poetry was unpalatable
to both the aristocracy and the 'middling' class of readers. Byron was
aware of this change and the return to Pope was his way of measuring
it.[49]

Malcolm Kelsall's brilliantly revisionary reading of Byron argues that
throughout his career, his political effectiveness was shackled by old Whig
compromises: 'the retention in *Don Juan*, however vestigially, of the ideals
of the Whig constitution and the great country house indicates that their
influence has not yet been displaced'.[50] I think, however, that there is evidence of a difference between Byron's classicism in 1820–1 and 1822–3.
Quite simply, the heroic couplet no longer upholds the same sort of heroism as, in the winter of 1822–3, Byron seemed to become increasingly
disillusioned with the aristocratic English elite.

When Sir James Wedderburne Webster arrived in Genoa in December
1822, Byron observed that he 'has been made a knight for writing against
the Queen ... He talked a deal of skimble skamble stuff', but he noted

that little had changed about the man except his new wig and 'that his
countenance rather more resembled his *back*side'.[51] Although he owed
Byron a thousand pounds (from a loan made ten years earlier), Webster
made no offer to pay back even the interest, thus contributing to the impression of a morally and financially bankrupt aristocracy which shaped
both the later cantos of *Don Juan* and *The Age of Bronze*.[52] Sir Timothy
Shelley's initial determination to 'do nothing' on Mary Shelley's be-
half afforded a bleak reminder of the unyielding character of hereditary
pride.[53] Between November 1822 and February 1823, the Portsmouth /
Hanson scandal was reported in the newspapers, exposing the squalid
horse-trading and brutalities which could occur unchecked in the 'great
country house'.[54] After years of rumour, an 1823 commission of lunacy
found that Portsmouth had been insane since 1809. The widely reported
evidence for this verdict included the peer's obsession with 'Black Jobs'
(his term for funerals) and his bloodthirsty ill-treatment of servants and
horses. The precision of his slaughter-house fetish (he would strike at
the cattle with an axe, shouting, 'serves them right, ambitious toads')
revealed a disturbing urge to dominate others, and was returned with interest by Portsmouth's second wife and her sisters.[55] Unfortunately, Byron
had been responsible for giving away this bride (his solicitor, Hanson's,
daughter) when Portsmouth married and had signed an affidavit in 1814
testifying to Portsmouth's sanity.

   Byron protested to Hobhouse: 'I could not foresee *Lunacy* in a Man
who had been allowed to walk about the world five and forty years as
Compos – of voting – franking – marrying – convicting thieves on his
own evidence – and similar past times which are the privileges of Sanity.'
Repeating the story to Lady Hardy he added, 'nor did he seem to me
more insane than any other person going to be married'.[56] Clearly,
the age of chivalry had gone. Although the Portsmouth affair was a
source of gruesomely amusing anecdotes throughout March 1823, it
also contributed to Byron's critical awareness of a corrupted strain in
his aristocratic Whig background. In the months which preceded the
composition of *The Age of Bronze* and *The Island*, Byron's letters also evince
a less hostile attitude to 'non-genteel reformers'. In particular, he appears
more ready to accommodate the radical aims and affiliations of the
Hunts.

   The evidence for this claim is finely balanced. Byron's attempts to
extricate himself from *The Liberal* are well known.[57] In October 1822,
besides, Byron duplicated the mistake he had made with Hobhouse, and
sent to Murray a patronising letter about Leigh Hunt's family which

was circulated and used gleefully against them. Hunt was wounded (as Hobhouse had been), but on 11 November 1822 he wrote to advise Byron:

Your Greek apothegm is indeed valuable with regard to men of his [Murray's] kind ... I am sure however, after all, that you wish me to think you mean kindly and respectfully to me at bottom. I am sure also that the Illiberals wish very much to the contrary, and that they could sow discord between us. I should like to disappoint them on that account.[58]

Byron did indeed disappoint the 'Illiberals'. He told Murray that he cared 'but little for the opinions of the English – as I have long had Europe and America for a Public', and he joked about the cost of 'becoming obnoxious to the Blue people'.[59] In letters to other friends he saluted the political courage of the Hunt brothers and their 'patriot paper', offered to come home to lend support in John Hunt's prosecution, declared that he wanted to leave more than a 'mere name' and asked Hobhouse to remember him to Burdett, one of the more radical Whigs who (like Hobhouse and Kinnaird) was out of favour with Holland House.[60] In the meantime, Byron's obsessive concern with his financial affairs indicated that he wished to make himself independent by the personal accumulation of wealth, rather than relying on social position.

Financial independence is a Popean characteristic which Byron had previously overlooked. In *English Bards and Scotch Reviewers* he had disdained the professional writer, and in his defences of Pope was careful to avoid all details of Pope's dedicated professionalism. But by 1822, letters to Kinnaird about funds and insurance policies flow thick and fast:

You will smile at all this tirade upon business – but it is time to mind it – at least for me to mind it – for without some method in it where or what is independence? the power of doing good to others or yourself. (*BLJ*, x, p. 43)

The obtrusive attention to financial matters in *The Age of Bronze* (especially the repeated rhyming on the word 'rent') completes a dialogue with Douglas Kinnaird, who was (after Hobhouse) Byron's closest confidant in England. Kinnaird was on the radical left, and his sexual politics were far less repressed than Hobhouse's. It was Kinnaird who coined the phrase about there being an 'Eleventh Commandment imposed upon the female part of our Island' not to read *Don Juan*.[61] His forthright views come through in a letter of 15 October 1822 about the Russian cantos of *Don Juan*:

With regards to the new Cantos I am delighted with them – The Political Reflections, the address to Wellington & the Preface are admirable – But why Call the <u>Katherine</u> a whore? She hired or whored others – She was never hired or whored herself – why blame her for liking fucking? If she had canted as well as cunted, then call her names as long as you please – But it is hard to blame her for following her natural inclinations ... I looked for more liberality from you – You must not turn against rogering – even tho' you practice it seldomer. (MS., John Murray Archive)

Kinnaird was (with Hobhouse) a correspondent who kept Byron's politics under close scrutiny. When he was asked to stand as candidate for Westminster, Kinnaird had declared himself in favour of annually elected parliaments, universal suffrage and same-day balloting.[62] Since the Westminster election of 1818 which had divided Hobhouse, Kinnaird and Burdett from the moderate Holland House Whigs, Kinnaird had been urging Byron to political action: 'Your Radicalism shall be written down', he told Byron on 8 October 1819, 'You shall not only find a welcome, but any charge of Horse or other that you may aspire to.'[63] Kinnaird was keen to detach Byron from the Whigs in the House of Lords ('that deceitfull [sic] arrogant Party'), and sent him throughout 1819 and 1820 urgent and dramatic accounts of Whig factionalism and national crisis:

We have batter'd the Whigs to a mercury – Their features are disfigur'd into one mass of deformity – The People will more readily get at the Government ... (8 October 1819)

Discontent & Distrust do actually disfigure the face of this land – Were the House of Commons shut up – men would in all classes begin to think for themselves – At present they do not ... (April 1820)

The Whigs as usual have been trimming ... (22 August 1820)

There is nothing too base for the nobility of this Country not to bear or do ... (27 October 1820)

Rely upon it the Country Gentlemen will bear a great deal more yet ... (28 March 1821: MS., John Murray Archive)

On 1 February 1823 Byron sent to Kinnaird an extended attack on the 'Country Gentlemen', to be inserted in *The Age of Bronze*. He received it enthusiastically: 'I am delighted at your attack on the Country Boobies & half-witted rogues.'[64] This addition to the satire suggests how closely Byron was now working with the discourse of the radical Whigs rather than the rhetoric of Holland House. Following the electioneering of 1819, Hobhouse repeatedly told Byron about the 'treacherous' behaviour of 'your friends the Whigs'.[65] Holland House, he protested 'has completely besotted the party – My lady sent her bastard [Charles Fox] to hiss me on the hustings, so we are at open war.'[66] Lord Holland held Byron's proxy vote for the 1818 session, but after that it was not renewed, ostensibly because of parliamentary regulations, but also because of an increasing political gulf between Byron and Holland.

As we saw in Chapter Three, the years 1820–1 witnessed a struggle between different English political and cultural factions to own Byron's poetry. In 1820 Hobhouse challenged Byron with the view: 'I am convinced that the proudest of all politicians & the most uncondescending is the man of principle, the real radical reformer.'[67] In February 1820 Byron wrote to Murray that he had always been 'a friend to and a Voter for reform'.[68] Belatedly and with some misgiving, in the winter of 1822–3 Byron's digressive textuality assumed the colours of this more radical agenda. When he said that *The Age of Bronze* was for 'the reading part of the Million', it is clear that he was directing it to the educated left. John Hunt's explanation of the change in Byron's readerly appeal makes this shift of political identity explicit. In a letter of 13 April 1823 John Hunt acknowledged that the likely sale of 3,000 copies of *The Age of Bronze* was much less than the 20,000 or more copies sold of *The Corsair*:

But your Lordship had not then, I believe, given so many deadly blows to Corruption and Bigotry ... there was 'no offence' in the Corsair, political or religious – and it must likewise be remembered, that the subject of the poem was one which addressed a much wider circle of readers than the Age of Bronze. Your Lordship's last labour of the Island will afford a better test of the state of opinion. (MS., John Murray Archive)

Byron's ostensible motives for writing had also changed. Writing from Greece in December 1823 he checked with Kinnaird about the publication of *Don Juan* and *The Island*: 'I am particular on this point only – because a sum of trifling amount even for a Gentleman's *personal* expences in *London* or *Paris* – in Greece can arm and maintain hundreds of men.'[69]

This shift in financial priorities can be coupled with Byron's explicit attacks on English high life as intrinsically and hypocritically '*intrigante* and profligate'.[70] It is also of a piece with the revision of his views on Hobhouse's radicalism. When Hobhouse visited Byron in Pisa in September 1822, Byron finally expressed support for his break with the moderate Whigs: 'B told me that he had been against me at my election at first because he knew nothing about the matter now he was anti-Whig.'[71] It appears that the Whigs at home knew this, and in 1823 Byron stated with equanimity: 'What *I* have done to displease my aristocratic connections I can quite understand.'[72] These exchanges are a vital part of the compositional context for *The Age of Bronze, Don Juan* and *The Island*,

and help to explicate the differences between works which were composed within a short space of time.

In an isolated *ottava rima* stanza, 'On Southey. Detached Thought',
tentatively dated by McGann to spring 1822, Byron ordered and ar-
ranged the distinctions between himself and Robert Southey:

> With you I have nought in common, nor would have –
>   Nor fame, nor feelings, nor the very Earth;
> So let us be divided by the grave
>   As we have been by thought and life and birth.
> And when the hungry worms their carrion crave,
>   When they alone can calculate your worth,
> When all your bones are rotten as your heart,
> May both our tombs and names be kept apart.
>
> (CPW, VI, p. 516)

The effect of the ababab section of this stanza is to allow tension to mount
before the last couplet forces Byron and Southey together in order to
separate them eternally: with the word 'apart', closure and separation
arrive together. The ruthlessness of the concluding couplet anticipates
the sustained intensity of *The Age of Bronze* in which the satiric targets
are allowed no room to breathe because they have taken over the whole
world.

The first section of *The Age of Bronze* advertises its proximity to the
process of *Don Juan* by forming a division of eight lines. Thereafter,
the couplets work as paragraphs, running lines on every so often to
remind us that form can be broken if the will is there.[73] Byron begins by
gesturing to the '"good old times"', and then withdraws certainty from
the idea by suggesting that all historical perspectives are conditioned
by relativity: 'all times when old are good' (ll. 1–2). Pope's stable moral
world based on divine order is questioned by displacing the voice of
moral authority in *Measure for Measure*: 'I know not if the angels weep',
and setting in play a repetition ('but men, / Have wept enough – for what?
to weep again') which builds throughout the poem to create 'history's
fruitless page' (l. 243). 'All is exploded' (l. 9) begins the second section in
which Byron again gestures to the political 'Titans' Pitt and Fox 'with a
dashing sea / Of eloquence between' now shrunken to 'a few feet / Of
sullen earth' to 'divide each winding sheet' (ll. 15–20). The image of the
tomb which 'preserves its form' (l. 26) stands from the beginning of the
poem as a reminder of terminal formal constraint. The couplets in this
work produce neither decorous restraint nor epigrammatic polish, but
a relentless legislative chartering. 'Lotted' is the word used by Byron to

suggest that – like Napoleon's rations – human existence is controlled by Congress. Rhymes (especially quasi-hudibrastic ones) force the reader to count every syllable of that constraint.

The dynamics of the Southey stanza, like odd moments in *Don Juan* canto XII, reveal why at this point in his career Byron exchanged *ottava rima* for the couplet:

> But now I'm going to be immoral; now
>   I mean to show things really as they are,
> Not as they ought to be: for I avow,
>   That till we see what's what in fact, we're far
> From much improvement with that virtuous plough
>   Which skims the surface, leaving scarce a scar
> Upon the black loam long manured by Vice,
> Only to keep its corn at the old price.
>
> (XII. 40)

The run of monosyllabic words in this stanza emphasises the hardening of tone and a restriction of the playful dynamics of *ottava rima*. The desire to show 'what's what in fact' demands that little or no room be left for readerly discrimination. Skimming the surface is the readerly process that Byron's poetry usually invites, but in late 1822 the decision to publish 'on his own account' necessitated a more authoritative gesture (however hollow that authority became in transmission). Canto XII is punctuated with digressions which signal a reinvigorated authorial independence and an awareness of new beginnings:

But now I will begin my poem (XII. 54)

>   You'll attack
> Perhaps this new position – but I'm right;
> Or if I'm wrong, I'll not be ta'en aback
>   (XII. 71)

> Here the twelfth Canto of our introduction
> Ends. When the body of the book's begun,
> You'll find it of a different construction
> From what some people say 'twill be when done.
>   (XII. 87)

The digressions of canto XII draw attention to the discrepancy between liberation on a small scale (from 'customers among the Orthodox') and economic enslavement on a larger scale (as the ramifications of '"Political Economy"' grow more pressing). This narrative technique highlights the construction of systems and how they are sustained – such as parliament:

"Tis not mere splendour makes the show august / To eye or heart – it is the people's trust' (xii. 83). Likewise, Byron acknowledges the reader's independence of his system: 'I can't oblige you, reader! to read on; / That's your affair, not mine' (xii. 87). As Malcolm Kelsall has pointed out, the interrogation of all systems carries within it the possibility of terminal irony. The poem, however, is aware of this nihilistic path and chooses another form.

The turn to heroic couplets in *The Age of Bronze* and *The Island* represents the working out of a corrosive irony that might otherwise have pervaded *Don Juan* much in the way Kelsall describes. Canto xiii continues the wry view of parliament as the home of meaningless utilitarian abstraction, but at the same time it alerts us to the danger of producing in both reader and poet a tendency to let idealism lapse into careless comedy, and like Cervantes, allow 'noblest views' to become 'mere Fancy's sport' (xiii. 10):

> I should be very willing to redress
>   Men's wrongs, and rather check than punish crimes,
> Had not Cervantes in that too true tale
> Of Quixote, shown how all such efforts fail.
>
> Of all tales 'tis the saddest – and more sad,
>   Because it makes us smile: his hero's right,
> And still pursues the right; to curb the bad,
>   His only object, and 'gainst odds to fight,
> His guerdon: 'tis his virtue makes him mad!
>   But his adventures form a sorry sight; –
> A sorrier still is the great moral taught
> By that real Epic unto all who have thought.
>
>   (xiii. 8–9)

In this way, Byron's wry consideration of Cervantes is more complex than Ruskin's accusation that either *Don Juan* or *Don Quixote* killed idealism:

If you were to ask me who of all powerful and popular writers in the cause of error had wrought most harm to their race, I should hesitate in reply whether to name Voltaire, or Byron, or the last most ingenious and most venomous of the degraded philosophers of Germany [Schopenhauer], or rather Cervantes, for he cast scorn upon the holiest principles of humanity – he, of all men ... helped to change loyalty into license, protection into plunder, truth into treachery, chivalry into selfishness.[74]

Ruskin imagines that culture is entirely in the hands of the poet while Byron sees it resting with his readers ('all who have thought'). His playful questioning about how meaning is constructed coexists within a narrative which only continues by mutual consent:

> And is there not Religion, and Reform,
>> Peace, War, the taxes, and what's called the 'Nation'?
> The struggle to be Pilots in a storm?
>> The landed and the monied speculation?
>>>> (XIII. 6)

Characteristically, the narrator of *Don Juan* will always 'leave the matter' where he finds it (XII. 80); but *The Age of Bronze* does not permit the space for reflection of *Don Juan*'s ababab lines and is more insistent that readers should come to the point of the satire. When stanza 13 turns to 'noble Albion', the frequency of marked digressive interruption forces the reader into a position of troubled vigilance. Doubt is cast on the long list of clichéd British achievements by quoting them and then interrupting the citation:

> 'And Waterloo – and trade – and – (hush! not yet
> A syllable of imposts or of debt) –
> And ne'er (enough) lamented Castlereagh,
> Whose pen-knife slit a goose-quill t'other day –
> And "pilots who have weathered every storm" –
> (But, no, not even for rhyme's sake, name reform).'
>>>> (ll. 536–41)

It is in line with the anger of *The Age of Bronze* that the quotation of Canning's praise of Pitt is signalled where it is not in *Don Juan*: Popean satire represents an obligatory sharpening of the reader's 'affair' with the poem while *Don Juan* allows the reader to forget, if he or she wishes. Throughout its 780 lines, *The Age of Bronze* is more fretful and unforgiving about lapses of attention. Its use of a quickly changing dialogue within the heroic couplets recalls the impatient Pope of the 'Epilogue to the Satires' (1738), while the sustained ironic concentration on civilisation's facade draws some of its strength from Churchill's 'Dedication to the Sermons'. Pope's satire on paper credit in the 'Epistle to Bathurst' ('Pregnant with thousands flits the Scrap unseen, / And silent sells a King, or buys a Queen' (ll. 77–8)) allows us to hear, however, the difference between their economic critiques.

As Reuben A. Brower remarks about Pope: 'ugly actualities ... gain force by the surface elegance of the diction'.[75] Byron's verse in *The Age of Bronze* deliberately eschews this surface elegance; stanza 15 on 'real paper or imagined gold' adopts a coarse register of body parts and a disturbingly reductive portrait of Jewishness.[76] Although we can recognise Byron's forefathers in the Juvenalian tone of the satire, Nina Diakonova is right to observe that in *The Age of Bronze* Byron is 'both disciple and iconoclast, rising from classicist abstractions to a realistic satirical portrayal of social psychology and the laws of its evolution'.[77] *The Age of Bronze* invokes Pope to implicate readers in the achievement of modern civilisation. All the generalised critical qualities associated with Popean satire – polish, versatility, feminine control – are present in a corrupted form in the Congress system itself.

Whereas Pope had deployed an antithetical style to dance between two clearly defined parties, 'Papist or Protestant, or both between, / Like good *Erasmus* in an honest Mean, / In Moderation placing all my Glory, / While Tories call me Whig, and Whigs a Tory' (Sat. II. i, ll. 65–8), Byron used Popean couplets in this late poem to embody a claustrophobic mediocrity without the lively paradoxical implications of Pope's 'isthmus of a middle state'.[78] Napoleon's heroic extremity is now diminished to existence in 'this middle state, / Between a prison and a palace' (ll. 72–3); he is one who can only 'flit between a dungeon and a throne' (l. 259), and his former wife 'flits amidst the phantoms of the hour' (l. 735). Similarly, Russia's enlightened despot is presented 'Now half dissolving to a liberal thaw, / But hardened back whene'er the morning's raw' (ll. 440–1). Seemingly everything is caught 'between those shifting rocks, / The new Symplegades – the crushing Stocks' (ll. 660–1) – which Byron's letters reveal to have caught him as well. *The Age of Bronze* offers the sound of a saw cutting off the seesaw on which the poet is sitting. Inbetweenness is the object of the satire, rather than its elegant solution.[79]

Pope had used couplets for discrimination, judgement, measuring the distance between things and framing an intelligible, connected order. In *The Age of Bronze*, Byron worked across the space of the couplet to collapse contemporary political distinctions (the Sovereigns are 'alike, / A common coin as ever mint could strike' (ll. 708–9)), and to demean legends by cramping their gestures. Historical allusions are invoked only to be re-embodied as pathetically limited physical entities.[80] Weinbrot, Brower and Tillotson praise Pope's synthesis of former traditions, the moral purpose of his compound texture and the importance of connection in his variety.[81] Byron disconnects Pope's smooth assimilation of culture: Cleopatra enters the poem as a piece of cargo and even the memory of her amorous conquest is tarnished ('Though Cleopatra's mummy cross the sea, / O'er which from empire she lured Anthony' (ll. 29–30)). The eagle that was Napoleon is 'Reduced to nibble at his narrow cage' (l. 56). In discussing *Don Juan*, Paul Curtis provides a helpful summary of the way in which the concept of organisation changes between Pope's and Byron's writing:

> The neo-classical poetry of Pope depends upon the image of time as a linear (and spatial) construct.... Pope's wit enables him firstly to see (to know) time and the literary tradition at a glance, and secondly to arrange artfully images of temporal import ... Byron dismantles the eighteenth-century aesthetic of allusion as exemplified in the poetry of Pope.[82]

Any homage to Pope in *The Age of Bronze* is indeed ironised as the poem wrenches lines from their untroubled celebration of sterling worth into a new world of obfuscation and compromise. The mercurial brilliance of Pope's friend Peterborough becomes the dubious fluctuation of Montmorency's career ('He falls indeed, perhaps to rise again / "Almost as quickly as he conquered Spain" ' (ll. 725–6)), and the erotic tenderness of 'Eloisa to Abelard' becomes an index of the power of international banks who 'waft a loan "from Indus to the Pole" ' (ll. 679). The poem is therefore caught between a yearning for the clear definition of heroic value which beacons from Pope's language and a knowledge that Pope's ability to order and energise culture antithetically is outdated. *The Age of Bronze* borrows Pope's disappointment at the failings of his own time and adds its layer of exasperation at the shrinking relevance of a Popean voice under a global political system which is crushing the cultural basis for identity and difference.

Pope used couplets in *The Dunciad* to belittle mediocrity. In *The Age of Bronze*, the same couplets are deployed to measure how mediocrity reproduces itself (as Shelley saw).[83] It is a hyper-self-conscious, doubly ironic use of form. All the sparkling patterns of repetition which Pope perfected to vary his lines are redeployed to mark the inescapable ironies of tamed existence like Napoleon's ('smile' (l. 57); 'But smile (l. 81); 'How must he smile (l. 91); 'How must he smile (l. 99); 'the better-seeing shade will smile' (l. 119)). The use of formal accomplishment to define the horrors of the Congress's 'vast design' is emphasised through triplets as linguistic skill is debased:

> There Chateaubriand forms new books of martyrs;
> And subtle Greeks intrigue for stupid Tartars;
> There Montmorency, the sworn foe to charters,
> Turns a diplomatist of great eclât,
> To furnish articles for the 'Debâts;'
>
> (ll. 716–20)

The rocking-horse motion which Hazlitt detected in Pope has become expressive of the wearisome predictability of 'kind[ling] souls within degraded flesh' (l. 269) as the ashes of old heroes are reheated. Repetition, the mode of the poem, marks a nauseating cultural condition. Masculine rhymes and monosyllables limit the amount of time spent with this debased currency while feminine and ludicrous strained double rhymes underline the inescapable lunacy of the system.[84]

Frederick Beaty argues that the 'desultory thoughts of this poem are unified largely by the section on Napoleon' (*Byron the Satirist*, p. 174). On the other hand, McGann finds that 'its centre is located in the passage where Diogenes is invoked ... as B's classical surrogate and alter-ego' (*CPW*, VII, p. 120). It may be, however, that Pope's couplets are recalled in order to highlight the lack of any centre or unifying heroic figure. *The Age of Bronze*, *The Island* and *The Deformed Transformed* all use multiple plot lines, doubling heroes and plots that become shadowed by alternative action, as if to debar the possibility of a single hero ever emerging.

In *The Age of Bronze*'s endless recycling of declines and falls, the reflexes of digression offer the reader the possibility of a fresh start, only to remove it again. A significant proportion of stanzaic paragraphs begin with 'But' (III, VI, VII, VIII, XII, XVII), others begin 'And what', or 'Or turn', or 'Enough of this' (XI, XV, XVII). These are all verbal cues for digressive interruption that we recognise from other poems; but in *The Age of Bronze*, the idea of a liberating break away from the main plot is rendered impossible by the weight of economic liabilities which hold everything in place. Freedom's awakened spark in the 'infant world' and Greece and Spain is confined between sections on the 'girded' Napoleon and the 'animated logs' (l. 407) of Congress who are 'crushing nations with a stupid blow' (l. 409). The almost partyless Canning offers a glimpse of independence (which is not the same as aristocratic individualism), but the romantic ideal of Canning's 'poetic flame' (l. 551) is thwarted when he is shown to be not fully in control of his royalist Pegasus: 'The unwieldy old White Horse is apt at last / To stumble, kick, and now and then stick fast' (ll. 564–5).[85] In this way, he is yet another unsatisfactory alter-ego, like Napoleon, and an example of how the satire, having identified a possible sign of promise, identifies the political inevitability of it stalling and grinding to a halt.

Balked movement is a recurrent device in the poem. Enjambed couplets begin to flow more freely in order only to be brought up short. Pope's vigorous intestinal wars harden into 'no movement' between courses; the walls of Verona girding their royal guests shrink to the kilt that girds Sir William Curtis; monuments of patriotism and freedom are fitted round the 'gross sirloin' (l. 776) of globalisation as it appeared in 1822. Coleridge had criticised the heroic couplets of Erasmus Darwin as 'the Russian palace of ice, glittering, cold and transitory'.[86] That is exactly what Byron insisted on as the form of *The Age of Bronze*: 'this is a *temporary* hit at Congress &c', Byron told Kinnaird, insisting that the poem must 'appear *alone*'.[87]

The effectiveness of the texture the poet created is suggested by Elizabeth Barrett Browning's response to his depiction of Napoleon's ex-wife as she recalled the passage in a letter to Miss Mitford in 1837: 'Do you remember Lord Byron's bitter lines, said bitterly while Marie Louise leant upon the arm of Napoleon's conqueror? . . . They have never past from my memory since I read them. There is something hardening, I fear, in power – even if there is not in pomp!'[88] Her sense of redoubled bitterness tells us that Byron succeeded in turning Popean polish into an unyielding brassy hardness encasing both a personal and public disillusionment.[89] For a moment, The *Age of Bronze* solidified Byron's digressive play into the shining contours of an urn. It needs, however, to be read in dialogue with the other poems of the same period if we are to be alert to the urgent variability of Byron's art in the months before he, like Prospero, relinquished his books.

The Island was begun just after Byron had sent *The Age of Bronze* to Mary Shelley for copying. After the roughened and masculinised Popean couplets of *The Age of Bronze*, this later poem uses its opening lines to signal a change of course: 'the vessel lay / her course, and gently made her liquid way' (ll. 1–2). *The Island* is explicitly about a feminine course of action, moving through a methodical consideration of different male heroes (Bligh, Christian, Torquil) towards the resourceful heroism of 'this daughter of the Southern Seas, / Herself a billow in her energies' (ll. 141–4).[90] Whereas *The Age of Bronze* deploys the cynical voice of the male libertine wit (Cleopatra 'lured' Anthony (l. 30)), *The Island* exemplifies Byron's ability to write sympathetically about individual women who were not known to him, but imagined.[91] Byron took care that his retelling of the story of *The Mutiny of the Bounty* should not fall into a predictable anti-revolutionary reception. He wrote to answer Leigh Hunt's comments on the work in progress:

I have two things to avoid – the first that of running foul of my own 'Corsair' and style – so as to produce repetition and monotony – and the other *not* to run counter to the reigning stupidity altogether – otherwise they will say that I am eulogizing *Mutiny*. – This must produce tameness in some degree – but recollect that I am merely trying to write a poem a little above the usual run of periodical poesy. (*BLJ*, x, p. 90)

None of the poem's most recent commentators examines its relationship to *The Age of Bronze* or considers how Byron turns between different communities of reader for each poem. Often read as an escapist idyll, *The Island* separates itself from Byron's famous narrative of female rescue in *The Corsair* through a poetic surface that promises pleasant songs and liquid lays, but does not, quite, lull its readers into escapist reverie.[92] Fragments of *The Age of Bronze* keep turning up to shadow the carefree islanders with trouble. The 'lovely . . . forms' (II. l. 59) of Toobonai are placed in the past, 'Before the winds blew Europe o'er these climes' (II. l. 66), and the poet insists that readers should identify an elegiac, rather than escapist melody: 'Who such would see, may from his lattice view / The Old World more degraded than the New, – / Now *new* no more' (II. ll. 73–5). Torquil is introduced as a potential hero:

> Placed in the Arab's clime, he would have been
> As bold a rover as the sands have seen,
> And braved their thirst with as enduring lip
> As Ishmael, wafted on his desart-ship;
> Fixed upon Chili's shore, a proud Cacique;
> On Hellas' mountains, a rebellious Greek;
> Born in a tent, perhaps a Tamerlane;
> Bred to a throne, perhaps unfit to reign.
>
> (II. ll. 179–86)

His various alter-egos begin with general, mythic allusions but gradually edge closer to home. With the mention of hereditary monarchs 'perhaps unfit to reign', the contemporary allusions of satire begin to make incursions on the shores of the idyll, especially if readers catch the echoes of this passage from *The Age of Bronze*:

> The Athenian wears again Harmodius' sword;
> The Chili chief abjures his foreign lord;
> The Spartan knows himself once more a Greek;
> Young Freedom plumes the crest of each Cacique;
> Debating despots, hemmed on either shore,
> Shrink vainly from the roused Atlantic's roar.
>
> (ll. 276–81)

In *The Island* the sound of idealistic philhellenism works to rupture the charm of its Edenic seclusion. An ironic awareness that we have been sucking on 'pamby' pleasures is enhanced a few lines later by direct authorial interpolation: 'Thou smilest, . . . Thou smilest? – Smile; 'tis better thus than sigh' (II. ll. 196–201). Byron's digressive interruptions to his narrative's celebration of natural harmony and love were noted by reviewers. More than one was upset by the intrusion of Ben Bunting's pipe-smoke into the poem and the sudden descent into nautical swearing; others, however, recorded their determination not to be 'surprised' by Byron's irregularities. Having found *The Age of Bronze* to 'bear the features' of Byron's muse ('careless and unequal, vigorous and caustic'), *The Monthly Review* took it for granted that there would be 'many blemishes of style' in *The Island* and duly singled out examples of the 'prosaic and bad'.[93] The *New European* objected to

> examples of doggrel, and incongruity, and bathos, and carelessness, which are crowded into almost every page ... Low jokes and bad jesting, imitations of Crabbe, and morbid misanthropy, now usurp the places of better feeling, and elegant Poesy. The spectres only of former successful exploits now flit athwart his pages. (*RR*, B: v, p. 1870)

This sense of being haunted by earlier poems is, as we have seen, part of the digressive texture of Byron's late works. With the exception of the *New European* which was wholly critical, reviewers of *The Island* attempted to isolate Byron's 'beauties' from contamination by strange contrasts and abruptness. Throughout his career, Byron's textual rendition of multiplicity baffled his readers. Almost as an answer to the 'system' which his reviewers perceived, Byron's last poems create still further a digressive palimpsest in which the controversies of his years of fame are juxtaposed with multiple future identities. *The Island* imagines various ends for its heroes: Bligh dreams of 'Old England's welcome shore' (I. l. 19) before the mutiny which translates him into the avenging wrath of English law. Christian contemplates his end: '"I am in Hell"' (I. l. 164) before his suicidal plunge from 'wounded, weary form' into formlessness (IV. l. 337). Torquil wonders whether he has been brought by Neuha to the rock to die before he plunges into the sea and (for his pursuers) melts into legend. Finally he is welcomed 'as a son restored' (IV. l. 408), the image of Byron's heroic return that both Kinnaird and Hobhouse treasured, but never saw.

    The Island is a verse romance that keeps interpolating other frames of reference so as to keep the reader awake with '*uncommon* place'. Christian's violent death shatters the language of natural harmony associated with the island (the rocks below received like glass / His body crushed into one gory mass' (IV. ll. 341–2)) until the last traces of human trouble are effaced ('But calm and careless heaved the wave below, / Eternal with unsympathetic flow' (IV. ll. 367–8)). In this way, the undertow of the couplet measures even as it resists 'the clock's funereal chime / Which deals the daily pittance of our span' (II. ll. 349–50). The reader is not allowed to settle into one perspective. Fantasy and practicality are entwined in the cave section as the poem offers its readers the 'fantastic shell' of Mermen and the tasty flesh inside the turtle shell (possibly the same turtle we watched hatching from its shell at the beginning of the canto: IV. ll. 99; 171–2; 21). Disconcertingly, the rapturous embrace of Torquil and Neuha is shadowed by the stark loss and deprivation of Pope's 'Eloisa to Abelard':

> enough that all within that cave
> Was Love, though buried strong as in the grave
> Where Abelard, through twenty years of death,
> When Eloisa's form was lowered beneath
> Their nuptial vault, his arms outstretched, and prest
> The kindling ashes to his kindled breast.
>
> (IV. ll. 221–6)

This allusion breaks into the illusion of their young love, not only by reminding the reader of mutilation and separation, but also because it holds an uncanny echo of the mordant view of revolutionary hope in *The Age of Bronze*:

> The infant world redeems her name of '*New*'.
> 'Tis the *old* aspiration breathed afresh
> To kindle souls within degraded flesh.
>
> (ll. 267–9)

'Kindling' is a preoccupation of both *The Age of Bronze* and *The Island*: it represents that moment when form changes and is, of course, associated most strongly with sparks of freedom. Byron's use of it in both these poems may be inflected by Eloisa's erotic resistance: 'I view my crime, but kindle at the view' (l. 185). *The Island* plays with the mood of unrepentant transition, teasing the reader by drawing out the moment before the turn (whether in the plot, or in the line) as with the mutineer who enacts Byron's habit of digressive interruption:

> – at times would stand, then stoop
> To pick a pebble up – then let it drop –
> Then hurry as in haste – then quickly stop –
> Then cast his eyes on his companions – then
> Half whistle half a tune, and pause again –
> And then his former movements would redouble,
> With something between carelessness and trouble.
> This is a long description, but applies
> To scarce five minutes past before the eyes;
> But yet *what* minutes! Moments like to these
> Rend men's lives into immortalities.
>
> (III. ll. 110–20)

Manfred's consciousness of being 'plough'd by moments, not by years' is here revisited in the context of self-reflexive narrative rather than mental theatre. Byron's use of caesuras emphasises an urgent and self-regarding discontinuity. The half-whistled tune recalls the half untold tale in *The Age of Bronze*. Both poems thematise the uncertainty which is also Byron's poetic texture.

As the line endings shift from masculine to feminine rhymes, the poem itself reflects on a moment which is also a turning point in the poet's career. 'The Island is much admired & if you choose ever to come back into our cloudy country I have no doubt you may carry all before you', Hobhouse wrote to Byron in July 1823.[94] But while Byron's verse experiments played out different versions of the future, he had selected another course (albeit one always shadowed with the other possibilities). The main characters in *The Deformed Transformed* – Caesar, Arnold, Bourbon – play with the role of leader, and the various versions of the future Byron offers his readers are literally rendered in the scene where Arnold chooses his new (old) form. *The Age of Bronze* lays Napoleon to rest only to rake over his ashes one more time: '(. . . But no, – their embers soon will burst the mould)' (l. 756). In the penultimate stanza of *The Island*, Neuha sees a sail and imagines another ending: 'With fluttering fear, her heart beat thick and high, / While yet a doubt sprung where its course might lie: / But no! it came not' (iv. ll. 379–80).[95] Perpetually haunted by other possibilities, the idyllic resolution of the poem remains strangely inconclusive.

The speed at which Byron was composing and the verbal overlaps between these last works encourage us to read them as digressive off-shoots from each other. He translates the 'common ark' in which 'Church, state, and faction, wrestle in the dark' (ll. 648–9) into Bligh's 'ark' and then into the 'slender ark' of Neuha and Torquil. Their feast in the 'yet infant world' at the end of *The Island* is reconfigured in the Whig banquets in the last cantos of *Don Juan*, in which Byron multiplied the possibility of a female hero by three, and continued, as the *Monthly Review* lamented, 'without much regard to that censure of the kind of colouring, expression, hint, and allusion in which the author indulges, that has been bestowed on this poem by the public'.[96]

But readerly responses to Byron's poetry might, in a curious way, have been more regarded than the reviewers thought. *Galignani's Messenger* for 22 October, 1822 (no. 2384) carried a long extract from *The Siege of Corinth* which ended with these words:

'Tis still a watch-word to the earth:
When man would do a deed of worth,
He points to Greece and turns to tread,
So sanctioned, on the tyrant's head; [*Macbeth IV. 3. l. 45]
He looks to her, and rushes on
Where life is lost or freedom won.

This was not the only time that Byron's early poetry returned in the context of the Greek struggle for independence; 'The Isles of Greece' lyric from *Don Juan* was also extracted from its rather negative context, and reprinted to encourage their readers' sympathy with the liberation movement. We cannot gauge what Byron's response to the re-emergence of his early verse might have been, but his lyric 'On this day I complete my thirty sixth year' gives us some indication of how far his philhellenism in 1824 oscillated between irony and idealism:

Awake ! (*not* Greece – She is awake!)
    Awake my spirit – think through whom
Thy life blood tracks its parent lake
    And then strike home!

The digressive aside which interrupts this lyric yields a penultimate instance of Byron's refusal to succumb entirely to abstraction. The parenthesis is a sudden reminder of another more matter-of-fact perspective which the poem opens even as it seems to be withdrawing from its readers. The throwaway remark is actually working very hard: the words offer the reflex of Romantic irony's check on lyric exaltation, assurance (to Hobhouse and the Greek Committee), a challenge (to the Illiberals of *The Courier*) and a rueful aside to a Greek boy who would probably never read the poem. At once ironically detached and committed to a world of particular accidents and delights, they epitomise the way in which Byron's digressions allow us to enjoy the exquisite performance of historical uncertainty – 'something between carelessness and trouble' or, 'like a system coupled with a doubt' (XVI. 9), *Don Juan*'s last glass of champagne.

Notes

INTRODUCTION

1 *BLJ*, VII, p. 219; *CPW*, IV, p. 1.
2 HLRO, Proxy Book 1816, vol. 91, p. 17.
3 Stuart Curran, *Poetic Form and British Romanticism* (New York: Oxford University Press, 1986).
4 *Edinburgh Review* 50 (1829–30), 32–47.
5 *The Globe and Traveller*, no. 6733 (30 June 1824). The final stanza was later revised to emphasise a singular instant of finality: 'an awful tale of greatness o'er' (*The Poetical Works of Elizabeth Barrett Browning* (London: Henry Frowde, 1904), pp. 53–4).
6 *The Works of Mrs Hemans with a Memoir of her Life by her Sister*, 7 vols. (Edinburgh and London: Blackwood and Cadell, 1839), IV, p. 179. For a reading of the feminised poetics of the poem, see Jerome J. McGann, *The Poetics of Sensibility: A Revolution in Literary Style* (Oxford: Clarendon Press, 1996), pp. 160–4.
7 Jerome J. McGann, *Fiery Dust: Byron's Poetic Development* (Chicago and London: University of Chicago Press, 1968), p. 278.
8 *The Works of Anna Laetitia Barbauld with a Memoir by Lucy Aikin*, 2 vols. (London: Longman, 1825), II, pp. 96–7.
9 See, for example, Philip W. Martin, *Byron: A Poet Before His Public* (Cambridge University Press, 1982).
10 Nigel Leask: *British Romantic Writers and the East: Anxieties of Empire* (Cambridge University Press, 1992), p. 28.
11 Ibid., p. 60.
12 Jerome Christensen, *Lord Byron's Strength: Romantic Writing and Commercial Society* (Baltimore and London: Johns Hopkins University Press, 1993).
13 Ibid., p. 327.
14 McGann, *Fiery Dust*, p. 289; *Don Juan in Context* (London: John Murray, 1976), p. 116.
15 McGann, *Don Juan in Context*, p. 118.
16 Ibid., pp. 70; 83.
17 Ibid., p. 130.

18 James Chandler, *England in 1819: The Politics of Literary Culture and the Case of Romantic Historicism* (Chicago and London: University of Chicago Press, 1998), pp. 373–4.

19 Ibid., p. 388.

20 William H. Galperin, *The Return of the Visible in British Romanticism* (Baltimore and London: Johns Hopkins University Press, 1993), p. 246.

21 Ibid., p. 271.

22 Moyra Haslett, *Byron's* Don Juan *and the Don Juan Legend* (Oxford: Clarendon Press, 1997), p. 276.

23 Irving Babbitt, *Rousseau and Romanticism* (Boston and New York: Houghton Mifflin, 1919), pp. 265–6.

24 For a recent discussion of Romantic writers anticipating an audience, see Lucy Newlyn, *Reading, Writing, and Romanticism: The Anxiety of Reception* (Oxford University Press, 2000).

25 Anne K. Mellor, *English Romantic Irony* (Cambridge, Mass.: Harvard University Press, 1980), pp. 186; 188.

26 Ibid., p. 188.

27 Tilottama Rajan, *Dark Interpreter: The Discourse of Romanticism* (Ithaca and London: Cornell University Press, 1980), p. 266.

28 Frederick Garber, *Self, Text and Romantic Irony: The Example of Byron* (Princeton University Press, 1988), p. 295.

29 Ibid., pp. 265; 295.

30 Ibid., pp. 296; 312.

31 Ibid., pp. 166; 290.

32 William Empson, *Seven Types of Ambiguity* (1930; Harmondsworth: Penguin, 1961), p. 247.

33 Michael G. Cooke, *Acts of Inclusion: Studies Bearing on an Elementary Theory of Romanticism* (New Haven and London: Yale University Press, 1979), p. 120.

34 Hermione de Almeida, *Byron and Joyce Through Homer: Don Juan and Ulysses* (London and Basingstoke: Macmillan, 1981), pp. 3; 140.

35 Andrew Bennett, *Romantic Poets and the Culture of Posterity* (Cambridge University Press, 1999).

36 *CPW*, v, p. 769.

37 Frederick L. Beaty, *Byron the Satirist* (De Kalb: Northern Illinois University Press, 1985); Stephen C. Behrendt, *Shelley and His Audiences* (Lincoln and London: University of Nebraska Press, 1989); Steven E. Jones, *Shelley's Satire: Violence, Exhortation, and Authority* (De Kalb: Northern Illinois University Press, 1994); *Satire and Romanticism* (New York: St Martin's Press, 2000); Gary Dyer, *British Satire and the Politics of Style, 1789–1832* (Cambridge University Press, 1997).

38 Andrew Elfenbein, *Byron and the Victorians* (Cambridge University Press, 1995), pp. 3; 10.

39 Thomas Carlyle, *Sartor Resartus: The Life and Opinions of Herr Teufelsdröckh* (London: Chapman and Hall, 1897), pp. 26–7; *The Works of John Ruskin,*

(eds.) G.T. Cook and Alexander Wedderburn, 39 vols. (London: George Allen, 1903–12), XXXVI, pp. xxxiv–xxxv.

40 Edward Dudley Hume Johnson, 'Lord Byron in *Don Juan*: A Study in Digression' (unpublished doctoral dissertation, Yale University, 1939); William T. Ross, 'Digressive Narrator and Narrative Technique in Byron's *Don Juan*' (unpublished doctoral dissertation, University of Virginia, 1970); Joel Dana Black, 'The Second Fall: The Laws of Digression and Gravitation in Romantic Narrative and their Impact on Contemporary Encyclopaedic Literature' (unpublished doctoral dissertation, Stanford University, 1979).

41 Wolfgang Iser, *Prospecting: From Reader Response to Literary Anthropology* (Baltimore and London: Johns Hopkins University Press, 1989), pp. 3–41. See also Wolfgang Iser, 'Indeterminacy and the Reader's Response in Prose Fiction', in J. Hillis Miller (ed.), *Aspects of Narrative: Selected Papers from the English Institute* (New York: Columbia University Press, 1971), pp. 1–45.

42 John Whale, *Imagination Under Pressure, 1789–1832: Aesthetics, Politics and Utility* (Cambridge University Press, 2000).

43 Johnson, 'Lord Byron in *Don Juan*'; McGann, *CPW*, V, p. 742; Peter W. Graham, *Don Juan and Regency England* (Charlottesville: University of Virginia Press, 1990).

44 Caroline Franklin, *Byron's Heroines* (Oxford: Clarendon Press, 1992); Haslett, *Byron's Don Juan*; Susan J. Wolfson, '"Their She Condition": Cross-dressing and the Politics of Gender in *Don Juan*', *ELH* 54 (1987), 598–612.

45 See Marjorie Perloff, *The Poetics of Indeterminacy: Rimbaud to Cage* (Princeton University Press, 1981), pp. 4–28.

46 *BLJ*, VI, p. 46.

47 Julia Kristeva, *Desire in Language: A Semiotic Approach to Literature and Art*, (ed.) Leon S. Roudiez, (transl.) Thomas Gora, Alice Jardine and Leon S. Roudiez (Oxford: Basil Blackwell, 1980), p. 83.

48 See, for example, 'La – The (Feminine)' and 'The Book of Promethea', in *The Hélène Cixous Reader*, (ed.) Susan Sellers (London and New York: Routledge, 1994), pp. 59–67; 121–8; Luce Irigaray, 'This Sex Which is Not One', (transl.) Claudia Reeder, in *New French Feminisms: An Anthology*, (eds.) Elaine Marks and Isabelle de Courtivron (Brighton: Harvester, 1981), pp. 99–106.

49 Jerome J. McGann, *Towards a Literature of Knowledge* (Oxford: Clarendon Press, 1989), p. 56.

50 Ibid., p. 56.

51 Jacques Derrida, *Acts of Literature*, (ed.) Derek Attridge (London and New York: Routledge, 1992), p. 56. Although it does not discuss Byron, the critical neglect of texture in Romantic writing is addressed in the introduction to Thomas McFarland, *Romanticism and the Heritage of Rousseau* (Oxford: Clarendon Press, 1995).

52 Terry Eagleton, *The Significance of Theory* (Oxford: Basil Blackwell, 1990), p. 56; Frank Kermode, *History and Value*, The Clarendon Lectures and the Northcliffe Lectures 1987 (Oxford: Clarendon Press, 1988), p. 143.

53 Andrew Bowie, *Aesthetics and Subjectivity: From Kant to Nietzsche* (Manchester: Manchester University Press, 1990), p. 147.

54 J. Paul Hunter, 'Form as Meaning: Pope and the Ideology of the Couplet', in David H. Richter (ed.), *Ideology and Form in Eighteenth-Century Literature* (Lubbock: Texas Tech University Press, 1999), pp. 147–62; p. 161. I am grateful to Susan Wolfson for this reference.

1 'SCORCHING AND DRENCHING': DISCOURSES OF DIGRESSION AMONG BYRON'S READERS

1 See, for example, the Byron entry in Iain McCalman (ed.), *An Oxford Companion to the Romantic Age: British Culture 1776–1832* (Oxford University Press, 1999), p. 442.

2 For the readers' internalisation of contemporary reviews, see Jon P. Klancher, *The Making of English Reading Audiences, 1790–1832* (Madison: University of Wisconsin Press, 1987).

3 *Lara*, I, 130; W.B. Yeats quoting Mme Blavatsky. Cited in Geoffrey Hartman, *Beyond Formalism* (New Haven and London: Yale University Press, 1970), p. 304.

4 M.H. Abrams, *Natural Supernaturalism: Tradition and Revolution in Romantic Literature* (New York and London: W.W. Norton, 1971), p. 13.

5 Thomas Humphry Ward (ed.), *The English Poets: Selections with Critical Introductions by Various Writers*, 5 vols. (London: Macmillan, 1880; repr. 1911), IV, pp. 245–6.

6 For a discussion of juxtaposition in the expurgated stanzas, see Martin, *Byron: A Poet Before His Public*, pp. 9–29 and Beaty, *Byron the Satirist*, p. 6.

7 For a recent examination of critical discourse focusing on Byron's ability to enthral the public, see Ghislaine McDayter, 'Conjuring Byron: Byromania, Literary Commodification and the Birth of Celebrity', in Frances Wilson (ed.), *Byromania: Portraits of the Artist in Nineteenth- and Twentieth-Century Culture* (London and Basingstoke: Macmillan, 1999), pp. 43–62. My argument seeks to modify McDayter's contention that style was not a focus for hostility in Byron's early reviews (p. 49).

8 Maria Edgeworth, *Letters from England 1813–1844*, (ed.) Christina Colvin (Oxford: Clarendon Press, 1971), p. 339.

9 See James Beattie, *Essays* (Edinburgh: William Creech, 1776), p. 620.

10 *The Complete Works of William Hazlitt*, (ed.) P.P. Howe, 21 vols. (London: J.M. Dent, 1930–4), xx, pp. 352–3). For a discussion of the relationship between wit and allusion, see John Sitter, *Arguments of Augustan Wit* (Cambridge University Press, 1991), pp. 175–86.

11 *RR*, B: II, p. 707.

12 For a different reading of Byron's 'urbane Voltairean detachment' in his notes, see Marilyn Butler, 'The Orientalism of Byron's *Giaour*', in Bernard Beatty and Vincent Newey (eds.), *Byron and the Limits of Fiction* (Liverpool University Press, 1988), pp. 78–96 (p. 87).

13 Samuel Smiles, *A Publisher and His Friends: Memoir and Correspondence of the Late John Murray, with an Account of the Origin and Progress of the House, 1768–1843*, 2 vols. (London: John Murray, 1891), I, p. 208.

14 Dyer, *British Satire and the Politics of Style*, pp. 11; 3–4.

15 For Byron's political closeness to Lady Oxford, see David V. Erdman, 'Lord Byron and the Genteel Reformers', *PMLA* 56 (1941), 1065–94.

16 *Journal of the Hon. Henry Edward Fox (Afterwards Fourth and Last Lord Holland) 1818–1830*, (ed.) The Earl of Ilchester (London: Thornton Butterworth, 1923), p. 165.

17 Malcolm Kelsall has identified the proximity between Byron's poetic style and the traditional Whig rhetoric of 'checks and balances'. See Malcolm Kelsall, *Byron's Politics* (Brighton: Harvester, 1987), pp. 34–56.

18 *RR*, B: v, p. 2125; *BLJ*, III, p. 62.

19 John Barrell, *The Political Theory of Painting from Reynolds to Hazlitt* (New Haven and London: Yale University Press, 1986), p. 125.

20 Sir Joshua Reynolds, *Discourses on Art*, (ed.) Robert R. Wark (New Haven and London: Yale University Press, 1975), p. 123.

21 Chris Baldick, *In Frankenstein's Shadow: Myth, Monstrosity and Nineteenth-Century Writing* (Oxford: Clarendon Press, 1987), p. 10; Edmund Burke, *Reflections on the Revolution in France and on the Proceedings in Certain Societies in London Relative to that Event*, (ed.) Conor Cruise O'Brien (Harmondsworth: Penguin, 1968; repr. 1983), pp. 92–3.

22 Reynolds, *Discourses*, p. 124.

23 See pp. 38–40 below.

24 See George Cruikshank's 'Management – or Butts & Hogsheads' (December 1812), associating Byron with the political party of Lord Holland. The cartoon is discussed in Richard Lansdown, *Byron's Historical Dramas* (Oxford: Clarendon Press, 1992), p. 26.

25 In 'Edmund Kean and Byron's Plays', Peter J. Manning registers the similarity between the 'discontinuous effects' of Edmund Kean's acting and Byron's oriental tales (*Keats-Shelley Journal* 21–2 (1972–3), 188–206; p. 191).

26 *Lady Blessington's Conversations of Lord Byron*, (ed.) Ernest J. Lovell, Jr (Princeton University Press, 1969), p. 211.

27 Ugo Foscolo, 'Narrative and Romantic Poems of the Italians', (transl.) Francis Cohen, *Quarterly Review* 21 (1819), 486–56.

28 Palgrave was identified as the translator of Foscolo's article by R.D. Waller in his introductory essay to John Hookham Frere, *The Monks and the Giants* (Manchester University Press, 1926), p. 60.

29 Foscolo, 'Narrative and Romantic Poems', pp. 489–90. For discussion of Byron's influences in Italian medley verse, see Jerome J. McGann, '"Mixed Company": Byron's *Beppo* and the Italian Medley', in Kenneth Neill Cameron and Donald H. Reiman (eds.), *Shelley and his Circle 1773–1822*, 8 vols. (Cambridge, Mass.: Harvard University Press, 1973–86), VII, pp. 234–57.

30 Foscolo, 'Narrative and Romantic Poems', pp. 494–5.

31 Dyer, *British Satire and the Politics of Style*, pp. 139–67.

32 *The Notebooks of Samuel Taylor Coleridge*, (ed.) Kathleen Coburn, Bollingen Series 50, 4 vols. (Princeton University Press, 1957–90), I, 1814. See Robert W. Jones, *Gender and the Formation of Taste in Eighteenth-Century Britain: The Analysis of Beauty* (Cambridge University Press, 1998), pp. 78–116.

33 Foscolo, 'Narrative and Romantic Poems', p. 505.

34 MS., John Murray Archive. I am grateful to Andrew Nicholson for checking this and all my transcriptions from the Murray Archive. I am grateful to JOHN MURRAY for permission to quote from the archive.

35 For Holland's holding of Byron's proxy, see HLRO, Proxy Book 1817, vol. 92, p. 9 and HLRO, Proxy Book 1818, vol. 93, p. 12.

36 *The Quarterly Review* 21 (1819), p. 564.

37 MS., John Murray Archive. A transcript of this letter was published for the first time by Peter Cochran in 'Francis Cohen, *Don Juan* and Casti', *Romanticism* 4.1 (1998), 120–4.

38 See David Simpson, *Romanticism, Nationalism and the Revolt Against Theory* (Chicago and London: Chicago University Press, 1993); Clifford Siskin, 'The Year of the System' in Richard Cronin (ed.), *1798: The Year of the* Lyrical Ballads (London and Basingstoke: Macmillan, 1998), pp. 9–31.

39 James Joyce, *A Portrait of the Artist as a Young Man* (London: Granada, 1977; repr. 1983), p. 195.

40 G.M. Matthews (ed.), *Keats: The Critical Heritage* (London and New York: Routledge, 1971), p. 149.

41 Haslett, *Byron's* Don Juan, p. 191.

42 *RR*, B: I, p. 36.

43 *'Don John' or 'Don Juan Unmasked': Being a Key to the Mystery Attending that Remarkable Publication; with a Descriptive Review of the Poem and Extracts*, 3rd edn (London, 1819).

44 Peter W. Graham (ed.), *Byron's Bulldog: The Letters of John Cam Hobhouse to Lord Byron* (Columbus: Ohio State University Press, 1984), p. 257. Hobhouse's objections to *Don Juan* are discussed in Elizabeth French Boyd, *Byron's Don Juan* (London and New York: Routledge, 1945), p. 14.

45 *The Yale Edition of the Works of Samuel Johnson*, (eds.) E.L. McAdam Jr, with Donald and Mary Hyde, and others, 16 vols. (New Haven and London: Yale University Press, 1958–90), VII, p. 66.

46 Byron, *The Complete Miscellaneous Prose*, (ed.) Andrew Nicholson (Oxford: Clarendon Press, 1991), p. 150.

47 See Richard Cronin, 'Keats and the Politics of Cockney Style', *SEL* 36 (1996), 785–806; Nicholas Roe, *John Keats and the Culture of Dissent* (Oxford: Clarendon Press, 1997); Jeffrey N. Cox, *Poetry and Politics in the Cockney School: Keats, Shelley, Hunt and their Circle* (Cambridge University Press, 1998).

48 T.S. Eliot, *On Poetry and Poets* (London: Faber and Faber, 1957; repr. 1971), p. 201.

49 Presbyter Anglicanus, 'Letter to the Author of *Beppo*', *Blackwood's Edinburgh Magazine* 3 (1818), 323–29; p. 326.

50 Barrell, *The Political Theory of Painting*, p. 121.

51 Reynolds, *Discourses*, pp. 102; 183; 185.

52 Rollins (ed.), *The Letters of John Keats 1814–1821*, (ed.) Hyder Edward Rollins, 2 vols. (Cambridge, Mass., Harvard University Press, 1858; repr. 1972), II, p. 65.

53 For a detailed account of Moore as a biographer, see Joseph W. Reed Jr, *English Biography in the Early Nineteenth Century 1801–1838*, Yale Studies in English vol. 160 (New Haven and London: Yale University Press, 1966), pp. 102–26. For Hunt's use of psycho-biography when reviewing *Don Juan*, see *RR*, B: III, p. 1004.

54 *The Works of Lord Byron: With His Letters and Journals, and His Life*, (ed.) Thomas Moore, 17 vols. (London: John Murray, 1832–3), VI, pp. 235–7.

55 E.L. Griggs, 'Samuel Taylor Coleridge and Opium', *Huntington Library Quarterly* 17 (1953–4), 357–78; p. 372. I am grateful to Seamus Perry for supplying this reference.

56 William Butler Yeats (ed.), *The Oxford Book of Modern Verse, 1892–1935* (New York: Oxford University Press, 1936), pp. xxiv–xxv.

2 'BREACHES IN TRANSITION': EIGHTEENTH-CENTURY DIGRESSIONS AND BYRON'S EARLY VERSE

1 See Walter Jackson Bate, *From Classic to Romantic: Premises of Taste in Eighteenth-Century England* (New York: Harper & Row, 1961), pp. 38–9.

2 Mark Akenside, *The Pleasures of Imagination to which is Prefixed a Critical Essay on the Poem by Mrs. Barbauld* (London: T. Cadell Junior & W. Davies, 1794), p. 4.

3 Richard Terry, 'Transitions and Digressions in the Eighteenth-Century Long Poem', *SEL* 32 (1992), 495–510; p. 502.

4 *A Pindarique Ode, Humbly offered to the Queen to which is prefix'd a Discourse on the Pindarique Ode* (London, 1706), p. i.

5 The appeal to a 'secret connexion' was also made by Abraham Cowley whose talk of 'Invisible Connexions' was picked up by Coleridge. See Paul Magnuson, *Coleridge and Wordsworth: A Lyrical Dialogue*, (Princeton University Press, 1988), p. 17. See also H.J. Jackson, 'Coleridge's Lessons in Transition: The "Logic" of the "Wildest Odes"', in Thomas Pfau and Robert F. Gleckner (eds.), *Lessons of Romanticism: A Critical Companion* (Durham, N.C.: Duke University Press, 1998), pp. 213–24.

6 Beattie, *Essays*, p. 664.

7 Samuel Johnson, *The Rambler*, (eds.) W.J. Bate and Albrecht B. Strauss, 3 vols. (New Haven and London: Yale University Press, 1969), III, p. 77.

8 *The Art of Poetry on a New Plan, Illustrated with a Great Variety of Examples from the Best English Poets*, 2 vols. (London, 1762), II, p. 40.

9 Hugh Blair, *Lectures on Rhetoric and Belles Lettres*, 2 vols. (London, 1783), II, p. 356.

10 Jane Austen, *Northanger Abbey*, (ed.) Anne Henry Ehrenpreis (Harmondsworth: Penguin, 1972; repr. 1988), p. 240.

11 Johnson's campaign against the offences of 'lax and lawless versification' is saluted in Robert Potter, *An Inquiry into some Passages in Dr. Johnson's Lives of the Poets: Particularly his Observations of Lyric Poetry, and the Odes of Gray* (London, 1783), p. 11. See also Robert Potter *The Art of Criticism as Exemplified in Dr Johnson's Lives of the Most Eminent English Poets* (London, 1789). For a later defence of 'abruptness of transition, and a peculiar warmth of impetuosity and diction', see Nathan Drake, *Literary Hours or Sketches Critical and Narrative* (London, 1798), p. 278.

12 *The Life and Works of William Cowper*, (ed.) Robert Southey, 8 vols. (London: Henry G. Bohn, 1854), VII, p. xvi.

13 Naomi Schor, *Reading in Detail: Aesthetics and the Feminine* (New York and London: Methuen, 1987), p. 4.

14 For discussion of the links and connections of Sensibility, see David Fairer, 'Sentimental Translation in Mackenzie and Sterne', *Essays in Criticism* 49. 2 (1999), 132–51.

15 *An Inquiry Concerning the Human Understanding*, note to Section III, 'Of the Association of Ideas'; quoted in Martin Kallich, 'The Associationist Criticism of Francis Hutcheson and David Hume', *Studies in Philology* 43 (1946), 644–67; p. 663.

16 John Wolcot, *The Works of Peter Pindar . . . To which is prefixed Some Account of his Life*, 4 vols. (London: Walker and Edwards, 1816), I, p. 46.

17 For Helen Maria Williams's use of a 'desultory' form to feminise the history of Revolution, see Gary Kelly, *Women, Writing, and Revolution 1790–1827* (Oxford: Clarendon Press, 1993), pp. 192–233.

18 'New Morality' appeared in *The Anti-Jacobin, or Weekly Examiner* on 9 July 1798. See William Gifford, *The Anti-Jacobin, or Weekly Examiner (1799)*, 2 vols. (Hildesheim and New York: Georg Olms Verlag, 1970), II, p. 625.

19 James Mackintosh, *Vindiciae Gallicae. Defence of the French Revolution and its English Admirers, against the accusations of the Right Hon. Edmund Burke* (London: G.G.J. and J. Robinson, 1791), p. vii.

20 *CPW*, IV, p. 447.

21 See Bennett, *Romantic Poets*, pp. 179–88. Digressive similarities between Churchill and Byron are discussed briefly in Thomas Lockwood, *Post-Augustan Satire: Charles Churchill and Satirical Poetry 1750–1800* (Seattle and Washington: University of Washington Press, 1979), pp. 28–31.

22 *CPW*, IV, p. 447.

23 See Bennett's discussion of the way in which payment and repayment are bound up with the construction of posterity (*Romantic Poets*, pp. 185–9).

24 *RR*, B: II, p. 703.

25 Peter J. Manning, 'Byron's *English Bards and Scotch Reviewers*: The Art of Allusion', *Keats-Shelley Memorial Bulletin* 21 (1970), 7–11.

26 *The Poetical Works of Charles Churchill with Explanatory Notes and An Authentic Account of His Life*, (ed.) William Tooke, 2 vols. (London: C. & R. Baldwin, 1804), I, p. xiv.

27 Review of the 1804 edition of Churchill's poems by Robert Southey in the *Annual Review, and History of Literature*, (ed.) Arthur Aikin, Vol. III (1804; London: Longman, Hurst, Rees and Orme, 1805), pp. 580–5; p. 582.

28 Ibid. Southey quotes from Churchill's 'The Conference', ll. 213–15.

29 'Churchill wrote with great rapidity, and generally published his compositions directly they were finished. This may account for the involved sentences and lengthy parentheses, which are the most obvious, if not the worst, blemishes of his style' (*The Poetical Works of Charles Churchill, With a Memoir by James L. Hannay and Copious Notes by W. Tooke*, 2 vols. (London: Bell and Daldy, 1866), I, p. 219).

30 Ibid., I, pp. xxx; xxxi. Dyer discusses Churchill very briefly as a Neo-Juvenalian satirist in *British Satire and the Politics of Style*, pp. 21–2; 44; 102.

31 *The Poetical Works of Charles Churchill* (1804), I, pp. 4–5. There are differences between this edition and the 1866 Tooke edition, particularly in the way that literary allusions are signalled, suggesting that the reception of allusion changed in the course of the nineteenth century.

32 *The Poetical Works of Charles Churchill* (1804), I, pp. xxv; xxix.

33 *BLJ*, II, p. 207.

34 One notable exception to this general neglect is Lockwood, *Post-Augustan Satire*, pp. 27–8.

35 On the specificity of Byron's satire (of which quotations from other texts form a significant part), see Claude M. Fuess, *Lord Byron as a Satirist in Verse* (New York: Columbia University Press, 1912), p. 71.

36 Lockwood, *Post-Augustan Satire*, p. 60.

37 *The Poetical Works of Charles Churchill* (1804), II, p. 3. For a consideration of Churchill's stylistic excess and refusal to polish in the context of eighteenth-century formal verse satire, see Howard D. Weinbrot, *Alexander Pope and the Tradition of Formal Verse Satire* (Princeton University Press, 1982), pp. 346–52.

38 Tooke's negative assessment of *The Ghost* contrasts markedly with contemporary reviews of the poem which he quotes in his edition. The *Monthly Review* applauded 'this heterogeneous production of a sportive, wild, and arbitrary fancy . . . this Shandy in Hudibrastics' (*The Poetical Works of Charles Churchill* (1804), II, p. 143).

39 John Lennard, *But I Digress: The Exploitation of Parentheses in English Printed Verse* (Oxford: Clarendon Press, 1991); A.B. England, *Byron's* Don Juan *and Eighteenth-Century Literature: A Study of Some Rhetorical Continuities and Discontinuities* (London and Cranbury: Associated University Presses, 1975), especially pp. 161–86.

40 Lennard, *But I Digress*, p. 160.

41 Laurence Sterne, *The Life and Opinions of Tristram Shandy Gentleman*, (ed.) Graham Petrie, (introd.) Christopher Ricks (Harmondsworth: Penguin, 1967; repr. 1986), p. 397.

42 Ibid., p. 232; Jonathan Swift, *Gulliver's Travels and Other Writings*, (ed.) Louis A. Landa (Oxford University Press, 1976), p. 331.

43 Sterne, *Tristram Shandy*, p. 595.

44 See, for example, Churchill's interest in 'indelicate' terms in *The Ghost* III, ll. 281–6 and the *lucus a non lucendo* figure in *The Ghost* II, ll. 253–8 which Byron also enjoyed enough to use twice in *Don Juan* at VI. 55 and IX. 21.

45 John Mullan, *Sentiment and Sociability: The Language of Feeling in the Eighteenth Century*, 2nd edn (Oxford: Clarendon Press, 1988; repr. 1990), p. 159.

46 For a more extensive discussion of the complex relationships between satire and sentiment, see Claude Rawson, *Satire and Sentiment 1660–1830* (Cambridge University Press, 1994). In his brief discussion of Byron's poetry Rawson claims that its self-conscious or Shandean dimension 'is either a corrupted or debased form of Augustanism or something else altogether' (p. 99).

47 For a recent discussion of generic mixture in Prior's pastoral lyrics, see Faith Gildenhuys, 'Convention and Consciousness in Prior's Love Lyrics', *SEL* 35 (1995), 437–55. See also Germaine Greer, '*Hours of Idleness*: The Poet's Voice', *The Newstead Byron Society Review* (July 2000), 29–48.

48 *Alma; or the Progress of the Mind* I, ll. 513–22, in *The Poetical Works of Matthew Prior* (Edinburgh: James Nichol, 1858).

49 Gildenhuys, 'Convention and Consciousness', p. 439.

50 Blanford Parker, *The Triumph of Augustan Poetics: English Literary Culture from Butler to Johnson* (Cambridge University Press, 1998), p. 204.

51 Ibid., pp. 207–8.

52 For earlier considerations of stylistic tension in Byron's early verse, see McGann, *Fiery Dust*, pp. 18–19; 20–21, Beaty, *Byron the Satirist*, p. 18; Andrew Rutherford, *Byron: A Critical Study* (Edinburgh: Oliver and Boyd, 1962), p. 15; Willis W. Pratt, *Byron at Southwell: The Making of a Poet with New Poems and Letters from the Rare Books Collection of the University of Texas* (Austin: University of Texas Press, 1948), p. 44. See also Fuess, *Lord Byron as a Satirist in Verse*.

53 For a psychological discussion of Byron's deferred valedictions, see Paul Elledge, 'Chasms in Connections: Byron Ending (in) *Childe Harold's Pilgrimage* 1 and 2', *ELH* 62 (1995), 121–48.

54 These two lines in MS. M are missing from *CPW*. Their presence makes more sense of the following lines which were obviously intended as a crescendo: 'Be these the themes to greet his faithful Rib, / So may thy pen be smooth, thy tongue be glib!' The mention of the Pox was probably the reason for the omission of the lines from *Murray's Magazine*.

55 For the private sexual code of 'old Horatian way', see Louis Crompton, *Byron and Greek Love: Homophobia in 19th-Century England* (London: Faber and Faber, 1985), p. 146.

56 *The Poems of Alexander Pope*, (ed.) John Butt (London and New York: Routledge, 1963; repr. 1989), p. 501.

57 *BLJ*, II, p. 126; *CPW*, I, pp. 454–5.

58 'A Discourse Concerning the Original and Progress of Satire', in *The Essays of John Dryden*, (ed.) W.P. Ker, 2 vols. (New York: Russell and Russell, 1961), II, p. 105. The identification of Hudibrastic rhymes as a flaw in Byron's verse is exemplified by the *Eclectic*'s review of *The Siege of Corinth* (*RR*, B: II, p. 733).

59 *BLJ*, II, p. 20.

60 *BLJ*, I, p. 2.

61 Roger Lonsdale classes him as 'much less of a borrower' when it came to writing poetry. See, *The Poems of Thomas Gray, William Collins, Oliver Goldsmith*, (ed.) Roger Lonsdale (London: Longman, 1969; repr. 1976), p. xvii.

62 For the argument that allusion is a more 'powerful' figure than metaphor, see Michael Riffaterre, 'Compulsory Reader Response: The Intertextual Drive' in Michael Worton and Judith Still (eds.), *Intertextuality: Theories and Practices* (Manchester University Press, 1990), pp. 57–76. Riffaterre argues that the text controls closely the reader's response but that the 'lure' of transgressing the distance between the two texts of intertextuality offers the reader 'an enormous return for a modest investment' (p. 72). He identifies the 'lexical Janus' which holds the distance between the two texts by the figure of 'syllepsis': a word which has two mutually incompatible meanings (one in the context and the other in the intertext). It is this paradoxical force, according to Riffaterre, which allows allusion to outweigh metaphor. Metaphor cannot generate an equal dynamic of incongruity as it relies on something being in common to both tenor and vehicle (p. 71).

63 Jonathan Bate, *Shakespeare and the English Romantic Imagination* (Oxford: Clarendon Press, 1986), pp. 30; 33–4; 75. Bate discusses the currency of Shakespearean allusion in the visual arts in 'Shakespearean Allusion in English Caricature in the Age of Gillray', *Journal of the Warburg and Courtauld Institutes* 49 (1986), 196–210.

64 *The Dramatic Works of Richard Brinsley Sheridan*, (ed.) Cecil Price, 2 vols. (Oxford: Clarendon Press, 1973), II, p. 723, ll. 17–19.

65 See 'On Some of the Old Actors', in *The Works of Charles and Mary Lamb*, (ed.) E.V. Lucas, 7 vols. (London: Methuen, 1903–5), II, p. 140.

66 *BLJ*, II, p. 210.

67 Third Lord Holland, *Further Memoirs of the Whig Party 1807–21 With Some Miscellaneous Reminiscences* (London: John Murray, 1905), p. 163.

68 Ibid.

69 For the modifications to Byron's 'Address, Spoken at the Opening of Drury-Lane Theatre', see *CPW*, III, pp. 17–21 and notes and Lansdown, *Byron's Historical Dramas*, p. 19.

70 *CPW*, III, pp. 20; 18.

71 Curran has discussed genre as 'the most consistent conceptual syntax informing literature': see *Poetic Form and British Romanticism*, p. 4. See also Alastair Fowler, *Kinds of Literature: An Introduction to the Theory of Genres and Modes* (Oxford: Clarendon Press, 1982), pp. 25–31.

72 Thomas De Quincey, *Recollections of the Lakes and the Lake Poets*, (ed.) David Wright (Harmondsworth: Penguin, 1970; repr. 1985), p. 38.

73 *Shelley's Poetry and Prose,* (eds.) Donald H. Reiman and Sharon B. Powers (New York and London: W.W. Norton, 1977), pp. 347–8.

74 William Wordsworth, *The Excursion* (1814); facsimile of 1st edn (Oxford: Woodstock Books, 1991), p. xi.

75 Byron, *Complete Miscellaneous Prose,* p. 109.

76 Prose writers such as Charles Lamb and William Hazlitt did sustain a high frequency of signalled allusion. See George L. Barnett, *Charles Lamb: The Evolution of Elia* (Bloomington: Indiana University Press, 1964), pp. 216–30; Jonathan Bate, 'Hazlitt's Shakespearean Quotations', *Prose Studies* 7 (1984), 26–37; James K. Chandler, 'Romantic Allusiveness', *Critical Inquiry* 8 (1981–2), 461–87.

77 Peter J. Manning, *Reading Romantics: Texts and Contexts* (Oxford University Press, 1990), p. 195. Critical reviews of Byron's time were another discourse loaded with literary allusion.

78 Among the various accounts of different modes of allusion, I have found work by the following critics helpful: Herman Meyer, *The Poetics of Quotation in the European Novel,* (transl.) Theodore and Yelta Ziolkkowski (Princeton University Press, 1968). Meyer locates the 'charm' of the quotation 'in a unique tension between assimilation and dissimilation: it links itself closely with its new environment, but at the same time detaches itself from it, thus permitting another world to radiate into the self-contained world of the novel' (p. 6). Meyer's comments on the difference between the parodies of Immermann and Hoffmann are also highly suggestive: 'we sense that the quotation is dragged in much more at random and that, very much in contrast to Hoffmann, it accomplishes little or nothing functionally' (p. 156). This sense of disturbing arbitrary use of quotation is very close to my reading of *English Bards and Scotch Reviewers.* See also Carmela Perri, 'On Alluding', *Poetics* 7 (1978), 289–307. Perri builds on Meyer's work to offer a list of conventions used in literary allusion, stressing that the source text must be 'some discrete, recoverable property'. Although this idea is not developed in the article, the physicality of the other text is an important feature of Byron's digressive allusion. See also Lucy Newlyn, *'Paradise Lost' and the Romantic Reader* (Oxford: Clarendon Press, 1993). Newlyn's work on allusion as a focus for indeterminacy, qualifying the stability of the source text (in this case, *Paradise Lost*) has contributed to my understanding of the way allusion invites choice on the part of the reader, although the Romantic allusions discussed by Newlyn uncover an indeterminacy she believes to be already present in Milton's text rather than setting up a tension between source and new context.

79 For a discussion of Byron's satire, particularly its affinity with Gifford's criticism, see Mary Clearman, 'A Blueprint for *English Bards and Scotch Reviewers*: The First Satire of Juvenal', *Keats-Shelley Journal* 19 (1970), 87–99.

80 Fuess traces the allusive history of these lines from Young on Pope to Canning, Hodgson, and Byron on Gifford (*Lord Byron as a Satirist in Verse,* pp. 53–4).

81 Manning, *Reading Romantics*, p. 135.
82 Roland Barthes, *Roland Barthes* cited in Worton and Still, *Intertextuality*, p. 114.
83 Harold Bloom, *The Anxiety of Influence: A Theory of Poetry* (Oxford University Press, 1973; repr. 1975).
84 Harold Bloom, *The Visionary Company: A Reading of English Romantic Poetry* (Ithaca: Cornell University Press, 1971; repr. 1983), pp. 258; 260.
85 Bate, *Shakespeare and the English Romantic Imagination*, p. 4.
86 Bloom, *The Anxiety of Influence*, p. 15.

3 ERRING WITH POPE: *HINTS FROM HORACE* AND THE TROUBLE WITH DECENCY

1 For the eighteenth-century criticism of English mixed or monstrous genres, see Stuart M. Tave, *The Amiable Humorist, A Study on the Comic Theory and Criticism of the Eighteenth and Early Nineteenth Centuries* (Chicago and London: University of Chicago Press, 1960), pp. 182–5.
2 Alan B. Howes (ed.), *Sterne: The Critical Heritage* (London and New York: Routledge, 1974), p. 382.
3 Ibid., p. 40.
4 Michel de Montaigne, *The Complete Essays*, (ed. and transl.) M.A. Screech (Harmondsworth: Penguin, 1991; repr. 1993), p. 206.
5 *Horace on Poetry: The Ars Poetica*, (ed.) C.O. Brink (Cambridge University Press, 1971).
6 *RR*, B: III, p. 1246.
7 Reynolds, *Discourses*, p. 96.
8 Hazlitt, *Complete Works*, VIII, p. 31.
9 Graham, *Byron's Bulldog*, p. 133.
10 Bernard Blackstone, *Byron: A Survey* (London: Longman, 1975), pp. 54–6. See also Beaty, *Byron the Satirist*, pp. 51–9 and Mary Rebecca Thayer, *The Influence of Horace on the Chief English Poets of the Nineteenth Century* (New Haven and London: Yale University Press, 1916).
11 See, *BLJ*, II, pp. 42; 43; 45; 112.
12 For a discussion of imitations and allusions to Horace, see Jane Stabler, 'The Genesis of Byron's *Hints from Horace*', *Translation and Literature* 3 (1994), 47–65.
13 Thayer, *The Influence of Horace*, p. 39.
14 Mikhail Bakhtin characterises Horatian satirical and epistolary genres as 'novelistic' discourse but also links Horace with Aristotle and Boileau as the main advocates of 'organic poetics', writers who were 'permeated with a deep sense of the wholeness of literature and of the harmonious interaction of all genres contained within this whole. It is as if they literally hear this harmony of the genres' (*The Dialogic Imagination: Four Essays by M.M. Bakhtin*, (ed.) Michael Holquist, (transl.) Caryl Emerson and Michael Holquist (Austin: University of Texas Press, 1981), p. 5).
15 Here, I disagree with McGann's view of the poem's form as 'the perfection of modesty' and his claim that in the *Hints*, Byron '[effaces] himself' (McGann, *Don Juan in Context*, pp. 16–17).

16 Anne Barton, *Byron, Don Juan*, Landmarks of World Literature Series (Cambridge University Press, 1992), p. 79.

17 In *Childe Harold's Pilgrimage* canto III, references to the act of reading are frequent because of the poem's central concern with ruin and inscription, but see the note to stanza 91 on 'the difference between what we read of the emotions then and there produced, and those we ourselves experience in the perusal in the closet. It is one thing to read the *Iliad* at Sigaeum . . . and another to trim your taper over it in a snug library – *this* I know' (*CPW*, II, p. 310).

18 Lovelace Deposit 158, fol. 176; second epigraph.

19 Hazlitt, *Complete Works*, VIII, p. 32. An interesting discursive link between the *improvisatori* poets and Pope occurs in William Hazlitt's 'On the Past and Future'. Here Hazlitt records the dominance of rhyme over the mind of a performer: 'The rhymes keep running in their head in spite of themselves, and will not let them rest' (Ibid., VIII, p. 30).

20 For a sophisticated discussion of the continuities between Pope and Byron, see Bernard Beatty, 'Continuities and Discontinuities of Language and Voice in Dryden, Pope, and Byron', in Andrew Rutherford (ed.), *Byron: Augustan and Romantic* (London and Basingstoke: Macmillan, 1990), pp. 117–35.

21 *Mac Flecknoe*, ll. 100–1; *BLJ*, VIII, p. 68. I am grateful to an anonymous Cambridge University Press reader for suggesting this point.

22 The long prose note incorporating the '"alacrity of sinking"' of Southey's latest work, a trial of Southey and the *Edinburgh Annual Register* (*CPW*, I, pp. 439–40), was reduced in 1821 as Byron planned *The Vision of Judgement*.

23 *BLJ*, VII, p. 60. A concise account of these exchanges is available in Byron, *Complete Miscellaneous Prose*, pp. 358–60; 393.

24 See Byron's reference to Southey's 'quarterly overflowings political and literary' (Byron, *Complete Miscellaneous Prose*, p. 104).

25 *BLJ*, III, p. 179.

26 MS., John Murray Archive. See *BLJ*, VII, p. 35: 'I think my translation of Pulci will make you stare . . . you will see what was permitted in a Catholic country and a bigotted age to a Churchman on the score of religion.'

27 Hazlitt, *Complete Works*, XII, p. 127.

28 See p. 97 above.

29 *The Works of Beaumont and Fletcher with an Introduction and Explanatory Notes by Henry Weber, Esq.*, 14 vols. (Edinburgh: James Ballantyne & Co. , 1812), X, p. 133.

30 Ibid., I, pp. lxxxv-lxxxvi.

31 Murray shared Byron's reservations about Hobhouse's political affiliations. In a letter of 16 November 1819 (discussing *Don Juan* cantos III and IV), Murray had written: 'There is apprehension of Revolution I assure you – Reforms of various kinds we ought & must have – & Ministers can not stand more in their own light than by opposing themselves to the March of the Intellect – the progress of Society. – Hobhouse will make nothing of his politics I am afraid' (MS., John Murray Archive).

32 Letter of 21 April 1820; Graham, *Byron's Bulldog*, p. 290.

33 Hobhouse's journal in the Broughton Papers. BL Add. Ms. 56546, 106v.
34 MS. letter from Kinnaird to Byron (1820); John Murray Archive.
35 For the presence of the Italian Revolution in Byron's dramatic writing as a form of historical self-consciousness, see Lansdown, *Byron's Historical Dramas*, pp. 42–77.
36 Cronin, *In Search of the Pure Commonwealth*, p. 161.
37 See *CPW*, IV, pp. 165–7.
38 For recent analysis of the Pope/Bowles controversy, especially its impact on the constructions of Romanticism and nationalism, see James K. Chandler, 'The Pope Controversy: Romantic Poetics and the English Canon', *Critical Inquiry* 10 (1984), 481–509 and Robert J. Griffin, *Wordsworth's Pope: A Study in Literary Historiography* (Cambridge University Press, 1995).
39 Smiles, *A Publisher and His Friends*, I, p. 420.
40 MS., John Murray Archive. Another complicating factor was that Keats's death led Byron to instruct Murray to 'omit *all* that is said *about him* in any M.S.S. of mine – or publication' (*BLJ*, VIII, p. 163).
41 Gifford also began to express reservations about the continuation of the Pope/Bowles controversy. On 11 May 1821 Murray wrote to Byron to acknowledge safe receipt of

> the Second Letter on Pope – which I immediately sent to Mr. Gifford – upon whom I called this morning and he told me he thought it very interesting & exceedingly clever – there were parts certainly wch could not be published, but he desired me to get it set up instantly in print & then he would go over it with great care & give your Lordship his opinion. (MS., John Murray Archive)

> Gifford wrote his response to Murray from Pimlico on 26 May. On 29 May 1821, Murray extracted a passage in a letter to Byron:

> I have added a Copy of the Second Letter with Mr Giffords remarks – he says 'I hope however Lord B will not continue to squander himself away thus – when will he resume his majestic march, & shake the earth again.' (MS., John Murray Archive)

> The fuller context of Gifford's remarks are as follows:

> I send Lord B. with a good deal cut out – but it will be unsafe to publish it – a little more may yet be spared, but that he will probably see himself. The <letter> matter is not very refined, but it is vigorous & to the purpose. Bowles requires checking. I hope however Lord B. will not continue to squander himself away thus. (MS., John Murray Archive)

42 The *Hints* were eventually caught up in the row between Byron, Murray and John Hunt over the publication of *The Vision of Judgement*. The *Hints* were sent to Hunt, but 'Slips of Letters to Pope, Blackwoods &c' were 'mislaid' (Murray to Byron, 25 September 1822; MS., John Murray Archive).
43 Upali Amarasinghe, *Dryden and Pope in the Early Nineteenth Century; A Study of Changing Literary Taste, 1800–1830* (Cambridge University Press, 1962).
44 See Byron, *Complete Miscellaneous Prose*, p. 360 for the printer's query on the 1820 proofs about incorporating 'all that relates to Pope' from the Letter to Blackwood 'as a Note [at?] the first place where Pope is mentioned'.

45 William Crowe, *A Treatise on English Versification* (London, 1827), p. 164.
46 Samuel Taylor Coleridge, *Biographia Literaria; or, Biographical Sketches of My Literary Life and Opinions*, (eds.) James Engell and W. Jackson Bate, 2 vols. (London: Routledge and New York, 1983), II, p. 107; *The Letters of William and Dorothy Wordsworth*, (ed.) Ernest De Selincourt, 2nd edn, *The Middle Years, 1812–1820*, (rev.) Mary Moorman and Alan G. Hill (Oxford University Press, 1970), III. 2, p. 385.
47 Letter of 1 May 1821; MS., John Murray Archive.
48 Graham argues that Byron 'makes [the Horatian matter] peculiarly English, and peculiarly his own, by pinning a particular British identity (that of his publisher) on his reader, casting the matter in terms of English literature, and transforming the translation' (*Don Juan and Regency England*, p. 147).
49 *BLJ*, IX, p. 54.
50 Hugh J. Luke, Jr, 'The Publishing of Byron's *Don Juan*', *PMLA* 80 (1965), 199–209; p. 206.
51 *RR*, B: I, p. 165.
52 Ibid., p. 461.
53 Byron, *Complete Miscellaneous Prose*, p. 117.
54 *BLJ*, II, p. 90.
55 *BLJ*, VIII, pp. 200; 203.
56 Byron, *Complete Miscellaneous Prose*, p. 170.
57 Ibid., p. 169.
58 *Henry Crabb Robinson on Books and Their Writers 1775–1867*, (ed.) Edith J. Morley, 3 vols. (London: J.M. Dent, 1938), III, p. 415; Lovell, *Lady Blessington's Conversations of Lord Byron*, p. 203.
59 Byron, *Complete Miscellaneous Prose*, pp. 146–57.
60 'Concluding Observations on the Poetic Character of Pope'; quoted in Jacob Johan Van Rennes, *Bowles, Byron and the Pope-Controversy* (New York: Haskell House, 1966), p. 34.
61 Byron, *Complete Miscellaneous Prose*, pp. 130–1.
62 *Joseph Andrews*, (ed.) R.F. Brissenden (Harmondsworth: Penguin, 1977; repr. 1984), pp. 99–100.
63 Rev. William Bowles, 'Two Letters to the Right Honourable Lord Byron in answer to his Lordship's letter . . .' in *The Pamphleteer* 35 (1821), 330–53; p. 334.
64 See also Byron's anecdote about Johnson, Garrick and the samphire gatherer in *King Lear* in which he seizes on the interruption of human activity: 'I am speaking of a description in which nothing is introduced from life to break the effect' (Byron, *Complete Miscellaneous Prose*, p. 138).
65 Roland Barthes, *The Pleasure of the Text*, (transl.) Richard Miller (Oxford: Basil Blackwell, 1990), p. 10.
66 Byron, *Complete Miscellaneous Prose*, p. 134; Pope, *An Essay on Man*, I, l. 6.
67 Reynolds, *Discourses*, p. 192.
68 Barthes, *The Pleasure of the Text*, p. 14.

4 UNCERTAIN BLISSES: *DON JUAN*, DIGRESSIVE INTERTEXTUALITY AND THE RISKS OF RECEPTION

1 Andrew Rutherford (ed.), *Byron: The Critical Heritage* (New York: Barnes and Noble, 1970), p. 275.

2 Wilfred S. Dowden (ed.), *The Journal of Thomas Moore*, 6 vols. (Newark: University of Delaware Press, 1983–91), II, p. 443.

3 For the history of the quotation mark in English printing, see M.B. Parkes, *Pause and Effect: An Introduction to the History of Punctuation in the West* (Aldershot: Scolar Press, 1992).

4 Newlyn *'Paradise Lost' and the Romantic Reader*, pp. 31–2.

5 De Selincourt (ed.), *The Letters of William and Dorothy Wordsworth*, p. 385.

6 William Wordsworth, *The Prelude*: 1799, 1805, 1850, (eds.) Jonathan Wordsworth, M.H. Abrams and Stephen Gill (New York and London: W.W. Norton, 1979), III, ll. 276–82 (1805).

7 Elizabeth Barrett Browning, *Her Novel in Verse, Aurora Leigh and Other Poems*, (introd.) Cora Kaplan (London: The Women's Press, 1978; repr. 1993), I, ll. 705–7.

8 G. Wilson Knight, *Byron and Shakespeare* (New York: Barnes and Noble, 1966), p. 257.

9 Bate, *Shakespeare and the English Romantic Imagination*, p. 242.

10 Peter Manning, *Byron and his Fictions*, (Detroit: Wayne State University Press, 1978), p. 201. John Hollander, *The Figure of Echo: A Mode of Allusion in Milton and After* (Berkeley: University of California Press, 1981), p. 95. See also Chandler, 'Romantic Allusiveness', 461–87.

11 Bate, *Shakespeare and the English Romantic Imagination*, p. 243.

12 Ibid., p. 246.

13 Ibid., p. 240.

14 Anne Barton, '*Don Juan* Transformed', in Rutherford (ed.), *Byron: Augustan and Romantic*, pp. 199–220; p. 214.

15 *CPW*, v, p. 717; Barton, *Byron*: Don Juan, p. 55.

16 Truman Guy Steffan and W.W. Pratt (eds.), *Byron's Don Juan: A Variorum Edition*, 4 vols. (Austin and London: University of Texas Press, 1957; rev. edn, 1971), I, p. 219.

17 Ibid.

18 Barthes, *The Pleasure of the Text*, p. 32.

19 Barton, '*Don Juan* Transformed', pp. 216–17.

20 Ernest J. Lovell, Jr, (ed.), *Medwin's Conversations of Lord Byron* (Princeton University Press, 1966), p. 132.

21 See Wolfson, '"Their She Condition"', pp. 585–617.

22 Ibid., p. 591.

23 See *Othello* III. 3. ll. 353–4; III. 3. l. 453; v. 2. ll. 145–6.

24 Lovell, *Medwin's Conversations*, p. 134.

25 For the newspaper defences of Caroline as 'driven snow' in 1820, see *CPW*, v, p. 722. The 'driven snow' image recalls (ironically) Hermione in *The Winter's Tale*.

26 Trelawny was to play Othello and Mary Shelley Desdemona. See Ernest J. Lovell, Jr (ed.), *His Very Self and Voice: Collected Conversations of Lord Byron* (London and Basingstoke: Macmillan, 1954), p. 282 and *The Journals of Mary Shelley 1814–1844*, (eds.) Paula R. Feldman and Diana Scott-Kilvert (Baltimore and London: Johns Hopkins University Press, 1987; repr. 1995), p. 398.

27 Perri, 'On Alluding', pp. 289–307.

28 See Tim Fulford, 'Coleridge and the Royal Family: The Politics of Androgyny', in *Coleridge's Visionary Languages*, (eds.) Tim Fulford and Morton D. Paley (Cambridge: Brewer, 1993), pp. 67–82; pp. 68–9.

29 For a defence of Caroline that hinges on 'odd instances of strange coincidence', see *CPW*, v, p. 722.

30 For an opposing view of seduction as a dissolution of identity and difference in *Don Juan*' see Charles Eric Reeves, 'Continual Seduction: The Reading of *Don Juan*', *Studies in Romanticism* 17 (1978), 453–63.

31 Lovell, *Medwin's Conversations*, p. 134.

32 See Anthony Giddens, *The Consequences of Modernity* (Stanford University Press, 1990); another crucial result of modernity, according to Giddens, is 'the transformation of intimacy' which could also be explored through Byron's relationship with his female readers. See Anthony Giddens, *The Transformation of Intimacy: Sexuality, Love and Eroticism in Modern Societies* (Cambridge: Polity Press, 1992).

33 See Robert F. Gleckner, 'Gambling and Byron's Poetics', *Nineteenth-Century Studies* 1 (1987), 1–11.

34 Peter Cochran, 'Byron and Castelnau's *History of New Russia*', *The Keats-Shelley Review* 8 (1993–4), 48–70; p. 61. See also Manning, *Byron and His Fictions*, pp. 207–10.

35 Michael G. Cooke discusses the ambivalence of Byron's '– or –' constructions in *The Blind Man Traces the Circle: On the Patterns and Philosophy of Byron's Poetry* (Princeton University Press, 1969), p. 12.

36 W.H. Auden, *The Dyer's Hand and Other Essays* (London: Faber and Faber, 1963; repr. 1975), p. 274

37 *Galignani's Messenger*, no. 2309. For more detailed discussion of this newspaper, see Chapter Five.

38 Lovell, *Lady Blessington's Conversations of Lord Byron*, p. 204.

39 Unexpectedly we can see a similar treatment of scale in relation to chance in the writing of Mary Wollstonecraft. Her scathing attacks on the massive injustice of the arbitrary power of the monarchy or the 'hazard' of the criminal justice system contrasted with her loving remonstrance of Godwin's fallible 'chance-medley' system of contraception. See Mary Wollstonecraft, *Political Writings*, (ed.) Janet Todd (Harmondsworth: Penguin, 1994), p. 15; Mary Wollstonecraft, *A Short Residence in Sweden*, (ed.) Richard Holmes (Harmondsworth: Penguin, 1987), p. 168; Claire Tomalin, *The Life and Death of Mary Wollstonecraft* (Harmondsworth: Penguin, 1974; repr. 1992), p. 265.

40 See Bernard Beatty, 'Byron and the Paradoxes of Nationalism', in Vincent Newey and Ann Thompson (eds.), *Literature and Nationalism* (Liverpool University Press, 1991), pp. 152–62; p. 154.

41 See David Fairer's discussion of slime as a fleshly condition, the opposite of divine imaginative creativity, in *Pope's Imagination* (Manchester University Press, 1984), pp. 118–52.

42 *BLJ*, VII, p. 124.

43 *Shelley's Poetry and Prose* (eds.) Reiman and Powers, p. 421.

44 Minutes of Proceedings in the Westminster Election 1818. BL Add. Mss. 27845. 88v.

45 Virginia Woolf, *To the Lighthouse* (London: Collins, 1977; repr. 1988), pp. 120; 123; 124.

46 The importance of uncertainty in relation to a sense of stability in *Don Juan* is illuminated in Michael G. Cooke, 'Byron's *Don Juan*: The Obsession and Self-Discipline of Spontaneity', *Studies in Romanticism* 14 (1975), 285–302. See also the comparison between Byron and Shelley in John Watkins, 'Byron and the Phenomenology of Negation', *Studies in Romanticism* 29 (1990), 395–411.

5 'THE WORST OF SINNING': *DON JUAN*, MORAL ENGLAND AND FEMININE CAPRICE

1 Claude Rawson suggests that Byron's use of '"Gazette" carries reverberations of Scriblerian scorn of journalists' (Rawson, *Satire and Sentiment*, p. 121).

2 Garber discovers a 'play of semblance' in the harem cantos 'with the nature of language' which continues in the preface to cantos VI, VII and VIII (*Self, Text, and Romantic Irony*, pp. 269–71).

3 This source is noted, but not discussed in Carl Woodring, *Politics in English Romantic Poetry* (Cambridge, Mass.: Harvard University Press, 1970), p. 206.

4 *BLJ*, IX, p. 74. For ironic references to the paper's 'impartiality', see *BLJ*, IX, pp. 117; 170.

5 For Byron's frustration at 'irregularities' in the delivery of the paper, see *BLJ*, XIII, p. 56.

6 McGann supposes that 'Byron seems to have read the account in *Cobbett's Register*' (*CPW*, V, p. 719), but the quotation he supplies is not as close to Byron's preface as the *Galignani* report.

7 That Byron is out of date is the view in, for example, E.D.H. Johnson's dissertation, 'Lord Byron in *Don Juan*' (especially Chapter Five) and Graham's study, *Don Juan and Regency England*. See also, Leslie A. Marchand, 'Narrator and Narration in *Don Juan*', *Keats-Shelley Journal* 25 (1976), 26–42; pp. 36; 39.

8 Elizabeth French Boyd, *Byron's 'Don Juan'*, (London and New York: Routledge, 1945), p. 152.

9 The *British Critic* chose to depict Byron's topicality as a sign that he was out of touch with English taste. The reviewer sought to warn him 'that "in the

lowest deep there is a lower deep," and that certain allusions still pass for very scurvy jests in England, to say the least of them. We do not choose to quote, but shall only remark that the note to the preface is repeated in the 8th canto' (*RR*, B: I, p. 336). Byron's 'allusion' was to the Bishop of Clogher. Appeals by Byron for more news than he could find in *Galignani's* may be found in his letters, see *BLJ*, VI, p. 233 and *BLJ*, VII, p. 131.

10 Kelsall, *Byron's Politics*, p. 167.

11 These matters are raised in a sequence of issues of *GM*, see, for example, nos. 1878, 2178, 2196, 2207, 2208, 2216, 2264–77 (March 1821–June 1822).

12 *The Letters of Mary Wollstonecraft Shelley*, (ed.) Betty T. Bennett, 3 vols. (Baltimore and London: Johns Hopkins University Press, 1980–8), I, p. 281.

13 Boyd, *Byron's 'Don Juan'*, pp. 132–5.

14 See, for example, *GM*, nos. 1872, 1970, 2115.

15 For Byron's use of slang, see William St Clair, 'Bamming and Humming', *Byron Journal* 7 (1979), 38–47.

16 Graham argues that 'the imported word "Or Molu" (especially when spelled as Byron chooses to spell it) suggests, as *Ennui* and the many other French words in the English cantos do, two contradictory truths about the Great World and the culture it epitomises ... The weakness of the Great World's argot is its shallow cosmopolitanism, but one strength of English is its being a truly cosmopolitan tongue. So although the Great World's frivolous babble mocks a unity lost, it also suggests ... an integration gained' (*Don Juan and Regency England*, pp. 176–7).

17 For a recent discussion of these lines in relation to Byron's Napoleonism, see Diego Saglia, 'Matrimonial Politics: Two references to Marie Louise of Austria in Byron's Poetry', *Byron Journal* 26 (1998), 112–15.

18 McGann suggests that Byron viewed her as an analogue to his own wife (*CPW*, VII, p. 130).

19 For a list of actual responses by individual female readers, see Haslett, *Byron's Don Juan*, pp. 208–16.

20 Quoted in Theodore Redpath, *The Young Romantics and Critical Opinion 1807–1824* (London: Harrap, 1973) p. 293; *RR*, B: III, p. 1297.

21 See, for example, George M. Ridenour, *The Style of 'Don Juan'*, Yale Studies in English, vol. 144 (New Haven and London: Yale University Press, 1960); Robert F. Gleckner, *Byron and the Ruins of Paradise* (Baltimore and London: Johns Hopkins University Press, 1967); McGann, *Don Juan in Context*, pp. 23–31 and pp. 142–9; Newlyn, *'Paradise Lost' and the Romantic Reader*, pp. 182–91.

22 Peter Conrad, *Shandyism: The Character of Romantic Irony* (Oxford: Basil Blackwell, 1978), p. 57.

23 Ibid., p. 60.

24 Bernard Beatty, *Byron's Don Juan* (Totowa: Barnes and Noble, 1985), pp. 115; 118.

25 See Barton's argument that *Don Juan* 'is itself a type of "mobility" in that the narrator's mercurial involvement with the emotions and events of the

moment never allows him to lose touch with the poem's past, and this is also the way it should be read' (*Byron*: Don Juan, p. 80).

26 See Barton's account of the 'outrageous delaying tactics' in the narrative before Lambro's return. Ibid., pp. 37–40.

27 For a psychoanalytic reading of Byron's treatment of and identification with abandoned women, see Lawrence Lipking, *Abandoned Women and Poetic Tradition* (Chicago and London: University of Chicago Press, 1988), pp. 32–56.

28 Jane Austen, *Pride and Prejudice*, (ed. and introd.) Tony Tanner (Harmondsworth: Penguin, 1972; repr. 1978), p. 375.

29 *CPW*, v, p. 709.

30 In *Galignani's Literary Gazette*, nos. 73–4 (September 1819), an article on 'The Most Important Inventions and Discoveries of our Times' included Sir H. Davy's miners' safety lamp and discussed the way that men of science were 'endeavouring to discover a *perpetuum mobile*'. In *GM*, no. 2137 (3 January 1822), an extract from the *Yorkshire Gazette* described a piece of mechanism which almost produced perpetual motion.

31 See Peter Cochran, 'Mary Shelley's Fair Copying of *Don Juan*', *The Keats – Shelley Review* 10 (1996), 221–41.

32 Caroline Franklin, 'Juan's Sea Changes: Class, Race and Gender in Byron's *Don Juan*', in Nigel Wood (ed.), *Don Juan*, Theory in Practice Series (Buckingham: Open University Press, 1993), p. 75. See also Beatty 'Byron and the Paradoxes of Nationalism', pp. 152–62.

33 Compare with Byron's letter to Augusta of 26 July 1819:

> – the time passes – I am very fond of riding and always *was out* of England – but I hate your Hyde Park – and your turnpike roads – & must have forests – downs – or deserts to expatiate in – I detest *knowing* the road – one is to go, and being interrupted by your damned fingerposts, or a blackguard roaring for twopence at a turnpike. (*BLJ*, vi, p. 186)

The word 'expatiate' relates the pleasures of movement and the pleasure of expansive conversation, but it also suggests that English travel is fraught with interruption.

34 *The Poems and Fables of John Dryden*, (ed.) James Kinsley (Oxford University Press, 1958; repr, 1962).

35 Maria Edgeworth, *Letters for Literary Ladies to which is added an Essay on the Noble Science of Self-Justification*, (ed.) Claire Connolly (London: J.M. Dent, 1993), pp. 51–2. For a helpful discussion of Byron's satirising of Edgeworth in *Don Juan* canto I, see Franklin, *Byron's Heroines*, p. 122.

36 The same effect can be experienced in the prose notes and satirical interruptions to *Childe Harold's Pilgrimage* cantos I and II where Byron questions the morality of, for example, the treatment of 'our Irish Helots' (*CPW*, II, p. 211).

37 *Poems of Alexander Pope*, *The Rape of the Lock*, II, ll. 105–6.

38 Madame de Staël-Holstein, *The Influence of Literature Upon Society, Translated from the French of Madame de Staël-Holstein*, 2nd edn, 2 vols. (London: Henry Colburn, 1812), II, p. 174.

39 It is also the image Byron used in letters to describe the separation scandal of 1816, see *BLJ*, VII, p. 42.

40 For Byron's use of French to make a moral point about English spiritual apathy, see Manning, *Byron and His Fictions*, pp. 238–9.

41 Franklin, *Byron's Heroines*, p. 117.

42 Galperin provides an interesting Kristevan reading of this episode in canto IV in *The Return of the Visible*, pp. 262–70.

43 The allusive links between the marriage of the Amundevilles and the meditations of the narrator in *Childe Harold's Pilgrimage* canto III are anticipated in the description of the Norman abbey (XIII. 57–8) where the outlet from the lake 'dash'd into a steep cascade, . . . / until again subsiding / Its shriller echoes – like an infant made / Quiet'.

44 For Byron's creation of himself as 'the driven outsider', see Vincent Newey, 'Authoring the Self: *Childe Harold* III and IV', in Beatty and Newey, *Byron and the Limits of Fiction*, pp. 148–90; p. 157.

45 The unsignalled echo of *Hamlet* juxtaposes the moment which '[gives] us pause' in Hamlet's 'To be, or not to be' soliloquy with the reckless hopelessness of 'their she condition'.

46 William A. Stephenson, 'A Scott Echo in "Don Juan", XIII, 37–38', *Notes and Queries* 220 (1975), 394; *CPW*, v, p. 756; Amanda Gilroy, 'Lord Byron Borrows a Figure', *Byron Journal* 20 (1992), 89–91. For a different contextualisation of the image, see Gerald C. Wood, 'The Metaphor of the Climates and *Don Juan*', *Byron Journal* 6 (1978), 16–25.

47 *GM*, no. 1926 (27 April 1821), for example, carried a report of Hobhouse's speech on parliamentary reform and an attack on his 'piebald patchwork of rhetoric'.

48 *RR*, B: v, pp. 2048–55; p. 2050.

49 We can be almost certain that Byron read the *Galignani's* account because Hobhouse was staying with him in Pisa at the time and Hobhouse's journal for 19 September 1822 records: 'read a speech of Canning's in Galignani's Messenger – he cried at taking leave of his Liverpool friends – we shall see if he has taken leave – wrote journal – went out riding with Byron' (BL. Add. Ms. 56546, 112v).

50 Stephenson, 'A Scott Echo', p. 394.

51 *The Letters of Sir Walter Scott*, (ed.) H.J.C. Grierson, 12 vols. (London: Constable, 1932–7), VII, p. 233.

52 Bloom, *The Visionary Company*, p. 270.

6 'BETWEEN CARELESSNESS AND TROUBLE': BYRON'S LAST DIGRESSIONS

1 *CPW*, VII, pp. 117; 130.

2 For the relationship between this drama and *Don Juan*, see Anne Barton, '*Don Juan* Transformed', pp. 199–220.

3 Warton summarised Pope's achievement as follows: 'He is never above or below his subject. Whatever poetical enthusiasm he actually possessed, he

with-held and suppressed ... Hence he is a writer fit for universal perusal, and of general utility; adapted to all ages and stations' (*The Works of Alexander Pope*, (ed.) Joseph Warton , 9 vols. (London, 1797), I, p. lxix.

4 Beaty, *Byron the Satirist*, p. 176.

5 Letter of 11 November 1822; Luther A. Brewer, *My Leigh Hunt Library: The Holograph Letters* (Iowa City: University of Iowa Press, 1938), p. 122.

6 *BLJ*, x, p. 81.

7 Wordsworth, *Poetical Works*, (ed.) Ernest De Selincourt (Oxford and New York: Oxford University Press, 1936; repr. 1985), p. 745.

8 Leigh Hunt, *The Autobiography of Leigh Hunt; with Reminiscences of Friends and Contemporaries*, 3 vols. (London: Smith, Elder and Co., 1850), II, p. 171.

9 *BLJ*, VIII, p. 12.

10 Byron, *Complete Miscellaneous Prose*, p. 156. See also *BLJ*, VI, p. 46.

11 Hunt, *Autobiography*, II, p. 170.

12 Ibid., II, p. 171; *BLJ*, IV, p. 326.

13 See Chandler, 'The Pope Controversy', pp. 481–509.

14 *Examiner*, 20 August 1815, p. 542.

15 Amarasinghe, *Dryden and Pope in the Early Nineteenth Century*, p. 168; Hunt, *Autobiography*, II, p. 163.

16 Rollins (ed.), *The Letters of John Keats*, II, p. 67; I, p. 281. After Keats's early fashionable criticism of Pope he later showed a more creative response to Pope's images for being 'in a mist': see, for example, II, p. 14 where Keats borrows 'What is this absorbs me quite' from 'The Dying Christian to His Soul'.

17 See *Examiner*, 1 June and 13 July 1817.

18 For a detailed discussion of Pope's Whig allegiance, see J.A. Downie, '1688: Pope and the Rhetoric of Jacobitism', in David Fairer (ed.), *Pope. New Contexts* (Hemel Hempstead: Harvester Wheatsheaf, 1990), pp. 9–24.

19 Corrected on 26 March 1815.

20 Byron [with P.B. Shelley and Leigh Hunt], *The Liberal: Prose and Verse form the South*, 2 vols. (London: John Hunt, 1822–3), I, p. viii.

21 Ibid., II, pp. v; 125–8.

22 Byron, *Complete Miscellaneous Prose*, p. 162.

23 Ibid., pp. 128; 144; 151; 172.

24 *BLJ*, v, p. 265; VII, p. 63; Byron, *Complete Miscellaneous Prose*, p. 158.

25 For Pope's efforts to associate the style of his writing with masculinity, see Weinbrot, *Alexander Pope*, pp. 143–5 and Christa Knellwolf, *A Contradiction Still: Representations of Women in the Poetry of Alexander Pope* (Manchester University Press, 1988), pp. 33–5.

26 *BLJ*, x, pp. 83; 89.

27 Ibid., p. 28.

28 Ibid., p. 90.

29 Brewer, *My Leigh Hunt Library*, p. 127.

30 Letter of 19 April 1823: MS., John Murray Archive.

31 Letter of 21 March 1823: MS., John Murray Archive.

32 William Keach, 'Cockney Couplets: Keats and the Politics of Style', *Studies in Romanticism* 25 (1986), 182–96; p. 184.

33 Woodring, *Politics in English Romantic Poetry*, pp. 154; 164–5.

34 *BLJ*, VII, p. 121.

35 See Byron's earlier praise for Matthew Prior's independence: 'never trust entirely to Authorship . . . a truly constituted mind will ever be independent' (*BLJ*, II, p. 179). See also Tom Moore's exhortation to Byron regarding *The Liberal*, *'you must stand alone'* (*The Letters of Thomas Moore*, (ed.) Wilfred S. Dowden, 2 vols. (Oxford Clarendon Press, 1964), II, p. 502).

36 Malcolm Kelsall, 'Totemism and Totalitarianism: Pope, Byron and the Hanoverian Monarchy', *Forum* 30 (1994), 328–40; p. 339.

37 *BLJ*, x, p. 90. The preface dedicated this poem to Moore in 1814, celebrating the 'good old and now neglected heroic couplet' (*CPW*, III, p. 149). Byron used a quotation from Pope in a letter to Moore of 2 April 1823 as an oblique rebuke to Moore for his conciliatory attitude to orthodox 'bigots' (*BLJ*, x, p. 137).

38 Manning, *Reading Romantics*, pp. 195–207.

39 Wolfson, *Formal Charges*, pp. 134; 278; 141.

40 Cronin, *In Search of the Pure Commonwealth*, pp. 160–2.

41 Byron, *Complete Miscellaneous Prose*, pp. 159–60.

42 *BLJ*, XI, p. 147.

43 The poem is in couplets, ending, 'A cut that will conclude his capers / Good honest Murray, give us up the papers': MS., John Murray Archive.

44 MS., John Murray Archive.

45 When Hobhouse visited Byron in Pisa in 1822 he recorded in his journal: 'Lord Byron considered Leigh Hunt as a legacy left to him. L.H. induced Lord B. to agree to set up a journal with him but I endeavoured to persuade Lrd B. that he had better not engage in any such partnership and it appears that Lord B. has managed to give up the scheme' (BL Add. Ms. 56546, 106v).

46 Letter of 2 November 1823: MS., John Murray Archive.

47 *Elizabeth, Lady Holland to her Son 1821–1845*, (ed.) The Earl of Ilchester (London: John Murray, 1946), p. 20. Her lack of enthusiasm follows her reading of Byron's *Memoirs* (courtesy of Tom Moore): Byron thought the fact that Moore had shown them to her 'somewhat perilous' (*BLJ*, VIII, p. 164). Hobhouse had also suggested to Byron in 1821 that he should publish less: 'Take Doctor's advice – let your readers get up from you with an appetite – This is right with the best works and of course more right where there is any doubt as to the nature of the performance' (Graham, *Byron's Bulldog*, p. 314).

48 Leslie Mitchell, *Holland House* (London: Duckworth, 1980), p. 191. The Holland House preference for these writers was one reason why Byron's early satiric portrait of a quasi Grub-street assembling under their roof was such an embarrassment to both parties.

49 Beaty suggests that *The Age of Bronze* is produced as though 'to recapture some of the lost popularity of *Childe Harold's Pilgrimage'* (*Byron the Satirist*,

p. 176). Rather than an attempt to restore the years of fame, I think the poem is a conscious testing of changed audience relations.

50 Kelsall, *Byron's Politics*, p. 192.

51 *BLJ*, x, pp. 48; 57.

52 Byron maintained that there was a crucial difference in manners between those who inherited their titles and those who were 'promoted'. See *BLJ*, VII, p. 200.

53 *BLJ*, x, p. 77.

54 Mary Shelley referred to the scandal in a letter to Byron of 27 November 1822, see Shelley, *Letters*, I, p. 293.

55 See Marchand's note in *BLJ*, x, p. 119.

56 *BLJ*, x, pp. 125; 129.

57 See William H. Marshall, *Byron, Shelley, Hunt and* The Liberal (Philadelphia: University of Pennsylvania Press, 1960), pp. 164–9.

58 Brewer, *My Leigh Hunt Library*, p. 122.

59 *BLJ*, x, pp. 36; 52.

60 Ibid., pp. 57; 72; 88; 116–17.

61 Letter to Byron of 8 October 1819: MS., John Murray Archive.

62 BL Add. Ms. 27845, 8 r, Westminster Election 1818 Minutes of Proceedings.

63 MS., John Murray Archive. See *BLJ*, VI, p. 217.

64 MS., John Murray Archive.

65 Graham, *Byron's Bulldog*, pp. 276; 286,

66 Ibid., pp. 276–7.

67 Ibid., pp. 286–7.

68 *BLJ*, VII, p. 44.

69 *BLJ*, XI, p. 75.

70 *BLJ*, x, p. 116.

71 BL Add. Ms. 56546, 109 v.

72 *BLJ*, x, p. 117.

73 See ll. 3–4 and *Don Juan* XII. 89. Byron's use of couplets in verse paragraphs is closest to Pope's technique in *The Dunciad*. After the second verse paragraph which contains several instances of run-on couplets, instances of enjambement occur infrequently. There is however, an increasing tendency to use feminine para-rhymes as the poem progresses: faltering foe / flake of snow (ll. 187–8); laws are pure / no manure (ll. 470–1); milk and honey /ready money (ll. 672–3), culminating in harm in / 'Carmen' (ll. 779–80).

74 Lecture II on Architecture, 4 November 1853 (Ruskin, *Works*, XII, pp. 55–6).

75 Reuben A. Brower, *Alexander Pope: The Poetry of Allusion* (Oxford University Press, 1959; repr. 1968), p. 254.

76 For further discussion of this topic, see Michael Scrivener, '"Zion Alone is Forbidden": Historicizing Anti-Semitism in Byron's *The Age of Bronze*', *Keats-Shelley Journal* 43 (1994), 75–116.

77 Nina Diakonova, '*The Age of Bronze* and the Traditions of Classicism', *Keats-Shelley Journal* 41 (1992), 49–58; p. 56.

78 For readings of Pope which focus on his lack of Hegelian resolution, see David Fairer, 'Pope, Blake, Heraclitus and Oppositional Thinking' in Fairer (ed.), *Pope. New Contexts*, pp. 169–88; Hunter, 'Form as Meaning', pp. 147–62.

79 See Bernard Beatty's discussion in 'Continuities and Discontinuities of Language and Voice in Dryden, Pope, and Byron', in Rutherford, *Byron: Augustan and Romantic*, pp. 117–35; p. 131.

80 In this respect I disagree with Diakonova's argument that the allusions of the poem are deployed so that concrete events may be 'generalized, sublimated and, as it were, eternalized', see '*The Age of Bronze* and the Traditions of Classicism', p. 53.

81 See Weinbrot, *Alexander Pope*, p. 364; Brower, *Alexander Pope: The Poetry of Allusion*, p. 345; Geoffrey Tillotson, *On the Poetry of Pope* (Oxford: Clarendon Press, 1950), p. 159.

82 Paul M. Curtis, 'The Mystery of Distance: Berkeley and Byron', *Keats-Shelley Journal* 41 (1992), 59–75; p. 72.

83 See Shelley's letter to Byron about the Pope controversy, 4 May 1821: 'I certainly do not think Pope, or *any* writer, a fit model for any succeeding writer; if he, or they should be determined to be so, it would all come to a question as to under *what forms* mediocrity should perpetually reproduce itself' (*The Complete Works of Shelley*, (eds.) Roger Ingpen and Walter E. Peck, 10 vols. (London: Ernest Benn, 1965), x, pp. 265–6).

84 ll. 269. Woodring notes suggestively that 'the couplets rock in antithesis only when fitted to indifferent virtues in the subject' (Woodring, *Politics in English Romantic Poetry*, p. 222).

85 Canning had crossed swords with Hobhouse as described in Chapter Five, but in 1822 Kinnaird approved of his foreign policy.

86 Coleridge, *Biographia Literaria*, i, p. 20.

87 *BLJ*, x, pp. 94; 110.

88 *Elizabeth Barrett to Miss Mitford*, (ed.) Betty Miller (London: John Murray, 1954), p. 16.

89 *CPW*, v, p. 742 notes the influence of Thomas Love Peacock's novels on *Don Juan*, and it is likely that Byron was also aware of Peacock's image of the age of brass for contemporary poetry. Cowper's blank verse is seen to usher in the age of brass by divesting verse of the 'exquisite polish' it had with the silver age of Dryden, Pope, Goldsmith, Collins and Gray (*Peacock's Four Ages of Poetry*, (ed.) H.F.B. Brett-Smith (Oxford: Blackwell, 1972), p. 13).

90 This idea has been explored in relation to colonisation and maternity in Catherine Addison, '"Elysian and Effeminate": Byron's *The Island* as a Revisionary Text', *SEL* 35 (1995), 687–706. James McKusick has argued that the different male heroes are evidence of a 'schizophrenic' form of stylistics and politics which he claims as a utopian 'opening of English poetry to cultural diversity' ('The Politics of Language in Byron's *The Island*', *ELH* 59 (1992), 839–56; (pp. 841; 852). Carl Woodring only considers the three male

heroes and sees the poem as part of Byron's quest for 'a respectable cause' (*Politics in English Romantic Poetry*, p. 226).

91 For Pope's division between misogynist wit and sympathy for particular female friends, see Valerie Rumbold, *Women's Place in Pope's World* (Cambridge University Press, 1989), p. 269.

92 Jerome McGann reads *The Island* as the achievement of paradise in the present moment. This emphasis on an economy of love is, however, subordinated to the birth of the (male) hero: ' By choosing love before everything else, a man is born into a life that has value and meaning, and until he makes that choice he remains unborn' (*Fiery Dust*, p. 198).

93 *RR*, B: IV, pp. 1824; 1827; 1828.

94 Graham, *Byron's Bulldog*, p. 335.

95 The anxious scanning of the horizon for a sail recalls and then revises *The Corsair* 1, l. 502 and 4, l. 483.

96 *RR*, B: IV, p. 1829.

Bibliography

Abrams, M.H., *Natural Supernaturalism: Tradition and Revolution in Romantic Literature* (New York and London: W.W. Norton, 1971)

Addison, Catherine, '"Elysian and Effeminate": Byron's *The Island* as a Revisionary Text', *SEL* 35 (1995), 687–706

Addison, Joseph, *Essays Moral and Humorous, also Essays on Imagination and Taste* (Edinburgh: Chambers, 1839)

Akenside, Mark, *The Pleasures of the Imagination to which is Prefixed a Critical Essay on the Poem by Mrs. Barbauld* (London: T. Cadell Junior & W. Davis, 1794)

Almeida, Hermione de, *Byron and Joyce Through Homer: Don Juan and Ulysses* (London and Basingstoke: Macmillan, 1981)

Amarasinghe, Upali, *Dryden and Pope in the Early Nineteenth Century; A Study of Changing Literary Taste, 1800–1830* (Cambridge University Press, 1962)

Anglicanus, Presbyter, 'Letter to the Author of *Beppo*', *Blackwood's Edinburgh Magazine* 3 (1818), 323–9

Auden, W.H., *The Dyer's Hand and Other Essays* (London: Faber and Faber, 1963; repr. 1975)

Austen, Jane, *Pride and Prejudice*, (ed. and introd.) Tony Tanner (Harmondsworth, Penguin, 1972; repr. 1978)

   Northanger Abbey, (ed.) Anne Henry Ehrenpreis (Harmondsworth: Penguin, 1972; repr. 1988)

Babbitt, Irving, *Rousseau and Romanticism* (Boston and New York: Houghton Mifflin, 1919)

Bakhtin, Mikhail M., *Rabelais and His World*, (transl.) Helene Iswolsky (The Massachusetts Institute of Technology Press, 1968)

   Problems of Dostoevsky's Poetics, (transl.) R.W. Rotsel (Ann Arbor, Mich.: Ardis, 1973)

   The Dialogic Imagination: Four Essays by M.M. Bakhtin, (ed.) Michael Holquist, (transl.) Caryl Emerson and Michael Holquist (Austin: University of Texas Press, 1981)

Baldick, Chris, *In Frankenstein's Shadow: Myth, Monstrosity, and Nineteenth-Century Writing* (Oxford: Clarendon Press, 1987)

Barbauld, Anna Laetitia, *The Works of Anna Laetitia Barbauld with a Memoir by Lucy Aikin*, 2 vols. (London: Longman, 1825)

Barnard, John, (ed.), *Pope: The Critical Heritage* (London and New York: Routledge, 1973)

Barnett, George L., *Charles Lamb: The Evolution of Elia* (Bloomington: Indiana University Press, 1964)

Barrell, John, *The Political Theory of Painting from Reynolds to Hazlitt* (New Haven and London: Yale University Press, 1986)

Barthes, Roland, *The Pleasure of the Text*, (transl.) Richard Miller (Oxford: Basil Blackwell, 1990)

Barton, Anne, *Byron and the Mythology of Fact*, Nottingham Byron Foundation Lecture (Nottingham: Hawthorne, 1968)

  '*Don Juan* Reconsidered: The Haidée Episode', *Byron Journal* 15 (1987), 11–20

  '*Don Juan* Transformed', in Andrew Rutherford (ed.), *Byron: Augustan and Romantic* (London and Basingstoke: Macmillan, 1990), pp. 199–220

  Byron: Don Juan, Landmarks of World Literature Series (Cambridge University Press, 1992)

Bate, Jonathan, 'Hazlitt's Shakespearean Quotations', *Prose Studies* 7 (1984), 26–37

  'Shakespearean Allusion in English Caricature in the Age of Gillray', *Journal of the Warburg and Courtauld Institutes* 49 (1986), 196–210

  Shakespeare and the English Romantic Imagination (Oxford: Clarendon Press, 1986)

  The Romantics on Shakespeare (Harmondsworth: Penguin, 1992)

Bate, Walter Jackson, *From Classic to Romantic: Premises of Taste in Eighteenth-Century England* (New York: Harper and Row, 1961)

Beattie, James, *Essays* (Edinburgh: William Creech, 1776)

Beatty, Bernard, *Byron's* Don Juan (Totowa: Barnes and Noble, 1985)

  'Continuities and Discontinuities of Language and Voice in Dryden, Pope, and Byron', in Andrew Rutherford (ed.), *Byron: Augustan and Romantic* (London and Basingstoke: Macmillan, 1990), pp. 117–35

  'Byron and the Paradoxes of Nationalism', in Vincent Newey and Ann Thompson (eds.), *Literature and Nationalism* (Liverpool University Press, 1991), pp. 152–2

Beatty, Bernard and Vincent Newey (eds.), *Byron and the Limits of Fiction* (Liverpool University Press, 1988)

Beaty, Frederick L., 'Byron's Imitations of Juvenal and Persius', *SEL* 15 (1976), 333–55

  Byron the Satirist (De Kalb: Northern Illinois University Press, 1985)

[Beaumont, Francis,] *The Works of Beaumont and Fletcher with an Introduction and Explanatory Notes by Henry Weber, Esq.*, 14 vols. (Edinburgh: James Ballantyne & Co., 1812)

Behrendt, Stephen C., *Shelley and His Audiences* (Lincoln and London: University of Nebraska Press, 1989)

Benham, Allen R., 'Horace and his *Ars Poetica* in English: A Bibliography', *Classical Weekly* 49 (1955), 1–5

Bennett, Andrew, *Romantic Poets and the Culture of Posterity* (Cambridge University Press, 1999)

Bishop, Elizabeth, *The Complete Poems 1927–1979* (London: The Hogarth Press, 1984)

Black, Joel Dana, 'The Second Fall: The Laws of Digression and Gravitation in Romantic Narrative and their Impact on Contemporary Encyclopaedic Literature' (unpublished doctoral dissertation, Stanford University, 1979)

Blackstone, Bernard, *Byron: A Survey* (London: Longman, 1975)

Blair, Hugh, *Lectures on Rhetoric and Belles Lettres*, 2 vols. (London, 1783)
    'A Critical Dissertation on the Poems of Ossian', in *The Poems of Ossian, Translated by James MacPherson, Containing Dr. Blair's Three Celebrated Critical Dissertations and a Preliminary Discourse or Review of the Recent Controversy Relative to the Authenticity of the Poems*, 2 vols. (London: Lackington and Allen, 1806)

Bloom, Harold, *The Anxiety of Influence: A Theory of Poetry* (Oxford University Press, 1973; repr. 1975)
    The Visionary Company: A Reading of English Romantic Poetry (Ithaca: Cornell University Press, 1971; repr. 1983)

Bohls, Elizabeth A., *Women Travel Writers and the Language of Aesthetics 1716–1818* (Cambridge University Press, 1995)

Bowie, Andrew, *Aesthetics and Subjectivity: From Kant to Nietzsche* (Manchester: Manchester University Press, 1990)

Bowles, Rev. William Lisle, 'Two Letters to the Right Honourable Lord Byron in answer to his Lordship's letter . . .', in *The Pampleteer* 35 (1821), 330–53

Boyd, Elizabeth French, *Byron's 'Don Juan'* (London and New York: Routledge. 1945)

Brewer, Luther A., *My Leigh Hunt Library: The Holograph Letters* (University of Iowa Press, 1938)

Brink, C.O. (ed.), *Horace on Poetry: The Ars Poetica* (Cambridge University Press, 1971)

Brower, Reuben A., *Alexander Pope: The Poetry of Allusion* (Oxford University Press, 1959; repr. 1968)

Browning, Elizabeth Barrett, *The Poetical Works of Elizabeth Barrett Browning* (London: Henry Frowde, 1904)
    Elizabeth Barrett to Miss Mitford, (ed.) Betty Miller (London: John Murray, 1954)
    Her Novel in Verse, Aurora Leigh and Other Poems, (introd.) Cora Kaplan (London: The Women's Press, 1978; repr. 1993)

Burke, Edmund, *A Philosophical Enquiry into the Origin of Our Ideas of the Sublime and Beautiful, With an Introductory Discourse Concerning Taste, and Several Other Additions*, 6th edn (London: J. Dodsley, 1770)
    Reflections on the Revolution in France and on the Proceedings in Certain Societies in London Relative to that Event, (ed.) Conor Cruise O'Brien (Harmondsworth: Penguin, 1968; repr, 1983)
    A Philosophical Enquiry into the Origin of our Ideas of the Sublime and Beautiful, (ed.) Adam Phillips (Oxford University Press, 1990)

Butler, Marilyn, 'The Orientalism of Byron's *Giaour*', in Bernard Beatty and Vincent Newey (eds.), *Byron and the Limits of Fiction* (Liverpool University Press, 1988), pp. 78–96

Byron, George Gordon, Baron, [with P.B. Shelley and Leigh Hunt], *The Liberal: Prose and Verse from the South*, 2 vols. (London: John Hunt, 1822–3)

The Works of Lord Byron: With His Letters and Journals, and His Life, (ed.) Thomas Moore, 17 vols. (London: John Murray, 1832–3)

The Works of Lord Byron. Letters and Journals, (ed.) R.E. Prothero, 5 vols. (London: John Murray, 1898–1901)

The Works of Lord Byron. Poetry, (ed.) Ernest Hartley Coleridge, 7 vols. (London: John Murray, 1898–1904)

Byron's Don Juan: A Variorum Edition, (eds.) Truman Guy Steffan and W.W. Pratt, 4 vols. (Austin and London: University of Texas Press, 1957; rev. edn, 1971)

Byron's Letters and Journals, (ed.) Leslie A. Marchand, 13 vols. (London: John Murray, 1973–94)

The Complete Poetical Works, (ed.) Jerome J. McGann, 7 vols. (Oxford: Clarendon Press, 1980–93)

The Complete Miscellaneous Prose, (ed.) Andrew Nicholson (Oxford: Clarendon Press, 1991)

Calinescu, Matei, *Five Faces of Modernity: Modernism, Avant-Garde, Decadence, Kitsch, Postmodernism*, 4th edn. (Durham, N.C.: Duke University Press, 1993)

Cameron, Kenneth Neill and Donald H. Reiman (eds.), *Shelley and his Circle 1773–1822*, 8 vols. (Cambridge, Mass.: Harvard University Press, 1973–86)

Campbell, George, *The Philosophy of Rhetoric*, 2 vols. (London: W. Strachan & T. Cadell, 1776)

Carlyle, Thomas, *Sartor Resartus: The Life and Opinions of Herr Teufelsdröckh* (London: Chapman and Hall, 1897)

Chalmers, Alexander (ed.), *The Works of the English Poets from Chaucer to Cowper; including the Series, Edited with Prefaces, Biographical and Critical by Dr. Samuel Johnson, and the Most Approved Translations. With Additional Lives by A Chalmers*, 21 vols. (London, 1810)

Chandler, James K., 'Romantic Allusiveness', *Critical Inquiry* 8 (1981–2), 461–87

'The Pope Controversy: Romantic Poetics and the English Canon', *Critical Inquiry* 10 (1984), 481–509

England in 1819: The Politics of Literary Culture and the Case of Romantic Historicism (Chicago and London: University of Chicago Press, 1998)

Chew, Samuel C., *Byron in England: His Fame and After-Fame* (London: John Murray, 1924)

Childers, William. 'Byron's *Waltz*: The Germans and their Georges', *Keats–Shelley Journal* 18 (1969), 81–95

Christensen, Jerome, *Lord Byron's Strength: Romantic Writing and Commercial Society* (Baltimore and London: Johns Hopkins University Press, 1993)

Churchill, Charles, *The Poetical Works of Charles Churchill with Explanatory Notes and An Authentic Account of His Life*, (ed.) William Tooke, 2 vols. (London: C. & R. Baldwin, 1804)

The Poetical Works of Charles Churchill, With a Memoir by James L. Hannay and Copious Notes by W. Tooke, 2 vols. (London: Bell and Daldy, 1866)

Cixous, Hélène, *The Hélène Cixous Reader*, (ed.) Susan Sellers (London and New York: Routledge, 1994)

Clancy, Charles J., 'A Review of *Don Juan* Criticism 1900–1973', Romantic Reassessment No. 40 (University of Salzburg, 1974)

Clearman, Mary, 'A Blueprint for *English Bards and Scotch Reviewers*: The First Satire of Juvenal', *Keats–Shelley Journal* 19 (1970), 87–99

Cochran, Peter, 'Byron and Castelnau's *History of New Russia*', *The Keats-Shelley Review* 8 (1993–4), 48–70

'Mary Shelley's Fair Copying of *Don Juan*', *The Keats-Shelley Review* 10 (1996), 221–41

'Francis Cohen, *Don Juan* and Casti', *Romanticism* 4.1 (1998), 120–4

Coleridge, Samuel Taylor, *Biographia Literaria; or, Biographical Sketches of My Literary Life and Opinions*, (eds.) James Engell and W. Jackson Bate, 2 vols. (London and New York: Routledge, 1983)

The Notebooks of Samuel Taylor Coleridge, (ed.) Kathleen Coburn, Bollingen Series 50, 4 vols. (Princeton University Press, 1957–90)

Congreve, William, *A Pindarique Ode, Humbly offered to the Queen to which is prefix'd a Discourse on the Pindarique Ode* (London, 1706)

Conrad, Peter, *Shandyism: The Character of Romantic Irony* (Oxford: Basil Blackwell, 1978)

Cooke, Michael G., 'The Restoration Ethos of Byron's Classical Plays', *PMLA* 79 (1964), 569–78

The Blind Man Traces the Circle: On the Patterns and Philosophy of Byron's Poetry (Princeton University Press, 1969)

Acts of Inclusion: Studies Bearing on an Elementary Theory of Romanticism (New Haven and London: Yale University Press, 1979)

'Byron's *Don Juan*: The Obsession and Self-Discipline of Spontaneity', *Studies in Romanticism* 14 (1975), 285–302

'Byron, Pope, and the Grand Tour', in Andrew Rutherford (ed.), *Byron: Augustan and Romantic* (London and Basingstoke: Macmillan, 1990)

Cooper, Anthony, Earl of Shaftesbury, *Characteristicks of Men, Manners, Opinions, Times*, 5th edn, 3 vols. (Birmingham: Baskerville, 1773)

Cowper, William, *The Life and Works of William Cowper*, (ed.) Robert Southey, 8 vols. (London: Henry G. Bohn, 1854)

Cox, Jeffrey N., *Poetry and Politics in the Cockney School: Keats, Shelley, Hunt and their Circle* (Cambridge University Press, 1998)

Crompton, Louis, *Byron and Greek Love: Homophobia in 19th Century England* (London: Faber and Faber, 1985)

Cronin, Richard, *Shelley's Poetic Thoughts* (London and Basingstoke: Macmillan, 1981)

'Mapping *Childe Harold* I and II', *Byron Journal* 22 (1994), 14–30

'Keats and the Politics of Cockney Style', *SEL* 36 (1996), 785–806

In Search of the Pure Commonwealth: The Politics of Romantic Poetry (London and Basingstoke: Macmillan, 2000)

Cronin, Richard (ed.), *1798: The Year of the Lyrical Ballads* (London and Basingstoke: Macmillan, 1998)

Crowe, William, *A Treatise on English Versification* (London, 1827)

Curran, Stuart, *Poetic Form and British Romanticism* (New York: Oxford University Press, 1986)

Curtis, Paul M., 'The Mystery of Distance: Berkeley and Byron', *Keats–Shelley Journal* 41 (1992), 59–75

Damrosch, Leo (ed.), *The Profession of Eighteenth-Century Literature* (Madison: University of Wisconsin Press, 1992)

Deporte, Michael V., *Nightmares and Hobbyhorses: Swift, Sterne, and Augustan Ideas of Madness* (San Marino: Huntington Library Press, 1974)

De Quincey, Thomas, *Recollections of the Lakes and the Lake Poets*, (ed.) David Wright (Harmondsworth: Penguin, 1970; repr. 1985)

Derrida, Jacques, *Acts of Literature*, (ed.) Derek Attridge (London and New York: Routledge, 1992)

Diakonova, Nina, '*The Age of Bronze* and the Traditions of Classicism', *Keats–Shelley Journal* 41 (1992), 49–58

Dowden, Wilfred S., 'A Jacobin Journalist's View of Lord Byron', *Studies in Philology* 48 (1951), 56–66

Dowden, Wilfred S., (ed.), *The Letters of Thomas Moore*, 2 vols. (Oxford: Clarendon Press, 1964)

    The Journal of Thomas Moore, 6 vols. (Newark: University of Delaware Press, 1983–91)

Downie, J.A., '1688: Pope and the Rhetoric of Jacobitism', in David Fairer (ed.), *Pope. New Contexts* (Hemel Hempstead: Harvester Wheatsheaf, 1990), pp. 9–24

Drake, Nathan, *Literary Hours or Sketches Critical and Narrative* (London, 1798)

Dryden, John, *The Essays of John Dryden*, (ed.) W.P. Ker, 2 vols. (New York: Russell and Russell, 1961)

    The Poems and Fables of John Dryden, (ed.) James Kinsley (Oxford University Press, 1958; repr. 1962)

Dyer, Gary, *British Satire and the Politics of Style, 1789–1832* (Cambridge University Press, 1997)

Eagleton, Terry, *The Significance of Theory* (Oxford: Basil Blackwell, 1990)

Edgeworth, Maria, *Letters from England 1813–1844*, (ed.) Christina Colvin (Oxford: Clarendon Press, 1971)

    Letters for Literary Ladies to which is added an Essay on the Noble Science of Self-Justification, (ed.) Claire Connolly (London: J.M. Dent, 1993)

Edmonds, Charles (ed.), *Poetry of the Anti-Jacobin* (Aberdeen University Press, n.d.)

Elfenbein, Andrew, *Byron and the Victorians* (Cambridge University Press, 1995)

Eliot, T.S., *On Poetry and Poets* (London: Faber and Faber, 1957; repr. 1971)

Elledge, Paul, 'Never Say(ing) Goodbye: Mediated Valediction in Byron's *Don Juan* XI', *Byron Journal* 20 (1992), 17–26

    'Chasms in Connections: Byron Ending (in) *Childe Harold's Pilgrimage* 1 and 2', *ELH* 62 (1995), 121–48

Empson, William, *Seven Types of Ambiguity* (1930; Harmondsworth: Penguin, 1961)

England, A.B., *Byron's* Don Juan *and Eighteenth-Century Literature: A Study of Some Rhetorical Continuities and Discontinuities* (London and Cranbury: Associated University Presses, 1975)

Erdman, David V., 'Lord Byron and the Genteel Reformers', *PMLA* 56 (1941), 1065–94

Fairer, David, *Pope's Imagination* (Manchester University Press, 1984)
  'Sentimental Translation in Mackenzie and Sterne', *Essays in Criticism* 49.2 (1999), 132–51

Fairer, David (ed.), *Pope. New Contexts* (Hemel Hempstead: Harvester Wheatsheaf, 1990)

Fielding, Henry, *Joseph Andrews*, (ed.) R.F. Brissenden (Harmondsworth: Penguin, 1977; repr. 1984)

Foscolo, Ugo, 'Narrative and Romantic Poems of the Italians', (transl.) Francis Cohen, *Quarterly Review* 21 (1819), 486–556

Fowler, Alastair, *Kinds of Literature: An Introduction to the Theory of Genres and Modes* (Oxford: Clarendon Press, 1982)

Fox, Henry, *Journal of the Hon. Henry Edward Fox (Afterwards Fourth and Last Lord Holland) 1818–1830*, (ed.) The Earl of Ilchester (London: Thornton Butterworth, 1923)

Franklin, Caroline, '"Quiet Cruising o'er the Ocean Woman": Byron's *Don Juan* and the Woman Question', *Studies in Romanticism* 29 (1990), 603–31
  Byron's Heroines (Oxford: Clarendon Press, 1992)
  'Juan's Sea Changes: Class, Race and Gender in Byron's *Don Juan*', in Nigel Wood (ed.), *Don Juan*, Theory in Practice Series (Buckingham: Open University Press, 1993), pp. 57–85

Frere, John Hookham, *The Monks and the Giants*, (ed.) R.D. Waller (Manchester University Press, 1926)

Fuess, Claude M., *Lord Byron as a Satirist in Verse* (New York: Columbia University Press, 1912)

Fulford, Tim, 'Coleridge and the Royal Family: The Politics of Androgyny', in *Coleridge's Visionary Languages*, (eds.) Tim Fulford and Morton D. Paley (Cambridge: Brewer, 1993), pp. 67–82

Fulford, Tim and Morton D. Paley (eds.), *Coleridge's Visionary Languages* (Cambridge: Brewer, 1993)

Galignani, (ed.), *Galignani's Messenger*, nos. 1829–2442 (Paris, 1821–2)
  Galignani's Weekly Repertory, or Literary Gazette, and Journal of the Belles Lettres, nos. 1–244 (Paris, 1818–22)

Galperin, William H., *The Return of the Visible in British Romanticism* (Baltimore and London: Johns Hopkins University Press, 1993)

Garber, Frederick, *Self, Text, and Romantic Irony: The Example of Byron* (Princeton University Press, 1988)

Gay, John, *Poetry and Prose*, (eds.) Vinton A. Dearing and Charles E. Beckwith, 2 vols. (Oxford: Clarendon Press, 1974)

Giddens, Anthony, *The Transformation of Intimacy: Sexuality, Love and Eroticism in Modern Societies* (Cambridge: Polity Press, 1992)

The Consequences of Modernity (Stanford University Press, 1990)

Gifford, William, *The Satires of Decimus Junius Juvenalis Translated with Notes and Illustrations* (London, 1802)

The Anti-Jacobin, or Weekly Examiner (1799), 2 vols. (Hildesheim and New York: Georg Olms Verlag, 1970)

Baviad and Maeviad, 8th edn (London: John Murray, 1811)

Gildenhuys, Faith, 'Convention and Consciousness in Prior's Love Lyrics', *SEL* 35 (1995), 437–55

Gilroy, Amanda, 'Lord Byron Borrows a Figure', *Byron Journal* 20 (1992), 89–91

Gleckner, Robert F., *Byron and the Ruins of Paradise* (Baltimore and London: Johns Hopkins University Press, 1967)

'Gambling and Byron's Poetics', *Nineteenth-Century Studies* 1 (1987), 1–11

Goldsmith, Oliver (ed.), *The Art of Poetry on a New Plan, Illustrated with a Great Variety of Examples from the Best English Poets*, 2 vols. (London, 1762)

Graham, Peter W. *Don Juan and Regency England* (Charlottesville: University of Virginia Press, 1990)

Graham, Peter W. (ed.), *Byron's Bulldog: The Letters of John Cam Hobhouse to Lord Byron* (Columbus: Ohio State University Press, 1984)

Gray, Thomas, *The Poems of Thomas Gray, William Collins, Oliver Goldsmith*, (ed.) Roger Lonsdale (London: Longman, 1969; repr. 1976)

Greer, Germaine, '*Hours of Idleness*: The Poet's Voice', *The Newstead Byron Society Review* (July 2000), 29–48

Griffin, Robert J., *Wordsworth's Pope: A Study in Literary Historiography* (Cambridge University Press, 1995)

Griggs, E.L., 'Samuel Taylor Coleridge and Opium', *Huntington Library Quarterly* 17 (1953–4), 357–78

Hartman, Geoffrey, *Beyond Formalism* (New Haven and London: Yale University Press, 1970)

Haslett, Moyra, *Byron's* Don Juan *and the Don Juan Legend* (Oxford: Clarendon Press, 1997)

Hazlitt, William, *The Complete Works of William Hazlitt*, (ed.) P.P. Howe, 21 vols. (London, J.M. Dent, 1930–4)

The Spirit of the Age (1825), facsimile edition (Oxford: Woodstock Books, 1989)

Hemans, Felicia, *The Works of Mrs Hemans with a Memoir of her Life by her Sister*, 7 vols. (Edinburgh and London: Blackwood and Cadell, 1839)

Hobhouse, John Cam, *Imitations and Translations together with Original Poems* (London: Longman, 1809)

A Journey through Albania and other Provinces of Turkey, Europe, and Asia to Constantinople during the Years 1809 and 1810, 2nd edn (London: J. Cawthorne, 1813)

Holland, Lady, *Elizabeth, Lady Holland to her Son 1821–1845*, (ed.) The Earl of Ilchester (London: John Murray, 1946)

Holland, Lord, *Further Memoirs of the Whig Party 1807–21 With Some Miscellaneous Reminiscences* (London: John Murray, 1905)

Hollander, John, *The Figure of Echo: A Mode of Allusion in Milton and After* (Berkeley: University of California Press, 1981)

Home, Henry, Lord Kames, *Elements of Criticism*, 5th edn, 2 vols. (Edinburgh, 1774)

Hone, William, '*Don John*' *or* '*Don Juan Unmasked*': *Being a Key to the Mystery Attending that Remarkable Publication; with a Descriptive Review of the Poem and Extracts*, 3rd edn (London, 1819)

Horn, András, *Byron's* Don Juan *and the Eighteenth Century Novel*, Swiss Studies in English No. 51 (Bern: Francke Verlag, 1962)

Howes, Alan B., *Yorick and the Critics: Sterne's Reputation in England 1760–1868* (New Haven and London: Yale University Press, 1958)

Howes, Alan B. (ed.), *Sterne: The Critical Heritage* (London and New York: Routledge, 1974)

Hume, David, *Four Dissertations* (London: A. Millar, 1757)

Hunt, Leigh, *The Autobiography of Leigh Hunt; with Reminiscences of Friends and Contemporaries*, 3 vols. (London: Smith, Elder and Co., 1850)

Hunter, J. Paul, 'Form as Meaning: Pope and the Ideology of the Couplet', in David H. Richter (ed.), *Ideology and Form in Eighteenth-Century Literature* (Lubbock: Texas Tech University Press, 1999), pp. 147–62

[Inchbald, Elizabeth], *The British Theatre; or A Collection of Plays which are acted at the Theatres Royal, Drury Lane, Covent Garden, and Haymarket . . . with Biographical and Critical Remarks by Mrs. Inchbald*, 25 vols. (London, 1808)

Irigaray, Luce, 'This Sex Which is Not One', (transl.) Claudia Reeder, in *New French Feminisms: An Anthology* (eds.), Elaine Marks and Isabelle de Courtivron (Brighton: Harvester, 1981), pp. 99–106

Iser, Wolfgang, 'Indeterminacy and the Reader's Response in Prose Fiction', in J. Hillis Miller (ed.), *Aspects of Narrative: Selected Papers from the English Institute* (New York: Columbia University Press, 1971), pp. 1–45

Prospecting: From Reader Response to Literary Anthropology (Baltimore and London: Johns Hopkins University Press, 1989)

Jackson, H.J., 'Coleridge's Lessons in Transition: The "Logic" of the "Wildest Odes"', in Thomas Pfau and Robert F. Gleckner (eds.), *Lessons of Romanticism: A Critical Companion* (Durham, N.C.: Duke University Press, 1998), pp. 213–24

Johnson, Edward Dudley Hume, 'Lord Byron in *Don Juan*: A Study in Digression' (unpublished doctoral dissertation, Yale University, 1939)

Johnson, Samuel, *A Dictionary of the English Language: in which Words are Deduced from their Originals, and Illustrated in their Different Significations by Examples from the Best Writers*, 2 vols. (London, 1755), facsimile edition (London: Longman, 1990)

The Yale Edition of the Works of Samuel Johnson, (ed.) E.L. McAdam Jr, with Donald and Mary Hyde, and others, 16 vols. (New Haven and London: Yale University Press, 1958–90)

The Rambler, (eds.) W.J. Bate and Albrecht B. Strauss, 3 vols. (New Haven and London: Yale University Press, 1969)

The History of Rasselas, Prince of Abissinia, (ed.) D.J. Enright (Harmondsworth: Penguin, 1976; repr. 1985)

Bibliography

Jones, Robert W., *Gender and the Formation of Taste in Eighteenth-Century Britain: The Analysis of Beauty* (Cambridge University Press, 1998)

Jones, Steven E., 'Intertextual Influences in Byron's Juvenalian Satire', *SEL* 33 (1993), 771–83

Shelley's Satire: Violence, Exhortation, and Authority (De Kalb: Northern Illinois University Press, 1994)

Satire and Romanticism (New York: St Martin's Press, 2000)

Joseph, M.K., *Byron the Poet* (London: Victor Gollancz, 1964)

Joyce, James, *A Portrait of the Artist as a Young Man* (London: Granada, 1977; repr. 1983)

Kallich, Martin, 'The Associationist Criticism of Francis Hutcheson and David Hume', *Studies in Philology* 43 (1946), 644–67

Keach, William, 'Cockney Couplets: Keats and the Politics of Style', *Studies in Romanticism* 25 (1986), 182–96

'Political Inflection in Byron's *Ottava Rima*', *Studies in Romanticism* 27 (1988), 551–62

Keats, John, *The Letters of John Keats 1814–1821*, (ed.) Hyder Edward Rollins, 2 vols. (Cambridge, Mass.: Harvard University Press, 1958; repr. 1972)

Kelly, Gary, *Women, Writing, and Revolution 1790–1827* (Oxford: Clarendon Press, 1993)

Kelsall, Malcolm, 'The Childe and the Don', *Byron Journal* 4 (1976), 60–73

Byron's Politics (Brighton: Harvester, 1987)

'Totemism and Totalitarianism: Pope, Byron and the Hanoverian Monarchy', *Forum* 30 (1994), 328–40

Kermode, Frank, *History and Value*, The Clarendon Lectures and the Northcliffe Lectures 1987 (Oxford: Clarendon Press, 1988)

Klancher, Jon P., *The Making of English Reading Audiences, 1790–1832* (Madison: University of Wisconsin Press, 1987)

Knellwolf, Christa, *A Contradiction Still: Representations of Women in the Poetry of Alexander Pope* (Manchester University Press, 1988)

Knight, G. Wilson, *Byron and Shakespeare* (New York: Barnes and Noble, 1966)

Kristeva, Julia, *Desire in Language: A Semiotic Approach to Literature and Art*, (ed.) Leon S. Roudiez, (transl.) Thomas Gora, Alice Jardine and Leon S. Roudiez (Oxford: Basil Blackwell, 1980)

Laclos, Pierre-Ambroise-François Choderlos de, *Dangerous Connections: or, Letters Collected in a Society, and Published for the Instruction of Other Societies*, 4 vols. (London: T. Hookham, 1748)

Lamb, Charles, *The Works of Charles and Mary Lamb*, (ed.) E.V. Lucas, 7 vols. (London: Methuen, 1903–5)

Lang, Cecil Y., 'Narcissus Jilted: Byron, *Don Juan*, and the Biographical Imperative', in *Historical Studies and Literary Criticism*, (ed.) Jerome J. McGann (Madison: University of Wisconsin Press, 1985)

Lansdown, Richard, *Byron's Historical Dramas* (Oxford: Clarendon Press, 1992)

Leask, Nigel, *British Romantic Writers and the East: Anxieties of Empire* (Cambridge University Press, 1992)

Lennard, John, *But I Digress: The Exploitation of Parentheses in English Printed Verse* (Oxford: Clarendon Press, 1991)

Lipking, Lawrence, *The Ordering of the Arts in Eighteenth-Century England* (Princeton University Press, 1970)

Abandoned Women and Poetic Tradition (Chicago and London: University of Chicago Press, 1988)

Lockwood, Thomas, *Post-Augustan Satire: Charles Churchill and Satirical Poetry 1750–1800* (Seattle and Washington: University of Washington Press, 1979)

Lovell, Ernest J., Jr (ed.), *His Very Self and Voice: Collected Conversations of Lord Byron* (London and Basingstoke: Macmillan, 1954)

Lady Blessington's Conversations of Lord Byron (Princeton University Press, 1969)

Medwin's Conversations of Lord Byron (Princeton University Press, 1966)

Luke, Hugh J., Jr, 'The Publishing of Byron's *Don Juan*', *PMLA* 80 (1965), 199–209

Mackintosh, James, *Vindiciae Gallicae. Defence of the French Revolution and its English Admirers, against the accusations of the Right. Hon. Edmund Burke* (London: G.G.J. and J. Robinson, 1791)

Magnuson, Paul, *Coleridge and Wordsworth: A Lyrical Dialogue* (Princeton University Press, 1988)

Manning, Peter J., 'Byron's "English Bards" and Shelley's "Adonais": A Note', *Notes and Queries* 215 (1970), 380–1

'Byron's *English Bards and Scotch Reviewers*: The Art of Allusion', *Keats-Shelley Memorial Bulletin* 21 (1970), 7–11

'Edmund Kean and Byron's Plays', *Keats–Shelley Journal* 21–2 (1972–3), 188–206

Byron and His Fictions (Detroit: Wayne State University Press, 1978)

'*Don Juan* and Byron's Imperceptiveness to the English Word', *Studies in Romanticism* 18 (1979), 207–33

Reading Romantics: Texts and Contexts (Oxford University Press, 1990)

Marchand, Leslie A., 'Narrator and Narration in *Don Juan*', *Keats–Shelley Journal* 25 (1976), 26–42

Marks, Elaine, and Isabelle de Courtivon (eds.), *New French Feminisms: An Anthology* (Brighton: Harvester, 1981)

Marshall, L.E., '"*Words are things*": Byron and the Prophetic Efficacy of Language', *SEL* 25 (1985), 801–22

Marshall, William H., *Byron, Shelley, Hunt, and* The Liberal (Philadelphia: University of Pennsylvania Press, 1960)

Martin, Philip W., *Byron: A Poet Before His Public* (Cambridge University Press, 1982)

'Reading *Don Juan* With Bakhtin', in Nigel Wood (ed.), *Don Juan*, Theory in Practice Series (Buckingham: Open University Press, 1993), pp. 92–118

Mathias, Thomas J., *The Pursuits of Literature: A Satirical Poem in Four Dialogues With Notes*, 8th edn (London: T. Becket, 1798)

Matthews, G.M. (ed.), *Keats: The Critical Heritage* (London and New York: Routledge, 1971)

McCalman, Iain (ed.), *An Oxford Companion to the Romantic Age: British Culture 1776–1832* (Oxford University Press, 1999)

McDayter, Ghislaine, 'Conjuring Byron: Byromania, Literary Commodification and the Birth of Celebrity', in Frances Wilson (ed.), *Byromania: Portraits of the Artist in Nineteenth- and Twentieth-Century Culture* (London and Basingstoke: Macmillan, 1999), pp. 43–62

McFarland, Thomas, *Romanticism and the Heritage of Rousseau* (Oxford: Clarendon Press, 1995)

McGann, Jerome J., '*Childe Harold's Pilgrimage* I–II: A Collation and Analysis', *Keats–Shelley Memorial Bulletin* 17 (1966), 37–54

  Fiery Dust: Byron's Poetic Development (Chicago and London: University of Chicago Press, 1968)

  'Milton and Byron', *Keats–Shelley Memorial Bulletin* 25 (1974), 9–25

  '"Mixed Company": Byron's *Beppo* and the Italian Medley', in Kenneth Neill Cameron and Donald H. Reiman (eds.), *Shelley and his Circle 1773–1822*, 8 vols. (Cambridge, Mass.: Harvard University Press, 1973–86), VII, pp. 234–57

  Don Juan in Context (London: John Murray, 1976)

  'Byron, Mobility, and the Poetics of Historical Ventriloquism', *Romanticism Past and Present* 9 (1985), 67–82

  The Beauty of Inflections: Literary Investigations in Historical Method and Theory (Oxford: Clarendon Press, 1985)

  Towards a Literature of Knowledge (Oxford: Clarendon Press, 1989)

  '"My Brain is Feminine": Byron and the Poetry of Deception', in *Byron: Augustan and Romantic*, (ed.) Andrew Rutherford (London and Basingstoke: Macmillan, 1990), pp. 26–51

  'Hero With a Thousand Faces: The Rhetoric of Byronism', *Studies in Romanticism* 31 (1992), 295–313

  The Poetics of Sensibility: A Revolution in Literary Style (Oxford: Clarendon Press, 1996)

McGann, Jerome J (ed.), *Historical Studies and Literary Criticism* (Madison: University of Wisconsin Press, 1985)

McKusick, James C., 'The Politics of Language in Byron's *The Island*', *ELH* 59 (1992), 839–56

Mellor, Anne K., *English Romantic Irony* (Cambridge, Mass.: Harvard University Press, 1980)

Meyer, Herman, *The Poetics of Quotation in the European Novel*, (transl.) Theodore and Yelta Ziolkkowski (Princeton University Press, 1968)

Miller, J. Hillis (ed.), *Aspects of Narrative: Selected Papers from the English Institute* (New York: Columbia University Press, 1971)

Milton, John, *Paradise Lost*, (ed.) Alastair Fowler, 2nd edn (London: Longman, 1968; repr. 1982)

Mitchell, Leslie, *Holland House* (London: Duckworth, 1980)

Montaigne, Michel de, *The Complete Essays*, (ed. and transl.) M.A. Screech (Harmondsworth: Penguin, 1991; repr. 1993)

Mullan, John, *Sentiment and Sociability: The Language of Feeling in the Eighteenth Century*, 2nd edn (Oxford: Clarendon Press, 1988; repr. 1990)

Newey, Vincent, 'Byron's "Prisoner of Chillon": The Poetry of Being and the Poetry of Belief', *Keats–Shelley Memorial Bulletin* 35 (1984), 54–70

'Authoring the Self: *Childe Harold* III and IV', in Bernard Beatty and Vincent Newey (eds.), *Byron and the Limits of Fiction* (Liverpool University Press, 1988), pp. 148–90

Newey, Vincent and Ann Thompson (eds.), *Literature and Nationalism* (Liverpool University Press, 1991)

Newlyn, Lucy, *'Paradise Lost' and the Romantic Reader* (Oxford: Clarendon Press, 1993)

Reading, Writing, and Romanticism: The Anxiety of Reception (Oxford University Press, 2000)

O'Neill, Michael, *Romanticism and the Self-Conscious Poem* (Oxford: Clarendon Press, 1997)

Parker, Blanford, *The Triumph of Augustan Poetics: English Literary Culture from Butler to Johnson* (Cambridge University Press, 1998)

Parkes, M.B., *Pause and Effect: An Introduction to the History of Punctuation in the West* (Aldershot: Scolar Press, 1992)

Peacock, Thomas Love, *Peacock's Four Ages of Poetry*, (ed.) H.F.B. Brett-Smith (Oxford: Basil Blackwell, 1972)

Perloff, Marjorie, *The Poetics of Indeterminacy: Rimbaud to Cage* (Princeton University Press, 1981)

Perri, Carmela, 'On Alluding', *Poetics* 7 (1978), 289–307

Pfau, Thomas and Robert F. Gleckner (eds.), *Lessons of Romanticism: A Critical Companion* (Durham, N.C.: Duke University Press, 1998)

Plett, Heinrich F., *Intertextuality: Research in Text Theory* (Berlin: Walter de Gruyter, 1991)

Pope, Alexander, *Poetical Works*, (ed.) Herbert Davies (Oxford University Press, 1966; repr. 1978)

The Poems of Alexander Pope, (ed.) John Butt (London and New York: Routledge, 1963; repr. 1989)

The Works of Alexander Pope, (ed.) Joseph Warton, 9 vols. (London, 1797)

Potter, Robert, *An Inquiry into some Passages in Dr. Johnson's Lives of the Poets: Particularly his Observations of Lyric Poetry, and the Odes of Gray* (London, 1783)

The Art of Criticism as Exemplified in Dr Johnson's Lives of the Most Eminent English Poets (London, 1789)

Pratt, Willis W., *Byron at Southwell: The Making of a Poet With New Poems and Letters from the Rare Books Collection of the University of Texas* (Austin and London: University of Texas Press, 1948)

Prior, Matthew, *The Poetical Works of Matthew Prior* (Edinburgh: James Nichol, 1858)

Punter, David, '*Don Juan*, or, the deferral of Decapitation: Some Psychological Approaches', in Nigel Wood (ed.), *Don Juan*, Theory in Practice Series (Buckingham: Open University Press, 1993), pp. 124–49

Rajan, Tilottama, *Dark Interpreter: The Discourse of Romanticism* (Ithaca and London: Cornell University Press, 1980)

Rawson, Claude, *Satire and Sentiment 1660–1830* (Cambridge University Press, 1994)

Redpath, Theodore, *The Young Romantics and Critical Opinion 1807–1824* (London: Harrap, 1973)

Reed, Joseph, Wayne, Jr, *English Biography in the Early Nineteenth-Century 1801–1838*, Yale Studies in English vol. 160 (New Haven and London: Yale University Press, 1966)

Reeves, Charles Eric, 'Continual Seduction: The Reading of *Don Juan*', *Studies in Romanticism* 17 (1978), 453–63

Reiman, Donald H. (ed.), *The Romantics Reviewed: Contemporary Reviews of British Romantic Writers*, 9 vols. (New York and London: Garland Publishing, 1972)

Rennes, Jacob Johan Van, *Bowles, Byron and the Pope-Controversy* (New York: Haskell House, 1966)

Reynolds, Sir Joshua, *Discourses on Art*, (ed.) Robert R. Wark (New Haven and London: Yale University Press, 1975)

Richter, David H. (ed.), *Ideology and Form in Eighteenth-Century Literature* (Lubbock: Texas Tech University Press, 1999)

Ridenour, George M., *The Style of 'Don Juan'*, Yale Studies in English vol. 144 (New Haven and London: Yale University Press, 1960)

'The Mode of Byron's *Don Juan*', *PMLA* 79 (1964), 442–6

Ridenour, George M. and Jerome J. McGann, 'On Byron', *Studies in Romanticism* 16 (1977), 563–87

Riffaterre, Michael, *The Semiotics of Poetry* (Bloomington: Indiana University Press, 1978)

Robinson, Charles, E., *Shelley and Byron: The Snake and Eagle Wreathed in Fight* (Baltimore and London: Johns Hopkins University Press, 1976)

Robinson, Henry Crabb, *Henry Crabb Robinson on Books and Their Writers 1775–1867*, (ed.) Edith J. Morley, 3 vols. (London: J.M. Dent, 1938)

Roe, Nicholas, 'Keats's Lisping Sedition', *Essays in Criticism* 42 (1992), 36–55

John Keats and the Culture of Dissent (Oxford: Clarendon Press, 1997)

Rollins, Hyder Edward (ed.), *The Keats Circle: Letters and Papers 1816–1878*, 2nd edn, 2 vols. (Cambridge, Mass.: Harvard University Press, 1969)

Ross, William T., 'Digressive Narrator and Narrative Technique in Byron's *Don Juan*' (unpublished doctoral dissertation, University of Virginia, 1970)

Rumbold, Valerie, *Women's Place in Pope's World* (Cambridge University Press, 1989)

Ruskin, John, *The Works of John Ruskin*, (eds.) G.T. Cook and Alexander Wedderburn, 39 vols. (London: George Allen, 1903–12)

Rutherford, Andrew, *Byron: A Critical Study* (Edinburgh: Oliver and Boyd, 1962)

Rutherford, Andrew (ed.), *Byron: The Critical Heritage* (New York: Barnes and Noble, 1970)

Byron: Augustan and Romantic (London and Basingstoke: Macmillan, 1990)

Saglia, Diego, 'Matrimonial Politics: Two references to Marie Louise of Austria in Byron's Poetry', *Byron Journal* 26 (1998), 112–15

Schor, Naomi, *Reading in Detail: Aesthetics and the Feminine* (New York and London: Methuen, 1987)

Scott, Walter, *The Letters of Sir Walter Scott*, (ed.) H.J.C. Grierson, 12 vols. (London: Constable, 1932–7)

Scrivener, Michael, '"Zion Alone is Forbidden": Historicizing Anti-Semitism in Byron's *The Age of Bronze*', *Keats–Shelley Journal* 43 (1994), 75–116

Shakespeare, William, *The Arden Shakespeare*, second series, (general eds.) Harold F. Brooks, Harold Jenkins and Brian Morris (London and New York: Methuen, 1951–82)

Shelley, Mary Wollstonecraft, *The Letters of Mary Wollstonecraft Shelley*, (ed.) Betty T. Bennett, 3 vols. (Baltimore and London: Johns Hopkins University Press, 1980–8)

The Journals of Mary Shelley 1814–1844, (ed.) Paula R. Feldman and Diane Scott-Kilvert (Baltimore and London: Johns Hopkins University Press, 1987; repr. 1995)

Shelley, Percy Bysshe, *The Poetical Works of Percy Bysshe Shelley*, (ed.) Mrs. Shelley (London: Edward Moxon, 1840)

The Complete Works of Shelley, (eds.) Roger Ingpen and Walter E. Peck, 10 vols. (London: Ernest Benn, 1965)

Shelley's Poetry and Prose, (eds.) Donald H. Reiman and Sharon B. Powers (New York and London: W.W. Norton, 1977)

Sheridan, Richard Brinsley, *The Dramatic Works of Richard Brinsley Sheridan*, (ed.) Cecil Price, 2 vols. (Oxford: Clarendon Press, 1973)

Simpson, David, *Irony and Authority in Romantic Poetry* (New York: Rowman and Littlefield, 1979)

Romanticism, Nationalism, and the Revolt Against Theory (Chicago and London: University of Chicago Press, 1993)

Siskin, Clifford, *The Work of Writing: Literature and Social Change in Britain, 1700–1830* (Baltimore and London: Johns Hopkins University Press, 1998)

'The Year of the System', in Richard Cronin (ed.), *1798: The Year of the* Lyrical Ballads (London and Basingstoke: Macmillan, 1998), pp. 9–31

Sitter, John, *Arguments of Augustan Wit* (Cambridge University Press, 1991)

Smiles, Samuel, *A Publisher and His Friends: Memoir and Correspondence of the Late John Murray, with an Account of the Origin and Progress of the House 1768–1843*, 2 vols. (London: John Murray, 1891)

Southey, Robert, Review of *The Poetical Works of Charles Churchill*, in *Annual Review, and History of Literature*, (ed.) Arthur Aikin, vol. III (1804; London: Longman, Hurst, Rees and Orme, 1805), pp. 580–5

Stabler, Jane, 'The Genesis of Byron's *Hints from Horace*', *Translation and Literature* 3 (1994), 47–65

Staël-Holstein, Anne Louise Germaine, Baronne de, *The Influence of Literature Upon Society, Translated from the French of Madame de Staël-Holstein*, 2nd edn, 2 vols. (London: Henry Colburn, 1812)

St Clair, William, 'Bamming and Humming', *Byron Journal* 7 (1979), 38–47

Stephenson, William A., 'A Scott Echo in "Don Juan", XIII. 37–38', *Notes and Queries* 220 (1975), 394

Sterne, Laurence, *The Life and Opinions of Tristram Shandy, Gentleman*, (ed.) Graham
    Petrie, (introd.) Christopher Ricks (Harmondsworth: Penguin, 1967; repr.
    1986)
Stone, P.K.W., *The Art of Poetry 1750–1820: Theories of Poetic Composition and Style
    in the late NeoClassical and Early Romantic Periods* (London and New York:
    Routledge, 1967)
Swift, Jonathan, *Gulliver's Travels and Other Writings*, (ed.) Louis A. Landa (Oxford
    University Press, 1976)
Symonds, John Addington, 'Lord Byron' in *The English Poets: Selections with Critical
    Introductions by Various Writers*, (ed.) Thomas Humphry Ward, 5 vols. (London
    and Basingstoke: Macmillan, 1880; repr. 1911), IV, pp. 245–55
Tave, Stuart M., *The Amiable Humorist: A Study on the Comic Theory and Criticism of
    the Eighteenth and Early Nineteenth Centuries* (Chicago and London: University
    of Chicago Press, 1960)
Terry, Richard, 'Transitions and Digressions in the Eighteenth-Century Long
    Poem', *SEL* 32 (1992), 495–510
Thayer, Mary Rebecca, *The Influence of Horace on the Chief English Poets of the
    Nineteenth Century* (New Haven and London: Yale University Press, 1916)
Tillotson, Geoffrey, *On the Poetry of Pope* (Oxford: Clarendon Press, 1950)
Tomalin, Claire, *The Life and Death of Mary Wollstonecraft* (Harmondsworth:
    Penguin, 1974; repr. 1992)
Vassallo, Peter, *Byron: The Italian Literary Influence* (New York: St Martin's Press,
    1984)
Walker, Keith, *Byron's Readers: A Study of Attitudes Towards Byron 1812–1832*
    Romantic Reassessment No. 88 (University of Salzburg, 1979)
Ward, Herman M., *Byron and the Magazines 1806–1824*, Romantic Reassessment
    No. 19 (University of Salzburg, 1973)
Ward, J.A., *The Critical Reputation of Byron's* Don Juan *in Britain*, Romantic Re-
    assessment No. 91 (University of Salzburg, 1979)
Ward, Thomas Humphry, *The English Poets: Selections with Critical Introductions by
    Various Writers*, 5 vols. (London and Basingstoke: Macmillan, 1880; repr.
    1911)
Warton, Joseph, *An Essay on the Genius and Writings of Pope*, 2nd edn, 2 vols.
    (London, 1762–82)
Warton, Thomas, *The History of English Poetry from the Close of the Eleventh to the
    Commencement of the Eighteenth Century*, 3 vols. (London, 1774–81)
    The Poetical Works of the late Thomas Warton, B.D., (ed.) Richard Mant, 2 vols.
    (Oxford, 1802)
Watkins, John, 'Byron and the Phenomenology of Negation', *Studies in Romanti-
    cism* 29 (1990), 395–411
Weinbrot, Howard D., 'History, Horace, and Augustus Caesar: Some Impli-
    cations for Eighteenth-Century Satire', *Eighteenth-Century Studies* 7 (1974),
    391–414
    Alexander Pope and the Tradition of Formal Verse Satire (Princeton University Press,
    1982)

Whale, John, *Imagination Under Pressure, 1789–1832: Aesthetics, Politics and Utility* (Cambridge University Press, 2000)

Wilson, Frances (ed.), *Byromania: Portraits of the Artist in Nineteenth- and Twentieth-Century Culture* (London and Basingstoke: Macmillan, 1999)

Wolcot, John, *The Works of Peter Pindar . . . To which is prefixed Some Account of his Life*, 4 vols. (London: Walker and Edwards, 1816)

Wolfson, Susan J., 'Keats's *Isabella* and the "Digressions" of "Romance"', *Criticism* 27 (1985), 247–61

'Couplets, Self, and *The Corsair*', *Studies in Romanticism* 27 (1988), 491–513

'"Their She Condition": Cross-Dressing and the Politics of Gender in *Don Juan*', *ELH* 54 (1987), 585–617

"A Problem Few Dare Imitate": *Sardanapalus* and "Effeminate Character"', *ELH* 58 (1991), 867–902

Formal Charges: The Shaping of Poetry in British Romanticism (Stanford University Press, 1997)

Wollstonecraft, Mary, *Political Writings*, (ed.) Janet Todd (Harmondsworth: Penguin, 1994)

A Short Residence in Sweden, (ed.) Richard Holmes (Harmondsworth: Penguin, 1987)

Wood, Gerald C., 'The Metaphor of the Climates and *Don Juan*', *Byron Journal* 6 (1978), 16–25

Wood Nigel (ed.), *Don Juan*, Theory in Practice Series (Buckingham: Open University Press, 1993)

Woodring, Carl, *Politics in English Romantic Poetry* (Cambridge, Mass.: Harvard University Press, 1970)

Woolf, Virginia, *To the Lighthouse* (London: Collins, 1977; repr. 1988)

Wordsworth, William, *The Excursion* (1814), facsimile of 1st edn (Oxford: Woodstock Books, 1991)

The Prelude: 1799, 1805, 1850, (eds.) Jonathan Wordsworth, M.H. Abrams and Stephen Gill (New York and London: W.W. Norton, 1979)

The Letters of William and Dorothy Wordsworth, (ed.) Ernest De Selincourt, 2nd edn, *The Middle Years, 1812–1820*, (rev.) Mary Moorman and Alan G. Hill (Oxford University Press, 1970)

Poetical Works, (ed.) Ernest De Selincourt (Oxford and New York: Oxford University Press, 1936; repr. 1985)

Wordsworth, William and Samuel Taylor Coleridge, *Lyrical Ballads*, (eds.) R.L. Brett and A.R. Jones (London: Methuen, 1963; repr. 1978)

Worton, Michael, and Judith Still (eds.), *Intertextuality: Theories and Practices* (Manchester University Press, 1990)

Yeats, William Butler (ed.), *The Oxford Book of Modern Verse, 1892–1935* (New York: Oxford University Press, 1936)

'Z', 'The Cockney School of Poetry, No. IV', *Blackwood's Magazine* 3 (1818), 519–24

Index

CAMBRIDGE STUDIES IN ROMANTICISM

general editors
MARILYN BUTLER
University of Oxford
JAMES CHANDLER
University of Chicago

8390298R00160

Printed in Great Britain
by Amazon.co.uk, Ltd.,
Marston Gate.